The handbook of

KCRM
Key Customer
Relationship
Management

The definitive guide to winning, managing
and developing key account business

KEN BURNETT

FINANCIAL TIMES
Prentice Hall

An imprint of **Pearson Education**

London • New York • San Francisco • Toronto
Sydney • Tokyo • Singapore • Hong Kong • Cape Town
Madrid • Paris • Milan • Munich • Amsterdam

PEARSON EDUCATION LIMITED

Head Office:
Edinburgh Gate
Harlow CM20 2JE
Tel: +44 (0)1279 623623
Fax: +44 (0)1279 431059

London Office:
128 Long Acre
London WC2E 9AN
Tel: +44 (0)20 7447 2000
Fax: +44 (0)20 7240 5771
Website: www.business-minds.com

First published in Great Britain in 2001

© Pearson Education Limited 2001

ISBN 0 273 65031 9

British Library Cataloguing in Publication Data
A CIP catalogue record for this book can be obtained from the British Library.

10 9 8 7 6 5 4 3 2 1

Designed by Claire Brodmann, Book Designs
Typeset by Northern Phototypesetting Co. Ltd, Bolton
Printed and bound in Great Britain by Biddles Ltd, Guildford & King's Lynn

The Publishers' policy is to use paper manufactured from sustainable forests.

Contents

4. How much do you *really* know about creating an effective KCRM organization? 103

5. How much do you *really* know about planning your business? 134

6. Do you *really* know how profitable your key customers are? 161

7. Do you *really* have a business plan for each of your key customers?

8. How much do you *really* know about selling your ideas?

9. How much do you *really* know about CRM information technology?

Figures

Tables

About the author

Ken Burnett, FIMC is a Management Consultant based in London specialising in management development, sales and marketing. He is a foremost authority, writer and seminar leader on the principles, practice and problems of constructively managing supplier–customer relationships.

After training as an accountant, his business baptism was with Procter and Gamble in the UK. His consultancy career spans over thirty years of which 60% has involved working as a profit-responsible line manager during crisis or growth assignments with client companies. Although much of his time nowadays is dedicated to management development and the design of training modules, he continues to act as a troubleshooter on behalf of venture capital groups.

Since starting his own consultancy in 1974 – the KGB Partnership – he has worked with almost 400 different industrial, consumer and service industry corporations in Europe, the Middle East, Asia, Australia and America. In addition, he has worked with the UK government to attract industrial development to depressed regions and implement change in public sector working methods. He is on the faculty of the Chartered Institute of Marketing, Management Centre Europe in Brussels and several European business training institutions.

He is a contributor to business programmes on BBC television and radio and has contributed to several books including *The real skills of Management* series (MTP Press). His last book, published by the Financial Times, on new trends in customer–supplier relationships, *Strategic Customer Alliances*, has been published in the UK, US, Italy, Spain and Indonesia in translation.

Over the last fifteen years he has been involved in helping companies to develop their systems and approaches to international business. In addition he has had a significant involvement in setting up a commercial organization in Eastern Europe for a world-class consumer company. This operation has extended to the Asia-Pacific region for which he has developed management training modules in seven languages. He is also involved in scripting the content of intranet web sites for staff training and schemes to create stronger links between business and universities.

During the past three years, he has been using his considerable experience to develop practical software systems in sales and marketing – particularly in the area of customer relationship planning and development. Whilst enthusiastic about the potential for business improvement, he believes that, too often, CRM systems are technology-driven rather than meeting the needs of customers and the employees who have to use them. CRM and the challenges of e-commerce are not merely addressed by new software but demand a dramatic review of the organization of, and the way we conduct, our business.

A dynamic seminar leader and conference speaker, he uses his significant experience both as a practitioner, consultant and trainer to make this book a necessary part of any performance-driven manager's development.

Acknowledgements

A book such as this represents the experiences, thoughts and ideas shared with many colleagues and client companies in hundreds of consultancy assignments in many different businesses. It is impossible to acknowledge individually their contribution to the development of this material, even though my debt to them is considerable, so I hope a general acknowledgement will go at least some way of the way to thanking them for this.

I wish to thank also the hundreds of participants in training programmes and conferences who have added to my knowledge of the subject matter and who, no doubt, will continue to do so for many years to come.

Finally, special mentions to Ron Springer of Arca Xytec Systems in Tacoma, Washington, who with his sales team – the 'wolf pack' – has always afforded me splendid American hospitality and wisdom, and to Jacqueline Cassidy at Pearson Education, who has played no small part in advising on the structure and presentation of this book.

Ken Burnett
Amersham,
Buckinghamshire
2000

Deciding on a title for this book was more difficult than nailing jelly to a wall. Specific words have so many different connotations for readers. Does one describe the purchaser of the product as an 'account' or a 'customer'? 'Account' has too much of a financial spin and might mislead some potential readers into expecting balance sheet analysis (although how to measure customer profitability is covered in Chapter 6). 'Key account management' has been hijacked by the sales-training writers and this book is not really about selling techniques (although Chapter 8 on executive presentations and Chapter 11 on negotiating are closely related).

'Customer relations' sounds too much like a manual about how to be nice to the customer (while breaking the news about the late delivery). 'Management' is a valid word to describe much of the content which includes sections on planning, organization, leadership, motivation, team building and strategy but it may not convey the essentially practical nature of the book and the word 'strategy' scares me to death. Strategy is about the art of war; strategy is about directing military movements so as to secure the most advantageous positions and combinations of forces; strategy is about the things you do that the enemy cannot see. Strategy is perpetrated by corporate planners or 'space cadets' as they were known affec-tionately at IBM. As a mere 'food-processor' (another affectionate old IBM term), I merely lunch the clients and muse on the tactics necessary to make some sense of the corporate plan. Strategy, too often, is good luck rationalized in hindsight.

This book *is* about developing, organizing and managing key customer operations. It is also about strategy, but the word has to be redefined – its purpose is to create synergy not to lay waste. In tradi-tional thinking the idea of working collaboratively with your customers on their needs implies the diversion of resources away from the vital task of continuously monitoring the enemy – your competitors; the new emphasis on customer relationships relocates the task of planning into the front-line and, in effect, disbands the marketing junta which has, for 40 years, attempted to lord its intellectual superiority over colleagues who merely make and sell the product. The corporate planner is dead; corporate planning is alive and well but now everybody can participate.

> Not knowing what we don't know is the first
>
> step to commercial failure.

In considering such title options, I realized that this book is about the application of *knowledge* – knowledge about your customers; their needs, wants and aspirations; their businesses and how they use your products and services; how they view and rate their suppliers; their priorities and motivations; their internal conflicts and collaborations; their processes, procedures and systems; how they make decisions and allocate their resources. This customer knowledge must be acquired, organized and used to create solid, mutually beneficial relationships aimed at retaining and developing the business. This knowledge must be customer-specific rather than some generic market research, and fortunately we are moving into a technological age that enables this. The more we accept the importance of such customer-specific knowledge, the more we realize how little we really know about our customers and this is at least one positive step forward. Not knowing what we don't know is the first step to commercial failure.

The last few years have spawned the term 'knowledge management', a variation of which is 'customer relationship management', or CRM, which is now more associated with software systems. Originally, these systems were 'contact management' programs or sales diary organizers, some of which developed into front-office 'sales automation' with order-processing facilities. The Internet has resolved early problems of real-time accessibility to company and customer information databases by remote users and made possible systems that truly integrate the back office (production, inventory, distribution, finance) with the front office (sales, service, marketing). Software vendors from both sides of the office are scrambling to merge or buy each other out by assembling packages of comprehensive, impressive technology under the generic name of 'customer relationship management'. Sadly, there is a high incidence of implementation failure and results that are below expectations. CRM is not a software package, it is a mindset. It involves a complete rethink of a company's organization and the way it does business. Although the best software now permits the customer to interface directly with the supplier's system, the emphasis is still mainly sales- rather than customer- oriented. It is more concerned with opportunity tracking and sales scripts than with enabling the customer's objectives to be achieved – the core issue at the heart of CRM. Furthermore, CRM is a selective process – you can only effectively manage a limited number of key customers or contracts. The software issue is reviewed in Chapter 9, but this book is about applying the concepts not the keystrokes and is about the targeted use of resources, which is why 'Key Customer Relationship Management' is probably the most apt description of the contents – thus giving birth to a new acronym, 'KCRM'.

> Looking for new products to sell to our existing customers is more cost effective than seeking new customers for our existing products.

The value of knowledge – in particular customer knowledge – is only just, as the twenty-first century dawns, being appreciated. The 'dot.com' revolution is spearheaded by companies whose worth is measured not by profits but by the extent of their customer databases and the opportunities to mine the information that has been enabled by advances in technology. We know that acquiring new customers can cost up to five times as much as keeping the existing ones; slowing down the average 20 per cent annual turnover of customers is a significant issue; looking for new products to sell to our existing customers is more cost-effective than seeking new customers for our existing products. Customer retention – particularly key customers – is the new mantra.

This revolution in supplier–customer relationships has considerable implications for many companies and will demand a dramatic reappraisal of their traditional business methods. Traditional commercial 'arm-wrestling' between customers and suppliers is giving way to more synergistic attitudes of openness, trust and co-operation.

The new order, triggered by the 'quality' revolution, is fuelled by advances in communication technology and the complex logistics of mega-corporations trying to do business on a global scale. Customers are forging closer working relationships with *fewer* suppliers; the lone salesperson is giving way to the account team – a multifunctional group drawn from all status levels within the company. The relationship management concept has major implications for all businesses in terms of organization structure, product design, control systems and monitoring of profit performance. This subject is an essential strategic issue for all chief executives, marketing managers, sales managers, commercial managers and key account executives who aspire to stay in business beyond the year 2000.

This book details the best practices of effective 'hands-on' key customer relationship management including:

- Self evaluation exercises at the beginning of each chapter help you to identify and clarify the KCRM issues within your own organization;
- the aims, implications, benefits and pitfalls of implementing KCRM;
- how to evaluate its relevance for your business;
- how to define, target and penetrate potential key customers;
- how to prioritize relevant sales effort and contract bids;
- how to structure a customer-driven organization;
- how to create a strategic selling and key customer development plan;
- how to organize key customer information systems;
- how to evaluate CRM software systems;
- how to analyze key customer profitability;
- how to develop synergistic key customer–supplier partnerships;
- how to analyze the political issues in key customer relationships
- how to negotiate effectively with professional purchasers

The central purpose of implementing KCRM is to win and retain profitable customers through relationships that create *stability and*

mutual gain. There are 11 components in the adoption and implementation of KCRM in your organization and Fig 0.1 shows you how
they fit together and where in this book they are addressed.

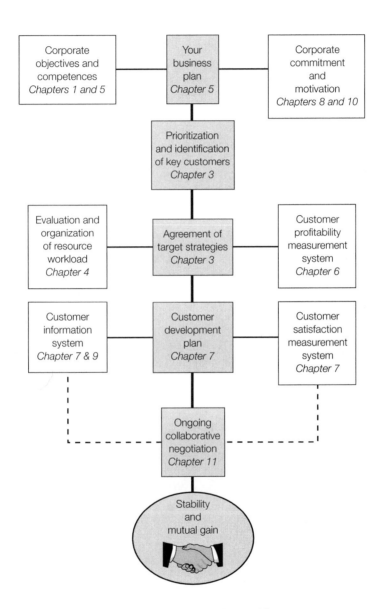

Figure 0.1   Implementing key customer relationship management

So how much do you really know about KCRM?

SELF EVALUATION

Firstly consider the following questions about your organization and key
customer relationship management (KCRM). The issues and implications
are discussed in Chapter 1.

Scale 1 = low/poor, 5 = high/good	1	2	3	4	5
1 How relevant are these market pressures to your business? – *too many competitors* – *new competitors/products* – *shorter product life cycles* – *need to adapt to more rapid changes* – *higher customer expectations of quality and service* – *greater customer purchasing power* – *changing channels of distribution*					
2 How do you rate your organization at – *identifying your different customers' needs?* – *customizing products/services to those needs?* – *identifying and focusing on key customers?*					
3 In your organization, how effective is – *internal communication of marketing strategy and business plans?* – *market intelligence feedback from sales and service?* – *the contribution of all personnel to the marketing strategy?*					
4 How do your customers rate the value they get from your products? – *How much of that value can your pricing capture as a percentage?* – *To what extent do you use differential pricing optimization strategies?*					

Scale 1 = low/poor, 5 = high/good	1	2	3	4	5
5 In your organization, are the primary objectives of KCRM					
– *to win new business?*					
– *to maintain existing business?*					
– *to gain market share?*					
– *to keep competition in check?*					
– *to reduce dependency on relatively few key customers?*					
– *to address operational supplier–customer problems?*					
6 In your organization, how significant will the impact of implementing KCRM be on					
– *financial, material and human resources?*					
– *the sales organization (internal and external)?*					
– *available skill requirements for managing key customers?*					
7 What degree of awareness is there about the pitfalls of KCRM?					
8 Overall, how relevant do you think KCRM is to your organization?					

HOW CAN KEY CUSTOMERS BE 'MANAGED'?

As a business philosophy Key Customer Relationship Management is, perhaps, the most significant development in the evolution of marketing since the 1960s. As a natural extension of market segmentation, it enables the marketing, sales and service functions to be truly integrated, company priorities to be clarified and resources to be more planned and cost-effectively deployed.

Perhaps we should now bury the word 'marketing', which has evolved into a business activity far more important than any one function or group of people in the business. Indeed, for many people the word 'marketing' has acquired enough negative implications to impede considerably progress towards the customer-driven thinking necessary to company survival and success beyond the year 2000.

To the customer, marketing may mean fancy packaging and inflated prices; to the production manager, marketing may be the force behind excessively complicated product ranges that change too frequently. To the salesperson, marketing may be the policy that is rationalizing out of existence the products that the customers depend on. To the financial controller, these people seem to think that money grows on trees!

> Customer-driven business management should be embraced
>> by *all* functions at *all* levels.

The paradox is that, in seeking to create an integrated market-driven philosophy, in many companies the marketing function has managed to un-integrate itself in a spectacular way. Customer-driven business management should be embraced by *all* functions at *all* levels. The full implications of customer relationship management could mean a dramatic shift in emphasis by the supplier from organization by function to an organization aligned to specific customers or groups of customers, which, in turn, means major changes in the structure of the business, the responsibilities and the relative status of the individuals in the business and maybe even the product itself.

The new emphasis on key customer relationship management

Customer-focus' will no longer be good enough. Growing customer power creates the need for the customer-driven organization. This concept is creating strong customer–supplier alliances and it is no small embarrassment that much of this new emphasis on relationships is being generated by customers rather than suppliers. What are the pressures which are forging these partnerships?

- *The glut economy*, with too much production capacity chasing too little consumption, creates pressure to differentiate the offering and to customize the product more to specific customer needs and, to do this, commitment is needed by both suppliers and customers.

- *New technologies* provide opportunities for new competitors with substitute products. Bethlehem Steel has almost defined itself out of business as a supplier to the automobile industry, which is increasingly using plastics in car assembly. Leapfrog technology is contributing to shorter product life cycles. Mr Gillette invented his safety razor blade in 1901 and had the better part of half a century to correct his mistakes and get the product right. Since the 1960s shavers of the world have been wooed by at least seven different hair-removal systems from the stainless steel windable coil to the disposable razor. Product managers no longer have the luxury of time to get it wrong and fix it. In some sectors of the hair-shampoo market you may enjoy a mere six weeks as brand leader. If the product, packaging, promotion or distribution is wrong, there's no time to undo the damage; your £5 million investment is wasted. The moral is sell it before you make it; for that you need a special kind of customer relationship and commitment.

■ *Shorter product life cycles* mean that customers now think in terms of buying in components, thus giving themselves the ability to respond quickly to their markets. Suppliers seek committed customers to safeguard investment returns on equipment and technology. Both parties, therefore, need stability in their relationships.

■ *The quality revolution* and 'just-in-time' production methods demand greater levels of collaboration and trust between customers and suppliers. In the UK, Marks & Spencer can claim almost to have invented the special relationship concept. Their attitude to suppliers was 'if you can't make a profit at that quality and that price ... we will show you how'. This offer of expertise was not always welcomed by blinkered, egocentric suppliers who resented the presumption on the part of Marks & Spencer that they would show them how to run their businesses. The more circumspect suppliers, for example, a luggage manufacturer in Cyprus, welcome the opportunity to plug in their businesses to Marks & Spencer's resources and know-how – 'Twenty per cent of my output goes to Marks & Spencer. If they can show me how to be more efficient, it is 100 per cent of my business that benefits'. However, the co-operative philosophy only works if it is successful. The more recent M&S history demonstrates that complacency has to be avoided, and that when survival is the issue, relationships are heavily challenged.

Advantages can be eroded quickly and the facility for identifying
changes with your customers and responding quickly is vital.

- *The accelerating dynamics* of the marketplace make it more
  difficult for established companies to maintain the advantages of
  size or experience. Competitors have details on 70 per cent of new
  products within a year; patenting usually fails to deter imitation;
  between 60 per cent and 90 per cent of process learning
  eventually diffuses to competitors; prices are readily matched and
  advertising moves are instantly countered because they are so
  visible. Competitors can 'buy into' the experience curve and
  customers can make your product themselves – offloading
  surpluses into the market at marginal prices. Advantages can be
  eroded quickly and the facility for identifying changes with your
  customers and responding quickly is vital. Eric von Hippel of
  Massachusetts Institute of Technology, analyzing innovation in
  the scientific instrument business, concluded that customers
  generated about 67 per cent of 'minor improvements', 85 per cent
  of 'major improvements' and nearly *all* major inventions. A
  McKinsey study suggests that high technology products coming
  to market six months late but on budget will earn 33 per cent less
  profit over five years than if they had been ready on time. In
  contrast, exceeding the budget costs by 50 per cent but coming out
  on time, will cut profits by only 4 per cent. Time and closeness to
  the customer are the new priorities.

- *Alliances, joint ventures and restructuring.* Many markets are
  presenting opportunities for customers to enter into alliances
  and/or develop international, or even global, organizations and
  strategies. The advantages of such strategies include:
  - the reduction of the risk of negative developments in individual
    markets;
  - lower costs, which may allow lower prices and more intensive
    marketing to expand the size of the targeted market segments;
  - improved profitability by spreading the fixed costs of the
    business across a larger unit volume.

The liberalization of trade policies, such as the reductions in
customs duties and other non-tariff barriers in Europe, provides

more compelling reasons for companies to think beyond traditional boundaries. All national companies must consider the
implications, for even if they have no ambition to extend
themselves, they must expect more intense competition in their
markets from outsiders. In the 1970s, the internationalization of
accountancy left five or six giants holding all the top audits. Some
pundits have forecasted that, within the next ten years, only ten
supermarket buying groups will exist in Europe. A similar rationalized future is predicted for the automobile industry.

If customers are going multi-national, they look for international suppliers and pan-European contracts. The negotiation and
implementation of such contracts across national boundaries
demands superlative customer relationships and co-ordination,
particularly between supplier service organizations, who may be
reluctantly living with contract terms negotiated outside their
'territory'.

■ *Channels of distribution* can no longer be managed positively
with a focus on avoiding conflict and reducing cost. As Lee
Iacocca declares, 'A company with the best distribution system
and the best service will win all the marbles – because you can't
keep an advantage in other areas for long'.

The challenge of managing distribution channels has always
been to balance responsiveness to the customer with costs and
control. The increasing emphasis on being close to the customer is
creating a potential shift in the balance of power between suppliers
and the middle men. Checkout technology means that the supermarkets probably know more about end-users than their suppliers
know.

Fragmentation and complexity of end-user markets afford a
proliferation of channel alternatives for suppliers but telemarketing and computer-to-computer ordering may demand
substantial capital investment by suppliers in order for them to
remain competitive. Whether by expanding the means of direct
access to the market or by acknowledging the new power of the
distribution channels, suppliers are forced into new levels of
commitment and resource allocation to stay close to the customer.

Such investment has to be guided and monitored by a more serious approach to customer relationship management than, perhaps, has been evident in the past.

Checkout technology means that the supermarkets probably know more about end-users than their suppliers know.

Embracing the concept of KCRM acknowledges these pressures, and implementing the principles outlined in this book, although sometimes politically challenging, demonstrates a positive approach that yields benefits for both the customer and the supplier.

Every customer is a market segment

The notion of key customer relationship management is a natural extension of market segmentation. In theory, every single potential customer is a market segment. In reality, businesses have to focus on specific market segments in which they believe that they can demonstrate *distinctive competence* and in which they can create a *sustainable competitive advantage*. The target segments must be accessible and have the potential to satisfy corporate objectives within viable cost parameters.

These identified market segments have to be translated into real live customers with names and addresses to be targeted by the sales team and turned into actual product deliveries, revenues and profits. Marketing success depends upon the integration of three activities:

- identification, analysis and selection of market segments
- creation of relevant products and services
- sales activity focused on key customers within the targeted segments.

For many companies, the effective co-ordination of these activities is jeopardized by:

- poor internal communication of marketing strategy

- inadequate channels for the feedback of market intelligence by sales and customer service

- the imposition of marketing strategy from the top down.

Poor internal communication results in salespeople trying to sell indiscriminately to any prospect who will listen; failure to sell means that they conclude that the product is over-priced or under-performs because, for much of the time, they may be addressing the wrong potential customers.

The lack of a channel for constructive feedback to the marketing people by the sales team means that there is no mechanism by which those who are talking directly with potential product users can contribute to product design or policy. Valuable daily dialogue with customers is not assimilated by corporate planners.

The top-down marketing philosophy practised in so many companies results in collaboration barriers between the marketing planners and those who actually have to implement the plan. Progressively the motivation and commitment to achievement is eroded by the limited participation in corporate planning that the latter are permitted.

There have been many highly motivational books and papers attempting to identify the recipe for company success but failing to convince on how it can be implemented. Customer relationship management concepts can, for many companies, provide the practical framework to make such things happen. The success of any supplier hinges upon the careful selection and management of relationships with key customers. In effect this means that there is a new dimension not only to the customer relationship management job, but to the way in which a company is structured, the development of its products, corporate objectives and the benchmarks by which results are measured.

In the 1990s there has been considerable progress in the implementation of customer relationship management principles. Usually, companies have identified their most important customers and organized their activities around them, although their prioritization processes are frequently unscientific and highly subjective. Key customer managers have been appointed but there may have been little thought given to this role in the overall organization structure of the business. The benefits of teamworking are increasingly recognized but teams are still more function-oriented than customer-centred. The most significant lethargy, however, is in the failure to rethink the traditional approach to performance measurement, particularly in recognizing that each specific key customer is a unique profit centre. For many companies the full implications and understanding of the customer relationship management concept may have been obscured, unfortunately, by the hijacking of the term as an upmarket title for sales and negotiation training.

WHAT WILL KCRM DO FOR YOUR COMPANY?

The prime purpose of organizing the company on a KCRM basis is to respond to a customer-driven environment and to develop your business overall in order to maximize the return on investment for shareholders. In any business, financial performance depends ultimately on creating capturable customer value (CCV) as efficiently as possible. The businesses that create most shareholder value are those that can capture the highest CCV, not merely the most efficient businesses. Figure 1.1 illustrates the cascade of value within Dell Computers, from the total CCV of the product ($10 000), to the actual value achieved ($2280) and the final shareholder value ($116) after increased efficiency benefits have been shared with stakeholders such as suppliers and employees.

In any business, financial performance depends ultimately on creating capturable customer value (CCV) as efficiently as possible.

When customers buy a PC from Dell, it is because they perceive a value in the benefits they can derive from the computer and the surrounding services offered by Dell, and this value depends both on the product/service and on the customers' needs. In some instances, a single PC could be crucial to solving a problem worth millions of dollars; usually the *perceived value of the benefits* it brings will be around $10 000.

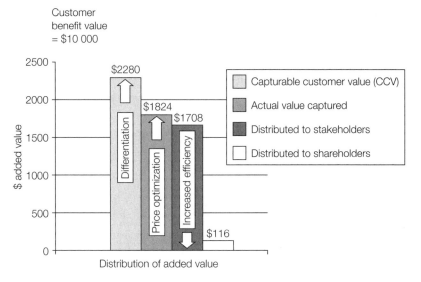

Figure 1.1 Value cascade – Dell Computers

Dell cannot hope to capture all of this value as revenue and in Dell's case, as in most businesses, the CCV will be significantly lower than the actual value of the products and services to the customer. Because there is a highly competitive market for the supply of PCs, there are well established guidelines for PC prices that are more closely related to the costs of supply than to the value of the benefits which customers can derive. PCs are almost commodity products, and the theoretically capturable value is usually in the range $1000 to $4000, depending upon the specification and competitive environment.

The more Dell can differentiate its products from competitors, the more CCV will be available to Dell. However, even in the case of a product that enjoys a monopoly position, the customer will not be prepared to pay for all of the theoretically capturable value. This is because there would then be no remaining *value for money* for the customer.

If Dell has a real understanding of its customers' perception of gross value and CCV, it can price in such a way as to leave customers perceiving excellent value for money, and itself with a high level of revenue. Dell's business model means that it can price for different segments with different value perceptions. Direct access to a large organization, with its fast response in building individual PCs to order, is a massive value-add in the minds of its customers. On average, it can capture around $1800 per PC and Dell has always sold PCs at a price premium. It has never positioned itself as offering a low-cost option.

Most of this revenue has to be paid out to other stakeholders in the business: employees; suppliers; landlords; providers of capital equipment, and so on. An efficient company can sustain high levels of customer value and revenue with less need to pay cash out to other stakeholders. Dell's direct-to-customer model is highly efficient, and removes the retail margin from the value cascade; even so around $1700 must be paid out to other stakeholders.

Finally, the cash which remains after all other stakeholders have been paid belongs to Dell's shareholders: about $116 per computer. This value cascade can also represent the lifetime expected value of the dividend flow to shareholders – the market capitalization of the business. In Dell's case, this is $56 billion. Similarly, the other columns reflect the total lifetime value of the value flows to other stakeholders ($825 billion) and to customers ($4 869 billion). The total stakeholder value which Dell will create over its lifetime is remarkable.

However, this broader strategy is made up of several more specific aims that are germane to company objectives. The main thrust of your KCRM effort may be to:

- *develop new product business* – to offset high research and development costs on new technology it makes good sense to collaborate with specific customers on applications, sometimes on a cost-saving basis. In Japan, it is usual for the researchers to spend almost 50 per cent of their time in the field discussing such applications directly with customers, rather than beavering away in the laboratories removed from the realities of business;

- *increase added-value*, the objective being to ensure that the product is designed to give added-value to the customer and that the customer is achieving these advantages so that part of that added-value is returned to the supplier in premium pricing

(KCRM, by its selective nature, focuses marketing effort onto the customers where this chemistry is possible, thus generating benefits for both parties);

- *gain market leadership* on the basis that market leadership = market share = volume = lowest unit costs as this can be a major source of *competitive advantage*, but, unfortunately, the full equation is not an automatic sequence and, if it is to work at all, has to be made to happen;

- *to spread risk and reduce vulnerability* – KCRM may be the means to expand the customer base if a supplier is too dependent on perhaps one or two major customers. Seasonality of demand and economic fluctuations in specific industries or countries may be problems best addressed by alliances with carefully chosen customers;

> Organizations lose 50 per cent of their customers every five years and it typically costs five times more to attract a new customer than to keep an existing one.

- *to maintain existing business* – sometimes the excitement of new customers and products overshadows the established core business. Complacency sets in, the existing business is taken for granted and not monitored but the usage of every product or application is constantly under challenge from competitors who are offering better ways to solve your customers' problems. It is claimed that organizations lose 50 per cent of their customers every five years and that it typically costs five times more to attract a new customer than to keep an existing one. As key customer managers, we have to be continuously in competition with *ourselves* to explore better ways to improve our customers' business and to maintain our competitiveness in the supply value chain;

- *to keep competition in check* – being close to your customers means that you are in a position to pre-empt, or at least counter, any competitive assault. By tying up key volume customers, you are limiting the competitor to the residue of the market and maintaining your cost leadership in the marketplace. This is especially relevant for distributors (Coca-Cola, for example, has been particularly successful in thwarting new entrants as big as Procter & Gamble by denying access to bottlers and channels of distribution);

■ *to address operational problems* – where specific customers are operating across regions or national boundaries, KCRM may be a necessary co-ordinating function for not only sales but pricing, technical support, customer service and distribution. The complications arising from such a situation are explored in Exhibit 1a at the end of this chapter;

■ *to define the business that you do not want* – too easily in the field of sales activity one is seduced into spending too much time and too many resources on a fascinating technical problem or the friendly customer with the wrong sort of business.

IS KCRM RIGHT FOR YOUR COMPANY?

The full implications of the KCRM concept affect far-reaching aspects of a company's organization, responsibilities, reporting, control monitoring and even product design. So what does the supplier company get out of all these changes? Is KCRM relevant to all organizations in all types of business? What are the cost implications of all these ideas? The backcloth to all these questions is the fact that, without it, you may not have a business in the twenty-first century.

The truth is that the KCRM concept is relevant to all companies selling goods and services ... to some extent. To what extent depends upon a number of factors as detailed above. However, to assess the practicalities of implementing KCRM, an organization must examine closely the drivers of capturable customer value (CCV) to determine whether, in their market, the benefits of KCRM are realistic. The key drivers of CCV are:

■ *the distinctiveness of the value delivered* – which is shaped by
  – the depth of your *customer knowledge*
  – the *tailorability* of your product/service

- *the value of the problem solved* – which is shaped by
  - the *frequency* of purchase and/or interaction
  - the *value* of the interaction
  - the *complexity* of your product/service.

Based on these criteria, Table 1.1 assesses the capturable customer value in various markets.

Table 1.1   Capturable customer value (CCV) drivers in various markets

Market	Tailorability	Frequency	Complexity	Value	CCV?
Petrol	Very low	Very high	Very low	Medium	= Low
Customized software	Very high	Low	Very high	High	= Medium
Tax advice	High	Medium	Very high	Very high	= High
Investment banking	Very high	Low	Very high	Very high	= High
Fast-moving consumer goods (FMCG)	Medium	Very high	Low	Very high	= Medium

It is apparent that basic commodity products such as petrol, despite high frequency of purchase and reasonably high value, will have relatively low CCV due to lack of perceived product differentiation – despite heavy brand advertising. Fast-moving consumer goods (FMCG) products, due to high value, frequency of purchase and ability to customize by wide ranges of product varieties, probably justify the high levels of promotion to maintain customer brand loyalty.

KCRM is *more relevant* to the business where:

- there is a strong *Pareto effect* in the market, that is, where there are a few customers dominating market demand, such as the top supermarket chains nationally or the major car manufacturers globally;

- there are significant *economies of scale* available to the supplier from dealing selectively with 'preferred' customers. These economies may be in production, distribution, promotion, training, packaging and, in turn, should permit unit costs to be low enough to enable the supplier to compete (or even determine) market prices;

- there is perceived *product/service differentiation* by the customer and enough added-value leverage possible to keep competition out. KCRM then ensures that the differentiation is maintained and converted to tangible benefits in terms of how the customer uses the product or service;

- there is a *complex decision-making unit* which transcends the supplier's usual geographically based allocation of responsibilities – for example, a customer where some decision-makers are located in corporate headquarters, while others may be at local branch level or even in other countries at international level;

- there are *multifunction contacts* between supplier and customer – for example, high-level technical or service support products;

- there is a *complex interactive product range* with the possibility of different product salespeople being involved with the same customer, maybe offering different solutions to the same problem;

- there are strong *creative opportunities* to tailor products to specific customer requirements and the relationship depends upon continuous trawling inside the customer's business for such opportunities;

- major customers are centralizing their operations;

- where competition is organising its activities along KCRM lines!

KCRM may be *less relevant* where:

- there is a highly fragmented market with few dominant customers;

- there is little product differentiation perceived by the customer and the customer's buying decisions are primarily based upon price (but beware of your assumptions in this situation);

- the product is not considered technically or financially significant by the customer;

- buying decisions are made at a low level in the customer's organization;

- there are few economies of scale – benefiting neither the customer nor supplier;

- the markets and customers in which you are involved are traditionally disloyal and do not value relationship building;

- you enjoy monopoly status in the market – you do not need to please the captive customer but, beware, this may reflect a rather cynical attitude and, anyway, is unlikely to prevail for very long.

What are the pitfalls of KCRM?

Taking fully on board the customer-driven ideas of KCRM may involve not only considerable change in the organization and its policies, but also the courage and risk of channelling resources towards a few carefully chosen customers. Some pitfalls will be self-evident:

- the increased dependence on relatively few customers and consequent vulnerability;
- the possibility of pressure on profit margins if a key customer chooses to abuse this preferred customer status;
- the likelihood that you will be dealing with more professional buyers who will be skilled in securing even more demanding standards of service and quality. (Customer service is a race without a finish.) In practice, however, the professional buyer is more likely to be an advantage to you rather than a disadvantage – it is the novices in purchasing who create the real problems in supplier–customer relationships.

Other pitfalls may be less obvious:

- The concentration on key customers may result in relative neglect of other customers, who may be the key customers of the future.
- Once the key customer relationship is established complacency may set in, and complacency comes shortly before crisis. KCRM is about investing resources in a *portfolio* of selected customers and, as with any investment, one is regularly monitoring performance, confirming investment decisions or possibly disinvesting. To sustain the freshness of the relationship an occasional turnover of people in the customer team should be encouraged and, although continuity must be maintained, working as a team on KCRM permits this.
- The team aspect is advantageous to KCRM in most situations – encouraging creativity, reducing stress and generating energy –

but not everybody relishes the loss of individual status that goes with the team concept. The praise and shot of adrenaline that goes with winning the big order might be diluted if it has to be shared with other team members and the high achiever might not always make the ideal customer co-ordinator.

What resources are needed?

Lastly, if KCRM is about the allocation of resources, the supplier has to have the resources to implement the plan. Ideally there should be a match between customer organizations and supplier organizations. Procter & Gamble in the United States has the resources to field a full team dedicated to Wal-Mart; Xerox in Belgium has a team focused solely on the European Union administration in Brussels. What, though, if you are a relatively small player in the league? You will have limited resources of people, time and money. The tendency then is to limit our ideas within resource barriers and thus constrain our creativity. Reputedly, the favourite question of Jack Welch, the Chief Executive of General Electric, to his managers at budget time is: 'What would you do if you had *twice* the money?'.

Let us start the planning on the basis of what we need to do rather than be shackled by the past and present practices.

We *never* have enough resources but, as with all planning, we have to start our approach to KCRM by asking '*ideally* what do we need and how can I justify that investment?'. Resources are not given – they are won or earned. Customer managers must have a vision of ideal resourcing and a plan for getting there. In the company, customer managers compete for resources with the catering manager who wants to refurbish the canteen and the data processing manager who wants to upgrade the hardware. Customer managers should have the advantage, because their need for resources impinges on the *external* potential of the company's operations. Investment in catering and data processing will produce greater efficiencies measured in £000s but the customer manager's use of resources could generate revenue calculated in £millions!

The lesson is – let us start the planning on the basis of what we need to do rather than be shackled by the past and present practices. For this we need information, facts and quantification. In the short-term, compromise may be necessary. In the long-term we need an organization which mirrors our customers' organizations and which meets their needs rather than our convenience.

Too often, in the pursuit of KCRM, suppliers and customers are preoccupied with the benefits of good relationships to *themselves*. It has to be realized that, in such a relationship, we can only achieve benefits if we help the other party to achieve their advantages. The accruing benefits of a collaborative relationship are mutually inter-dependent. The purpose of the relationship is to achieve our goals by helping customers achieve their goals. At all times, customer managers must be sensitive to the objectives of the people with whom they are dealing and motivated to find a way to enable these objectives to be achieved.

Table 1.2 summarizes the benefits of good, open, trusting, collaborative supplier-customer relationships.

HOW DOES KCRM AFFECT THE SALES FUNCTION?

The new emphasis on customer-driven KCRM has put the sales function back into the forefront of corporate strategy. However, the job of 'customer manager' differs from the conventional sales approach in some fundamental aspects.

■ *Prospecting*
  The traditional approach is based upon maximum coverage, identi-fying 'suspects' and 'qualifying' prospects, whereas KCRM is about determining ideal customer profiles, targeting specific actual or potential customers, and developing penetration strategies and mutually beneficial business plans in *partnership* with the customer.

■ *Product*
  Salespeople tend to sell the *standard* product and develop the customer's needs to fit but KCRM is about negotiating with the customer about a realistic basis for *customizing* the product to fit the customer's need.

Table 1.2 The benefits of collaborative supplier–customer relationships

For the customer	For the supplier
• continuity and stability of supply which extends to priority treatment in the occasional crisis	• long-run planned flows of work which lower production costs and enhance overall competitiveness
• lower unit costs by co-ordinating optimum production and delivery schedules, joint demand forecasting and guaranteed take-up of supply	• lower unit costs by co-ordinating optimum production and delivery schedules, joint demand forecasting and guaranteed take-up of supply
• access to technical developments in order to ensure maintenance and growth of competitive market share by the customer	• greater business stability by collaborative planning and commitment that means eventually that the supplier and customer need each other
• better identification of both market and product opportunities through coverage of the industry in greater depth (with the customer's knowledge) and breadth (with the experience of the supplier)	• planned achievement of company goals by selection of target customers who are able to provide the sort of business necessary to fulfil corporate objectives in aspects of growth, volume, margin and technical development
• well-defined lines of communication and influence through development of personal, named relationships which, on a team basis, are not dependent on single individuals	• image enhancement related to the status of the customer in the market place, for example, the kudos of being a supplier to Harrods
• joint-funding of research and development on specific projects (or marketing promotions in the retail context)	• possible backing of product development by joint funding or guarantees of volume usage by the customer.
• image enhancement, perhaps, if the supplier is perceived in the market place as synonymous with highly positive attributes, e.g. quality or design.	

■ *Organization*
The customer manager is more likely to be a good team leader than a high-powered salesperson. The job is to orchestrate a web of multi-level and multifunction contacts between the supplier's and the customer's organizations.

■ *Profile*
KCRM calls for total understanding of how business works – both the customer's and your own. The main thrust of the sales approach is usually product and application knowledge.

- *Style*

  managers are likely to spend more time persuading and negotiating for change within their own company than they do with the
  customer. The customer manager is the agent of change with the
  purpose of maintaining and developing profitable customer
  relationships by addressing customers' needs in specific terms.

- *Responsibility*

  The customer manager provides major creative input to the
  corporate plan and, unlike the salesperson, is not merely involved
  in implementation.

- *Authority*

  On the assumption that they may not be able to handle it, profit data
  is rarely given to salespeople, who may be allowed little latitude on
  pricing. Customer managers, though, have wide-ranging authority
  and financial information. Much of this authority will derive more
  from their personal relationships and powers of persuasion within
  their organization than from their job description.

- *Culture*

  KCRM is essentially *pro-active* in customer relationships in
  contrast with the more usually *reactive* nature of the sales
  function.

- *Competition*

  Whereas salespeople tend to use competition as the benchmark
  and meet rivals head-on from contract to contract, the KCRM
  approach is based on creating sustained competitive advantage
  and 'moving the ground' so that rivals find difficulty in substituting their process or product.

- *Targets*

  Rather than short-term revenue and volume, the KCRM focus is
  based upon profit and long-term stakeholder value.

WHAT ARE THE IMPLICATIONS FOR HUMAN RESOURCES?

Organizations have developed from being functionally based, through
the 'matrix-management' ideas of the 1970s, to the fashionable small,
autonomous profit-centres of the 1980s. In the 1990s, a new focus of

responsibility has emerged – the customer team – which embraces multifunctional members drawn from all status levels within the company. The new concept is strategic alliances *with customers*.

These changes have considerable impact on human resources development for the company. Not only will key customer managers need entrepreneurial skills in selling and negotiation, but the new order will demand positive participation by them in the marketing plans of both supplier and customer companies. This means total understanding of the implications of deals for both parties – financial, production, operational and profit implications. The customer manager will have to display, perhaps, more skills in influencing colleagues than customers. In short, the key KCRM function is that of *broker* between two great corporations that want to do business to mutual advantage. It may be compared to mating elephants – there is a high risk of being crushed.

Skill requirements of the key customer manager

The demands of the job may require most, if not all, of these attributes:

- *an understanding of how business works* – their own and that of their customers
- *an ability to counsel, advise and influence* – both within their own company and that of their customers
- *an ability to identify key result areas* with the greatest leverage between efforts and results
- *an ability to plan* and allocate resources cost effectively, judging where to focus the effort
- *an ability to orchestrate* supplier–customer contacts over a range of functions and organizational levels
- *an ability to negotiate* effectively in the best interests of their company and key customers
- *an ability to lead* a multidisciplinary team
- *an understanding* of interactive skills and, perhaps, international cultures.

The exact job specification will vary according to the industry and the geographical scope of the KCRM function, but it will be apparent that any person with such a combination of attributes is likely to be heading for a senior general management position in the future. Involvement in KCRM provides an excellent apprenticeship for the top job because it interrelates with all company activities. In some circumstances, it is a useful career path for the first-class salesperson who may be too impatient with less talented colleagues to be appointed into a staff-management role as sales force manager.

The potential key customer manager is most likely to have come from the sales team and, preferably, not have been recruited directly from outside as the job is likely to involve diplomacy and trade-offs with other people in the organization – it is useful to have somebody who already knows their way around. The financial, leadership and planning aspects do not preclude appointees from disciplines other than sales, but the job requires the 'people-influencing' skills which should be the hallmark of a successful salesperson.

Whoever is chosen, a carefully constructed development programme will be necessary to complement that individual's proven abilities. Salespeople may be weak in understanding finance and systematic forward planning; deficiency in these skills will be a considerable disadvantage for *any* modern professional.

Corporate objectives and the key customer manager

As key customer managers carry an important and maybe significant percentage of volume, revenue and profit, it is essential that they participate in the creation and evolution of their company's objectives – short term and long term. The manager will bring:

- *market intelligence* – knowledge of trends in products, technology, demand and competitive data
- *customer knowledge* – the plans and objectives of key customers
- *creative ideas* for new products and services and improvement of current standards
- *appreciation* of the implications of various resource allocation options.

The new generation of key customer managers will be involved in *longer-term* corporate objectives, not just the achievement of the current plan. Strategic customer relationships have, by their very nature, longer-term pay-offs.

HOW DO I MAKE KCRM WORK IN MY ORGANIZATION?

There are 11 steps in the adoption and implementation of KCRM concepts in your organization:

1 understand your *corporate objectives* and evaluate your *core competences*;

2 generate the overall business plan

3 prioritize your customer and prospect database and identify key customers;

4 agree development, maintenance and target strategies for your key customers;

5 calculate and organize your key customer workload resources;

6 get senior management commitment and motivate customer team members;

7 prepare detailed individual key customer development plans;

8 set up a key customer profitability measurement system;

9 establish a key customer information system;

10 establish key customer satisfaction measurement systems;

11 collaboratively negotiate the business for mutual stability and gain.

SUMMARY

The world of buying and selling is continuously evolving and some suppliers may have been rather slow to recognize what is happening in relationships with customers. The new customer thinking is to have fewer but preferred suppliers with more collaborative open dealings; the traditional tactical offensive by suppliers is disappearing. The extent to which KCRM is relevant to your organization will depend the value placed by your customer on your product/service together with a number of other factors, including frequency of interaction, product complexity and tailorability.

The aim of KCRM is to create stability and mutual gain in key customer relationships measured in terms of achieving the maximum capturable customer value. The new regime can mean growth and prosperity for those suppliers who embrace it: but it can also mean major changes – in organization, products and people – which go much further than most companies appreciate.

This chapter has examined the reasons, implications, benefits and pitfalls for the new emphasis on KCRM and how the investment of resources in strategic alliances with carefully chosen customers is a practical approach to achieving corporate objectives in terms of growth, profit, new business, market share, stability or product development. However, the skills and disciplines necessary to make KCRM work are at a substantial remove from traditional selling techniques.

Exhibit 1a

The pan-European contract

The names and some details in this case-study have been disguised and imply no criticism of any company or persons.

Numo is a German company which manufactures a specialized component used in production processing equipment all over the world. It is a market leader. Research, manufacturing and corporate headquarters are based in Frankfurt, but the company has sales and marketing companies in most European countries (as well as America, the Middle East, Far East and Australasia). These 'local' companies are relatively autonomous and each has responsibility for its own bottom-line.

The product involves considerable local technical support and servicing, all of which is a 'cost' to be set against the gross margin achieved by each national company. Prices are negotiated locally with customers and vary widely from country to country. If a substantial contract is at stake, the national company involved would negotiate a special deal on factory prices directly with Frankfurt.

One of Numo's key European customers is Philips, the electronics giant. Numo's components are used extensively in several of Philips' manufacturing centres located throughout Europe. Philips approached Numo with the intention of negotiating a pan-European contract to co-ordinate all purchases in all countries and replace the local arrangements which hitherto had prevailed. Philips, of course, were interested in using their purchasing power, regarding both price and servicing priorities.

Faced with this initiative from a major customer, Numo decided to delegate the responsibility for negotiating this pan-European contract to their Dutch national organization, because that is where the Philips corporate headquarters are located. A contract was agreed with Philips HQ on terms and conditions which *overall* gave the customer some financial concessions and which maintained Numo's business with this major customer with everything pointing towards a good share of new business in expanding manufacturing locations.

Unfortunately, almost 40 per cent of Numo's current business with Philips was with UK-based locations at a locally negotiated price which was 20 per cent *higher* than the prices in the new pan-European deal. The new contract prices substantially reduced the attractiveness of Philips' business to the UK company. As a result, Philips no longer held a position for high-priority service in the UK and within six months the customer was complaining about the deterioration of service since the new contract had been agreed.

'What am I supposed to do?' explained Bob Carter, the UK General Manager for Numo. 'I am responsible for the profitability of the operation; I have to optimize the use of my scarce technical support resources, which means giving priority to my best customers; Philips are no longer one of *my* priority customers since the deal, even though they are important to Frankfurt.'

The situation was exacerbated further by the fact that Philips' UK volume usage was in decline (although in other countries of Europe volume was increasing at *higher* than average prices since the new contract).

In summary, the results of the new contract were:

■ better prices for the customer

■ increased volume business for the supplier (overall)

■ lower profit in the UK (which at present is responsible for a declining 40 per cent of Numo's business with Philips)

■ lower service priority for Philips in the UK which may jeopardize the future of the total contract.

How might this outcome have been avoided?

1. It is regrettable that the first initiative had to be taken by the customer. One of the main justifications for having a customer-driven organization with key account management is to *anticipate* such actions and, indeed, take the *initiative* in such situations. In this way, the unfortunate results of Numo's stampeded reaction to Philips' initiative might have been anticipated and minimized, if not avoided.

2. Proactive policies depend upon the availability of information. In this case, individual account information was held in each respective national company and corporate headquarters in Frankfurt did not have a facility for monitoring customers on an international scale, let alone the terms and conditions operating on specific contracts. The existence of such an information system might have triggered a key account initiative on an international basis.

3. A co-ordinated information system might have indicated more clearly the implications and size of the UK company's business with Philips *before* the Dutch national manager was given the responsibility for negotiating the pan-European contract. Obviously the British manager should have been involved in these negotiations.

In the present climate of Europeanization, perhaps Numo should be moving towards a policy of price harmonization and/or ways of differentiating its product and service wherever necessary.

The problem is, how do you negotiate prices from corporate headquarters and still keep autonomous profit responsibility and motivation in the national organizations? Although the initiative was poorly handled by Numo, the reality of the situation is that the pan-European price negotiated with Philips would probably not be different if Bob Carter *had* been involved in the discussions. However, some forethought might have changed:

- the method of price implementation for the Philips contract
- the method of Numo's internal profit accounting for its national companies
- the contact responsibility for and co-ordination of the Philips' business.

The terms of the Philips contract

Two options may be considered:

1. The policy of different prices in different countries could continue as before but with an overall retrospective rebate, given quarterly by Numo headquarters, based on a pan-European price. This suits the Numo accounting system, but may not suit the individual Philips national organizations, who may not get the benefit of the centralized discount agreement. In addition, it might make local price negotiation somewhat meaningless.

2. A pan-European price could be agreed with variances for different volumes or service requirements in each national organization. In addition, a retrospective annual rebate could be sent from Numo headquarters to Philips' headquarters based on overall volume achieved.

   This might help the Numo organization's problems, but might be too complex for the Philips organization, which seeks standardization across Europe. It might even be advantageous for Philips to buy all Numo products in the cheapest country and ship them to other locations where they are more expensive.

Numo's method of internal profit accounting

This is probably the nub of the problem. After a decade of decentralized delegation of profit responsibility, the pan-European contract will impose prices on national organizations and undermine real, bottom-line responsibility. How can Numo maintain the responsibility and motivation of its national managers *and* respond to the demands of the marketplace? Here are four options.

1. *A subsidy from Numo headquarters to the national organization* might appear to be the easiest immediate solution, but might prove difficult to operate in future years. How could such a subsidy be calculated? It would have to be based on the difference between the *actual* Philips price and some *notional* market price. How would that notional price be calculated? Could it be the average market price or, perhaps, some fixed percentage of mark-up on the transfer price from factory to national organization?

2. *A special transfer price* from factory to national organization on Philips contracts. This could involve costly administration and would also affect the factory profit accounting system where allowances would have to be made.

3. *Local price less rebate*: the separate national organizations would invoice Philips at agreed *local price less a rebate* to bring the net price to the agreed pan-European price. The rebate would be *cross-charged internally* to Numo headquarters.

4. *Cross-charging installation and service costs*: the separate national organizations would have to live with the new pan-European prices on the basis that they each may benefit from other contracts negotiated elsewhere. However, the installation and service priorities would be maintained by allowing such costs to be cross-charged to a central installation and service budget maintained at Numo headquarters.

In practice, although the circumstances in each industry and with each key account will differ, the options that tend to be preferred are variations on 3 and 4 above. However, considerable political confusion arises when there are performance payments geared to profit performance in each national organization. In considering these problems, the potential solutions lie in the organizational structure for international key accounts.

Contact responsibility

Organization of international key account coverage is specific to each situation. A number of options might be considered:

A centralized key account team

The team is based in the supplier's corporate headquarters and wholly profit-responsible for international key accounts with locally incurred costs cross-charged to them by national organizations.

■ *Advantages*: high calibre people and excellent transnational co-ordination; simplification of local profit responsibility by exclusion of key account business.

■ *Disadvantages*: lack of proximity to customer; language problems; no incentive for local service or prioritization; may involve high sales cost (travel) and domestic inconvenience for account team members.

A key account manager in each national organization

The manager reports directly to the local national sales manager.

■ *Advantages*: good local co-ordination and motivation; close contact with customer end-user; no language difficulties.

■ *Disadvantages*: no overall international view or co-ordination; where is the international contract negotiated; what influence can be exerted on central key account policies?

The manager reports directly to an international key account manager at corporate headquarters.

■ *Advantages*: good international co-ordination; close contact with local customer; no language difficulties.

■ *Disadvantages*: alienation from local sales team; may have difficulties influencing local priorities and decisions.

Conclusion

In general terms, the centralised key account team tends not to be favoured, as it creates a 'them and us' culture in companies which affects standards of service to key customers, the responsibility for which is usually local.

The most common form of international key account structure is the key account manager based in the national organization (speaking that language) and reporting directly to the national organization manager with an indirect responsibility to a centrally based key account co-ordinator. International key account contracts are 'controlled' by the key account manager in whose national organization the corporate headquarters of that key account are situated. There are exceptions to this, when major purchasing decisions are made elsewhere in the customer's organization structure.

Negotiations are conducted with the assistance of the international key account co-ordinator and the national organization manager concerned. The key account co-ordinator will negotiate the implementation of the contract with other national organization managers who are affected by the terms of the new contract and ensure that the new deal is acceptable to all parties.

The many variables in a negotiation will impact on several functions in the supplier organization, and the national key account managers must have direct channels to the factories to negotiate commitments and, occasionally, special price deals that will benefit all parties. Traditional procedures with transfer prices based on fixed percentages must now be flexible enough to take into account all aspects of the deal, including volume opportunities and standard specifications, which could be very attractive to the factory in some circumstances.

Until recent times, most aspects of internal accounting have been designed for internal purposes and, frequently, have created short-sighted obstacles to fully meeting the needs of customers. Customer-driven organizations have external focus. Wealth is created *externally* and focusing on internal matters usually has much less impact on the bottom-line.

A distinction must be made between accounting for financial purposes and accounting for measurement or monitoring purposes. Too much energy is wasted in organizations trying to allocate the credit for sales between different individuals or teams. The team emphasis in key account management makes this impossible to calculate fairly and simply. By far the easiest way is to ensure that all involved receive 100 per cent credit. Double or even treble crediting should present no problem, provided everyone knows that is how the system works.

Is your organization *really* customer driven?

SELF EVALUATION

Firstly, consider the following statements about your organization; the issues and implications are discussed in Chapter 2.

		Always	Often	Sometimes	Rarely	Never
1	My company listens to what key customers tell it.					
2	The marketing department provides me with much specific help in dealing with key accounts.					
3	The technical/production/ operations people treat key customers with great care.					
4	The service department gives key customers priority.					
5	It is easy for key customers to deal with my company.					
6	We are well organized internally to suit the needs of our key customers.					
7	People in my company know the special needs of the key customers.					
8	Our information systems are designed to give comprehensive data about all aspects of our key accounts.					
9	My top management spends much time with key accounts.					
10	My company has clear objectives and strategies for major customers.					
	For each tick score	5	4	3	2	1
	Column totals					
	Overall total					

The maximum score is 50. If you score more than 35, then you probably get quite good support from your company. If you score less than 30, you probably spend too much time fighting the establishment.

EVOLUTION AND REVOLUTION

The status of any one individual or function in an enterprise at any specific moment may well be determined by the nature of the business problems and priorities of that company at that time. Over a period of some 70 years of business evolution, the engineering, production, sales and marketing people have all enjoyed the top status roles in their companies with, arguably, the accountants and the strategists edging them out of the top jobs more recently. Outside of retailing, the purchasing function has rarely made it to the boardroom – an oversight which is only now being addressed with the adoption of the customer management philosophy.

For the first half of the twentieth century in most industries of the Western world, demand exceeded supply. In the pursuit of productivity, the engineers and the production people held sway in the early days. The evolution of the large multi-nationals through merger and acquisition propelled the humble bookkeeper into a role of influence as the need to monitor the monies became more complex. One by one, the different business functions had their decade of influence until the mid-point of the century when supply began to overtake demand. When you have a warehouse full of product, *selling* assumes a new priority and, in the mid 1950s, the hitherto undistinguished salesman became the proud holder of a key to the executive washroom.

The selling style in the 1950s was raw and little more than verbal gymnastics. Whatever the customer said, the appropriate snappy answer could be found in the sales manual. Your hundred or more salespeople would discard their vehicles in the east car park of the Holiday Inn and, after the new product launch meeting, would exit into the west car park and scatter across the country in their new Ford Anglias, plastered with advertising and equipped with radio telephones to transmit their sales successes back to head office with minimum delay. Enthusiasm, energy and youth were used to move the product and 'push' was everything. Towards the 1960s, however, people began to realize that there might be better ways to run the business and the power of positive selling gave way to the basic marketing concept.

The marketing concept

The basic concept was simple: if you found out what the customer wanted and then made it, good business would follow. This simple philosophy was not without difficulties. In the US, Ford had lost $350 million on the notorious Ford Edsel, which had been conceived in 1952 to fill a specific medium-size car market niche that had all but disappeared by the time of its launch in 1957. This experience demonstrated the first complication of the marketing concept – if your product has a five-year gestation period you have to *anticipate* your customers' needs. Nowadays, one has to anticipate the customers' *latent* needs (for example, tactile buttons on car devices) to maintain a sustained competitive advantage in the market.

> If your product has a five-year gestation period you have
> to *anticipate* your customers' needs.

Nevertheless, the new marketing concept of the 1960s was the beginning of the customer-oriented organization, but the focus was still very much on suppliers' *internal* objectives, priorities and, perhaps, the exploitation of the market rather than collaborative synergy.

Marketing had been around before the 1960s. It dates from the time when mankind resorted to bartering instead of stealing to acquire goods. Barter evolved into trading and selling, which was, and still is, a fine art form in the oldest civilizations. In the middle of the nineteenth century, the International Harvester Company provided early evidence of modern marketing in the West with market research, pricing policies, spare part service and instalment credit. In the early 1900s, marketing was being taught in the University of Pennsylvania but it was in the context of an auxiliary function of the sales department. It has taken three-quarters of a century to percolate through consumer goods, consumer durables, industrial equipment, business-to-business and, eventually, service companies. Banking, insurance and stockbroking are more recent converts; museums, hospitals and other non-profit sectors of the economy are now interested.

The potential of the marketing concept was recognized at an early stage in the US; but was this really customer-orientated marketing?

US companies entered European markets in the 1950s with American products and advertising campaigns. Their failures are well documented; General Mills with Betty Crocker cake-mixes found Devil's Food far too exotic for British housewives; John Deere found European landscapes were very different to the endless, flat Kansas terrain for which their equipment was designed. These experienced marketers failed to appreciate that we need to start where the *customers* are, not where the *products* are.

In retrospect, marketing comes across as a methodology to persuade target customers to accept what we know is good for them; even in 1999 the media described the tactic used by package holiday companies of pressurizing customers into buying insurance as a 'marketing device'. It is a form of arrogance which has beset the large conglomerates of the world and made them vulnerable to smaller but rapidly growing, more user-friendly, competitors.

A case study in the *Harvard Business Review* (March 1988) illustrated this point. 'Buck' Rogers, IBM's much-respected former vice-president of marketing, was invited to suggest a solution to a hypothetical problem about a quality equipment supplier with a fixed-price policy reacting to a lower bid from the hungry foreign competitor on a contract with an established cost-cutting customer. The advice was unequivocally 'get closer to the customer – don't concede on price'. Whilst subscribing to the get-closer idea, the intransigence of the rest of this advice suggests the purpose of getting closer is to find a customer need that fits the supplier's solution. This is customer-orientation with a 'heads I win, tails you lose' philosophy and falls well short of the creative customer alliances generated in the 1990s. In 40 years, marketing has moved from being *customer-orientated* to *customer-focused* and now to being *customer-driven*.

Marketing in the 1960s was 'customer-oriented', generating easy-to-understand 'packaged' tools like the product life cycle, the marketing mix (the right product, in the right place, at the right price with the right promotion), together with substantial emphasis on market share. In the early 1970s, more sophisticated ideas on market segmentation and product positioning indicated a subtle shift towards becoming customer-focused. However, the dramatic impact of the 1973 oil crisis underlined the fact that, for all the analysis,

planning and control exerted *within* a company, there were significant factors *outside* the organization that could make or break it.
Currency fluctuations, political embargoes, leapfrog technology – all
could play havoc with expectations and forecasts. Five-year plans
became three-year plans, then one-year plans. Strength through size,
portfolio management and diversification were recurring themes,
blurring the focus on quality and specific customer needs.

> In 40 years, marketing has moved from being
> *customer-orientated* to *customer-focused*
> and now to being *customer-driven*.

In the 1980s the focus moved to competitive analysis. Substantial
resources were directed into forecasting and outguessing rival
strategies. Information technology opened up opportunities for data
storage and analysis and the readiness of managers to change
employers every few years facilitated this process. Marketing was
put onto a war footing against competition and, once again, the
reality was that companies were distracted from the major priority –
customer needs.

THE CHANGING FACE OF PURCHASING

Until the mid 1980s, the purchasing function had never been considered as a major player in twentieth-century business evolution.
The frustration of the professional buyer can be heard at any purchasing conference, where the recurring lament is heard: 'Our job is
seen only as the administration of light bulb purchases. All the major
expenditure decisions are taken out of our hands.'

In the 1990s, the true importance of the purchasing function has
been realized and is beginning to get deserved recognition. Of course,
the true impact of the purchasing task has been realized in retailing
for many years, but in industry the buyer has been the poor relation
for far too long and, like the salesperson, has had to shake off an
historic image dating from the 1960s of less aggressive price-focused
behaviour in business relationships.

> The emphasis now is not just on doing things right but on
>   making sure that the right things are being done in the first place.

The buying function has progressed through the jargon of 'materials management' in the 1970s and 'procurement logistics' in the 1980s to the new buzz words 'purchase marketing'. The buying function has been swept on the crest of the 'quality' movement wave to its present position where it plays an increasingly critical part in the commercial success of the enterprise. The emphasis now is not just on doing things right but on making sure that the right things are being done in the first place.

The new buyers are more proactive in developing relationships with preferred suppliers and in increasing efficiency by reducing the number of suppliers. The objective is to have closer business collaboration with fewer suppliers and more co-operative, creative idea sharing for mutual benefit.

The value of a healthy, constructive dialogue between supplier and customer is demonstrated by an example from the furniture industry. For four years, a veneer producer had been supplying an expensive white ash veneer to a large furniture manufacturer. The product was expensive because of a high rejection rate during processing due to black specks in the natural raw material. The move towards greater collaboration revealed that, in the finished furniture product, the veneer was painted over by the customer! Less waste, more efficient production and lower costs resulted from this belated discovery.

Some of the factors that have enhanced the role of purchasing management in the last decade include:

- direct and indirect material costs now account for between 50 and 80 per cent of total costs in manufacturing industries;

- the degree of vertical integration is gradually decreasing in manufacturing industries; policies are oriented less towards make and more towards buy;

- technological change is increasing rapidly and is a key competitive factor; therefore, manufacturing firms outsource technical development to specialist suppliers in order to stay in front technologically;

- the cost of capital has increased significantly since the first oil embargoes so capital tied up in raw material inventory now accounts for approximately ten per cent of the total balance sheet;

- quality is, today, perhaps the number one competitive weapon and, as a chain is never stronger than its weakest link, quality assurance starts with the supplier;

- the competitive structure in business today has become global so purchasing has to follow and monitor new suppliers on a worldwide basis.

At the same time, the purchasing task has become more complex because of:

- the rapid fluctuations in supply and demand due to considerable over-capacity and resultant high levels of supplier competition

- the price volatility of raw materials, due to political and ecological pressures

- constant innovation, new technologies and materials

- continuous shifts in currency values

- higher levels of government interference and legislation.

This ever-growing complexity of materials and supply sources means that the purchasing function needs to adopt the same sort of prioritization and selectivity procedures that sellers need to do to implement KCRM concepts. They need Supplier Relationship Management.

As with any function, the objective of purchasing is to use its resources, which mainly comprise staff and information, in the most cost-effective way to implement the policy of the company. In effect, this means that the purchasing department focuses its effort on components, materials and suppliers where there are the most significant *technical* and *financial* implications.

The Siemens, Nissan and Dow Corning operations (Exhibits 2a, 2b and 2c) are good examples of many of the current trends in purchasing strategy on a global level.

Exhibit 2a

Siemens' purchasing strategy

Siemens have 120 000 suppliers worldwide with nearly 2500 purchasing staff and 1500 frontline buyers in 256 purchasing departments. Twenty thousand of these suppliers are designated first choice and their data is stored in Siemens' internal electronic information system. In order to determine the focus of Siemens' purchasing activities, suppliers are classified under two headings:

1 *supply risk* – which is a measure of how dependent Siemens are upon that supplier in terms of *technical complexity* and *availability* of the supplier's component. It asks: 'What are the implications for Siemens if this supplier fails to meet performance standards?'. The criteria for measuring the supply risk of a given supplier will include factors such as:

■ how non-standard is the supply component?

■ what would be the costs if we were to change suppliers?

■ how difficult would it be for us to make this component ourselves?

■ how few supply sources are there for this component?

2 *profitability impact or purchasing value* – the bottom-line impact of the supplier relationship for Siemens is measured in terms of how much purchasing expenditure is tied up with this item.

The criteria of supply risk and profitability impact create an *evaluation matrix* with four possible supplier classifications:

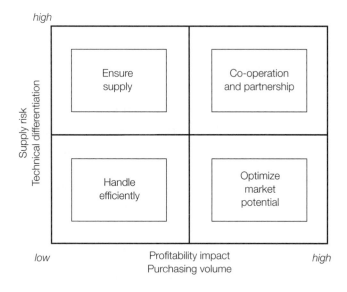

Figure 2.1 The purchasing matrix

1 *High-value products with high technical demand*, such as power supplies, coolers for central processing units (CPUs), customized gate arrays

2 *High-volume standard products*, such as printed circuit boards, memory integrated circuits (ICs), precious metals, zinc-plated tin sheets

3 *Low-value products with high technical demand*, such as parts for which tooling is necessary, relays, transformers

4 *Low-value standard products*, such as metals, chemicals, plastics, resistors, capacitors.

The intensity and nature of Siemens' relationships with its suppliers is determined by these four classifications.

Classification 1: high-value products with high technical demand

The purchasing strategy is technical co-operation characterized by:

- intense relationships with suppliers including technical support and jointly financed research and development
- long-term contracts
- joint efforts towards standardization and transfer of know-how
- focus on the manufacturing process and quality assurance procedures, such as in-house inspection
- optimization of communication and exchanges of information through electronic data interchange (EDI) and electronic mail

- possible support in dealing with bottlenecks of base material procurement.

Classification 2: high-volume standard products

The purchasing strategy is optimization of savings potential characterized by:

- global sourcing
- development of an international information system for purchasing
- worldwide search for relevant qualified suppliers
- second source policy
- allocation of best qualified and experienced buyers with international training.

Classification 3: low-value products with high technical demand

The purchasing strategy is guaranteed availability characterized by:

- quality audits and dedicated warehouse facilities
- inventory and requirements planning with built-in warning system
- strategic inventory (safety or buffer stock)
- consignment stock at supplier's premises
- particular emphasis on maintaining good relations with suppliers

Classification 4: low-value standard products

The purchasing strategy is efficient processing characterized by:

- reduction of purchase processing costs by electronic systems

- outsourcing to distributors or suppliers who will take over part of the usual logistic performance, such as warehousing, requirements planning, reporting and so on

- increasing the utilization of data processing and automated order placement systems

- just-in-time, ship-to-stock, ship-to-line procedures

- efforts to reduce number of suppliers and items.

In Classification 4, Siemens have conferred preferred status on three distributors out of a total of 80. This arrangement stipulates a 48-hour guaranteed delivery service, an agreed profit margin and that the distributor will be responsible for warehousing, forecasting and stock and volume reports to Siemens.

The implications of Siemens' strategy

It is apparent that any prospective supplier to Siemens must consider seriously how the customer classifies their products. Siemens' declared purchasing policy, as described, must have considerable implications on the relationship possibilities for a supplier. Any supplier manager who has Siemens as a key customer and whose product is in Classifications 2 or 4 may have difficulty in generating special relationships; it takes two to make a partnership. Somehow the perception of the product has to be elevated by differentiation to induce Siemens to enter into a preferred status relationship.

In addition to the usual tasks of a purchasing function, Siemens has a more specialized group of people who are designated *purchasing marketing*. One of their principal functions is to make Siemens a more attractive customer for potential suppliers. In this capacity, they are involved in market research, seeking out and evaluating new suppliers, as well as exploring new areas of collaboration with existing suppliers, which could be to their mutual benefit. For example, alignment of order quantities with the most cost-effect production batch quantities would be beneficial to both parties. On the other hand, the supplier might be invited to do a technical survey of Siemens' production design and methods, with a view to reducing the number of *special* components and increasing the number of *standard* components which are both easier to stock and produce. In this way, the supplier improves efficiency and, by passing on some part of the benefits of this efficiency, enables Siemens to compete favourably in its respective marketplace.

Siemens also take an interest in how its purchasing managers spend their time. They have ongoing monitoring as to how many hours it takes for each buyer to purchase DM100 000 of supplies classified in eight different categories. This will indicate, for example, how the purchasing manager in one production plant will spend 1.7 hours to purchase DM100 000 of integrated circuits, whereas a similar purchase in another plant may take three times that amount of buying time. This sort of analysis may not give answers, but it does prompt the right questions and focuses the allocation of buying resources in the right direction.

Exhibit 2b

Nissan (UK) purchasing strategy

In 1987 Nissan established a manufacturing plant in northern England with an integrated operation consisting of casting, pressing, plastic moulding and engine assembly employing more than 3000 people. Initially only one model was made there – the Bluebird – which eventually gave way to the Primera model, produced at the rate of 120 000 vehicles per year and exporting to 30 countries worldwide including Japan.

Nissan (UK) is an interesting case study in how the Japanese approach to buyer–seller relationships can be translated into a European environment. Traditionally the UK motor industry has been characterized by arms-length relationships, multiple sourcing and contracting on a job-by-job basis. The Japanese car industry, on the other hand, for many years has promoted a strong sense of mutual dependence, long-term commitment and shared benefits with its suppliers. In addition, the European car industry has had a much higher degree of *vertical integration* and works with a larger number of direct suppliers, with component purchasing policies still focused on a national, rather than international, basis. Surveys suggest that Japanese component makers achieve higher labour productivity and quality, faster design development and delivery cycles, more variety and lower product costs. In terms of quality, reject rates from Nissan suppliers in Japan have been reduced by a factor of 10 every ten years since 1960 and are currently less than 100 parts per million. UK suppliers to Nissan are currently operating at about 1000 parts per million reject rate, which is good by traditional standards but is still about a generation behind the Japanese.

Nissan have formed supplier development teams (SDT) that work with suppliers to reduce price over time. Pricing is not the dominant factor in supplier relationships. A fair margin is allowed and the aim is to offset inflation through productivity and to achieve long-term end-product pricing targets on a collaborative basis.

The relationship is maintained through close and frequent contacts at all levels and there is an informality of commitment that extends beyond the current model. Of 126 suppliers to the Bluebird model, only 14 were dropped when the Primera went into production. The new car has 80 per cent local content which has involved increasing the number of suppliers by 65. An SDT assessment regularly evaluates the supplier relationship on the basis of stock control, housekeeping, safety, morale, management, policy and communications, quality, delivery control and productivity.

Exhibit 2c

Dow Corning (Europe) purchasing strategy

Dow Corning operate a 'preferred supplier' system designated 'supplier quality management process' (SQMP). Preferred suppliers are those who 'most help us to be preferred suppliers to our own customers'.

A partnership between Dow Corning and its suppliers is described as a long-term alliance to which each company brings its maximum capabilities in order to generate the most profitable results for both parties.

The expectations and benefits cited from such alliances are:

- mutually set objectives
- mutual strategy for how to reach these objectives
- mutual risks – areas of risk defined and who is taking them, and optimization of investments
- increased flexibility of production programmes
- total quality assurance
- increased competitiveness for Dow Corning and improved market share for the preferred supplier.

This sort of special relationship is only possible with a limited number of selected suppliers who are capable of offering:

- product quality, consistency and performance

- a 'quality' culture
- sound organization of their own suppliers
- supply reliability – currently and with visible indications for the future
- viability of facilities
- raw material position
- shipping position
- operational technology
- research and development capability, innovation and development
- visible marketing strategy
- competitiveness: current and future through cost reductions from efficiency, productivity improvements or from technological breakthrough
- inventory management policy
- just-in-time capabilities
- profitability: long-term viability of the supplier company
- political and economical position
- financial health, ownership and stability of the supplier.

Dow Corning operate an elaborate evaluation system for suppliers based upon seven basic weighted criteria (the figures in parentheses indicate the weighting):

- supplier (10 per cent)
- product (30 per cent)

- delivery (30 per cent)

- packaging (5 per cent)

- labelling (5 per cent)

- paperwork (5 per cent)

- pricing (15 per cent)

Each of these criteria are further evaluated on the basis of a number of weighted factors, as follows:

- *supplier*

   access to information (10 per cent); technical and after-sales support (15 per cent); innovative spirit (10 per cent); commercial and technical reputation (10 per cent); past performance (20 per cent); financial situation (15 per cent); efficiency of internal organization (10 per cent); capabilities of salespeople (10 per cent)

- *product*

   conformity with specifications (40 per cent); quality assurance procedures (20 per cent); quality consistency (40 per cent)

- *delivery*

   requested material (40 per cent); requested quantity (30 per cent); requested time (5 per cent); requested location (20 per cent); requested documentation (5 per cent)

- *packaging*

   compliance with safety regulations (40 per cent); compliance with Dow Corning specifications (40 per cent); quality of packaging (20 per cent)

- *labelling*

   compliance with safety regulations (60 per cent); clear marking/warning codes (40 per cent)

- *paperwork accuracy*

   right price (25 per cent); right quantity (25 per cent); right location (10 per cent); right purchase order number (20 per cent); right shipping documents (20 per cent)

- *pricing*

   competitiveness based on long-term orientation, creativity and optimization of cost (100 per cent).

The delivery and paperwork factors are monitored by computer and, once a year, a composite rating, integrating the seven criteria, is assigned to all suppliers and determines the status of each supplier.

A rating score of 91+ per cent is deemed excellent and earns a letter of congratulations and a nomination for the award of 'Supplier of the Year'. A rating of 81–90 per cent is good and 71–80 per cent is average. Both classifications result in a jointly agreed improvement plan. A supplier who regularly scores a rating below 70 per cent, after a given period, may be removed from Dow Corning's list. The percentage split for Dow Corning's suppliers is: excellent, 29 per cent; good, 61 per cent; average, 9 per cent; unsatisfactory, 1 per cent.

Dow Corning have a declared policy of working closer with fewer but larger suppliers and reducing the supplier base. The aim is to achieve partnership relationships with major and strategic suppliers leading to mutual opportunities and shared benefits. The guidelines which Dow Corning issue to their purchasing agents stress:

- close cost control

- long-term relationships

- win-win mode negotiations
- promotion of the best possible Dow Corning image
- proactive pursuit of market knowledge
- in-depth knowledge of end-use applications.

The final aim is to turn the purchasing function into a source of profit and to contribute to the overall profitability of Dow Corning, while achieving the status of a 'preferred customer' from major suppliers with implied benefits of:

- supply security
- quality of products
- supplier, research, development and technical sources
- reliability of delivery and service
- highly competitive prices
- provision of market information
- high levels of attention.

'Dow Corning will provide products and services that meet or exceed the requirements of customers. Each employee and supplier must be committed to this goal of doing it right, first time.'

The policy statements and intentions indicated in these three examples of purchasing operations are praiseworthy and create high expectations for a brave new world of open, trusting customer–supplier relationships.

However, the truth is that there is still a significant percentage of solid but old-fashioned salespeople and buyers who have been brought up in a traditional adversarial climate of mistrust and opportunism. Many salespeople still bombard the customers with general information, features and benefits, hoping that some of it will be relevant. Many buyers still project an attitude of the-only-thing-that-matters-is-price.

Egos and the competitive instinct for winning distort the reality that buyers and sellers need each other. Salespeople ride on the coat-tails of successful customers by trying to get the highest prices possible, rather than exploring ways to make those customers more successful by helping them to compete successfully and grow their respective markets. Buyers squeeze the lowest prices out of suppliers and strangle the possibility of joint ideas and creativity that will generate added-value in their businesses.

The 'quality' movement and the realization that companies have enough to do fighting competitors without fighting suppliers or customers will, perhaps, kill off the dated, aggressive attitudes that are almost endemic. The key customer manager is in a unique position to seize this opportunity, which has primarily arisen from customer initiatives, and accelerate the new age of collaborative relationships which will be the means to prosperity beyond the year 2000.

How do purchasing policies impact on KCRM?

The first factor to be considered in developing an appropriate strategy for gaining preferred supplier status with a specific customer is to evaluate how significant your product or your service is to that customer, quantified in technical significance (supply risk) and financial significance (in the context of the customer's total purchasing budget). Although the size and nature of the transactions may be critical to the supplier, how does it rank in the customer's priorities? The customer may be a key customer to you but do you really matter to the customer?

> The customer may be a key customer to you but do you really matter to the customer?

The nature of the customer–supplier relationship will be determined by the supply risk and financial implication matrix described in purchasing strategy exhibit 2a. The four purchasing strategies detailed in the matrix suggest four distinctive selling strategies:

1 *technical co-operation* (high supply risk and high value): relationship-building a high priority; dedicated technical staff; long-term contracts; guarantees of supply; heavy involvement in manufacturing processes and quality assurance; joint research and development (on a shared cost basis); maintenance of entry barriers for competitors; network of customer contacts at all levels

2 *optimization of savings potential* (standard product and high value): relationship conditional upon pricing; aim to be the most efficient, lowest-cost producer in the industry; high levels of competitor analysis and monitoring; constant development of service elements around the core product; highest levels of negotiation skills

3 *guarantees of availability* (high supply risk and low value): relationship building a high priority; co-operation of quality audits; consignment and buffer stock agreements (which keep out competitors); joint demand forecasting; constant monitoring of raw material supplies

4 *efficient order-processing* (standard products and low value): relationships low priority; supplier to take over total sourcing administration; utilization of automated order placement, data processing and EDI; constant search for reduction of ancillary costs associated with the use of the product.

It will be obvious that selling strategies 1 and 3 lend themselves to close customer–supplier relationships and are particularly desirable positions from the supplier's point of view. Strategies 2 and 4, however, may be described as *commodity* situations where the relationship will depend more on factors outside the intrinsic nature of the product. All suppliers are selling 'augmented' products and services, that is, a total package which consists of a core functional product augmented by a number of relationship benefits such as service, guarantees, reputation and quality, which may be how each individual supplier is differentiated.

Suppliers who are perceived by purchasers as offering strategies 1 and 3 will usually have some core product differential which enhances the customer's need for close relationships. The less fortunate strategy 2 and 4 suppliers may not have many advantages in their core product but must strive to differentiate themselves with augmentations to their commodity product with the objective of raising the purchaser's perception of their priority.

REDEFINING THE CUSTOMER'S NEED

- *Example 1*

   The salesperson selling ingredients to the bakery trade discusses new recipes and formulations which not only make full use of the capabilities of the product, but increase the variety of merchandise for the customer's business. The strategy is to gradually replace the baker's older recipes with new recipes for mutual benefit. The recipes are built around the performance features of the products, which are no longer sold as mere substitutes for what the baker was using previously.

- *Example 2*

   The office furniture salesperson, instead of entering a Dutch auction for supplying a few supplementary desks and chairs, puts forward a plan for an

▶

entirely new office layout, which is built around a highly space-efficient and environmentally attractive workstation concept. The purchaser may not wish to make such a sweeping change every time, but the possibilities of winning the business are considerably improved by the strategy of redefining the need, rather than merely submitting a 'me-too' price quotation.

■ *Example 3*

A potential supplier of 'nuts and bolts' to a factory will survey how the product is stocked, shipped and used in the customer's factory. The potential supplier notices that, at present, the product is delivered with the nut and bolt screwed together in boxes which are fed directly to the assembly line. The operator needs to perform *three* actions (unscrew, insert, rescrew) to incorporate the bolt into the assembly. By arranging packaging in boxes that *separate* the nuts from the bolts, the assembly task is reduced to *two* actions – a 33 per cent increase in productivity!

The key customer manager selling essentially a commodity product has to search continuously for ways to differentiate the product from that of the competition – by packaging, service and usage. In addition because, by definition, the market is likely to be price-led, it is important to be able to match the highest levels of production efficiency and the lowest costs of production in the industry in order to exert influence on pricing levels.

THE INFLUENCE OF THE QUALITY MOVEMENT

The 1980s saw the movement of corporate thinking towards refocusing on the core business and divesting the portfolio businesses acquired in the previous 20 years. Striving for excellence was the keynote of the decade and the quality movement became a unifying link between all the business functions. The quality onus was moved onto the supplier and new forms of buyer–seller relationships began to emerge. In the 1990s this relationship was reflected in the new emphasis on key account management and, with new Internet technology, has now blossomed into customer relationship management. In many businesses, multifunction customer teams

have emerged as key influential elements in corporate politics –
teams dedicated to a small group of key customers or even a single
key customer. Every senior manager, irrespective of function, is
seconded to one or more of these teams. The emphasis has moved
from finding customers for products to finding products for
customers. The vision comes from the top, but the corporate plan is
put together bottom-up.

Customer-driven marketing

From 1960 to 1990, marketers struggled to define what they do. It is
interesting to note the subtle change of emphasis as marketing moved
along its own experience curve from a mechanistic approach to one
firmly rooted in human behaviour.

1960 'The performance of business activities that direct the flow of
goods and services from producer to user' (American
Marketing Association)

Product

1967 'The analyzing, organizing, planning and controlling of the
firm's customer-impinging resources, policies and activities
with a view to satisfying the needs and wants of chosen
customer groups at a profit.' (Philip Kotler, *Marketing
Management*, 1st edition, Prentice Hall, 1967)

Sales

1980 'The human activity directed at satisfying needs and wants
through exchange processes' (Philip Kotler, *Marketing
Management*, 4th edition, Prentice Hall, 1980)

channel

1985 'The process of planning and executing the conception,
pricing, promotion and distribution of ideas, goods and
services to create exchanges that satisfy individual and
organisational objectives' (American Marketing Association)

marketing

1990 'A social and managerial process by which individuals and
groups obtain what they need and want through creating,
offering and exchanging products of value with others'
(Philip Kotler, *Marketing Management,* 7th edition, Prentice
Hall, 1990)

Service

(handwritten: Customer)

1991 'The business task of establishing, maintaining and enhancing customer relationships at a profit' (Philip Kotler (conference quote, Brussels 1991))

GAINING AND SUSTAINING COMPETITIVE ADVANTAGE

The new dynamics of the successful company are fuelled by gaining and sustaining *competitive advantage* in the perceptions of our target customers. Relationship building with key customers depends not merely upon charismatic selling. In any marriage, even the power of love can be strained if basic tangible benefits are not evident. The customer continuously needs a solid justification for preferring you as a supplier; there has to be a perceived competitive advantage.

Competitive advantage is created in two ways:

- *cost leadership* permitting pricing policies that enable your target customers to compete in their markets;

- *distinctive competence* giving your target customers a competitive edge in their markets.

As described in Chapter 1, it is necessary for suppliers to *position* themselves according to their customers' purchasing strategies which, in turn, are determined by aspects of technical and financial significance. In practice this poses the question: does the supplier go for cost leadership or distinctive competence?

Cost leadership strategy

Cost leadership, resulting from production efficiencies, economies of scale, use of resources, value engineering and constant attention to driving down costs will enable suppliers to lead market pricing and, if necessary, beat those who erode the key customer base by price-cutting without necessarily selling cheap products or sacrificing their own added-values. We are all part of a much longer value chain that is only as strong as its weakest link and, in highly competitive industries, the strength of the chain is only as good as the realization of its members that they have to help each other – supplier and customer – to compete effectively, so that a supplier's cost leadership, reflected in their prices, enables *customers* to be the cost leaders in *their* marketplaces.

If cost leadership is to be your chosen strategic thrust, it is essential for key customer managers to understand the cost infrastructure of both customers and their own company. The aim is to provide acceptable quality at the lowest possible delivered cost and to use that cost efficiency to deter competitors from engaging in price-cutting penetration strategies. To these ends, it is vital to understand the main leverage points for cost advantage, which will differ from industry to industry and company to company. In general terms, the cost structure for a manufacturing company will differ greatly from a professional service company (see Table 2.1).

From the data in Table 2.1, it is not unreasonable to assume that, in the manufacturing industry, the main cost drivers will be found in the operational area, and factors of standard specifications and volume usage of plant capacity will loom large in any cost calculations to do with special partnerships with customers – both from the supplier's and customer's point of view.

The relevance to the customer's cost structure will determine the degree of importance attached to the supplier's product or service.

In professional services, attracting and keeping the best quality human resources assumes not only significant cost proportions but is

Table 2.1 Differences in company cost structures

Costs	Manufacturing company	Professional service company
Human resource development	2%	20%
Technology development	9%	8%
Procurement function	1%	–
Inbound logistics	3%	7%
Operations	68%	21%
Outbound logistics	1%	5%
Marketing and sales	6%	26%
After-sales service	1%	–
Corporate overhead	9%	13%
Total costs	100%	100%

critical to performance quality. Full utilization of these human resources and making sure that all their time is appropriately invoiced is one of the key success factors. In addition, with high sales and marketing costs, one is targeting high-frequency automatic repeat business, rather than the one-off short project that will probably require just as much time to sell and negotiate.

In both cases, manufacturing and professional services, the relevance to the customer's cost structure will determine the degree of importance attached to the supplier's product or service.

Of course, to be the cost leader supplier, you must know what your competitors' costs are. For many manufacturing companies, the most obvious route to this information is to buy their competitors' product, strip it down and evaluate the cost which, in fact, is common practice in the automobile industry. Indeed, the study of competition is now a commonplace mainstream activity, to the extent that many companies regularly run recruitment campaigns for the express purpose of securing business intelligence from rival concerns.

The major players will have people who eat, breathe and sleep their competitors; not only the products but the cultures and priorities. How much does competitor A need that contract? How far will they be prepared to go to get it?

No major player will go into a negotiation for a large contract without a simulation of their competitors' bids, prepared in detail by dedicated staff, and it is not uncommon for a major player to employ a 'spoiler' whose job it is to fill up competitors' capacity with low margin work by bidding down the price on contracts and then withdrawing.

> If you are the Goliath, it is dangerous to let the Davids get a
> foothold in your key customer's business.

A cost-leadership strategy will depend largely upon the size of the supplier and, although leapfrog technology can wipe out the experience curve overnight, production costs usually benefit from the economies of scale. However, a specialized small supplier, perhaps operating in a modest geographical area with a limited product range and lower overheads, may outperform the larger company on unit cost. The volume of business gained might be too insignificant relatively or too unattractive to result in price retaliation from the major supplier. If you are the Goliath in this situation, it is dangerous to let the Davids get a foothold in your key customer's business. Good principles of relationship management permit early detection of intrusion by the Davids.

Distinctive competence strategy

Distinctive competence results from innovation, responsiveness to customer needs and frequent small, but customer-driven, improvements. The customer perceives that the total 'augmented' package you offer is distinctively more advantageous than that offered by your competitor and therein lies the value of committed relationship management; your position as 'preferred supplier' places you on the inside track in a unique position to monitor and respond promptly to your customer's changing needs and you set the benchmark of performance by which any competitive marauder will be judged.

A differentiated position on competence may be achieved by superior service, better product quality, uniquely tailored products or services, innovative features, strong brand names or the strength of your distributor network. It may be internally driven by capitalizing on your core competences or correcting your areas of weakness; it may be externally driven by quick responses to customer needs or competitor developments.

A small but very customer-driven supplier of paper to printers in the UK gives selected customers – in an industry not famous for forward planning – a one-hour delivery promise. When warehouse pressures threaten this commitment, a loud red bell in the office summons all the staff, including the owner, accountant, secretary *et al.*, to help with moving paper into the vans. Only one telephonist remains upstairs. That is what being customer-driven means.

Amongst the customer-driven Goliaths, Mobil Oil, supplier of lubricants and greases to industry, when making overtures to a large customer uses golfing terminology in determining what it calls the 'bogey' figure – that is, the total current spend on competitor's products by that customer. Although Mobil's price per unit for their product may be higher than that of the competition, a detailed technical application plan is drawn up with the aim of 'beating the bogey' – that is, delivering a lower annual spend on lubricants for that customer. This is not achieved by price adjustment but by reviewing grades, specifications, logistics, frequency of application – optimizing the way the customer uses the product.

How much is distinctive competence worth to the customer?

Acknowledged distinctive competence permits premium prices but necessitates added costs and selective investment to achieve high leverage of sources of advantage. An airline targeting business travellers must demonstrate competitive capability in punctuality, reliability, appropriate flight times and instant availability of seats. The on-cost of meeting punctuality and reliability standards means having excess capacity standing by in the event of technical malfunctions. Appropriate flight times mean increased frequencies and flying, perhaps, smaller less cost-efficient planes every hour on a prime route, rather than once a day. Enabling the business traveller to book seats at short notice inevitably means accepting that you will fly with some empty, but available, space. In addition to all this, the business traveller requires flexibility, which means having a sophisticated global computer reservation system. It has been estimated that any one of these factors adds up to 15 per cent to an airline's operating costs, but they are necessary just to stay in the target market.

Over a period of time, profitability will depend in part on the sustainability of your competitive advantage. Sustainability depends on building relationships with the key customer and, if possible, creating exit barriers or switching costs to deter defection to competitors. In the case of the airlines, they lock in the frequent business traveller with promotions based on accumulated air mileage and selective membership of executive clubs with special lounge facilities. The car-rental companies attempt to get their plastic card in your wallet so that you go directly to *their* desk at airports, because they have all your personal details on file and much of that tedious form-filling is obviated. The supermarkets recognize good spenders through loyalty cards and can track and remind customers of their regular product purchases.

It is how the saving, be it time or money, is invested
that yields the real benefits for the customer.

Pursuit of competitive advantage, whether cost-driven or competence-driven, is a continuous process which, if well planned and successful, is self-reinforcing. Achieving advantage should generate customer loyalty, satisfaction and profitability which, in turn, make possible increased investment in superior skills and resources, which strengthen one's competitive position.

Such positioning, however, is not quite so simple. Competing on price and demonstrating distinctive competence are interdependent. For the customer the question is 'how much is distinctive competence worth?'. This combination of cost and competence may be described as 'value-driven'.

Value-driven strategy

A value-driven strategy is the key to stability and mutual gain with key customers. For this it is necessary to quantify what your product or service is worth to your customer – how much value the customer is getting over and above the price that is paid. The price is that part of the customer value that is capturable (CCV) and will depend on how your customer perceives what makes you different from your competitors.

With some products, it is not too difficult to demonstrate how better performance, fewer rejects, more accuracy and so on can yield financial advantages, but turning quality, service or reputation into numbers can be more difficult. Usually the main thrust of such advantages is the financial penalty of living with less reliable quality or service. In other words, a premium price is a form of insurance policy for the customer.

In attempting to put these matters in perspective, one should:

■ always use the customer's own data or estimates if one is going to extrapolate figures or put a price on possible mistakes;

■ focus on the effect on the customer's *revenues* rather than the *costs,* if appropriate: a new product that reduces a customer's machine downtime may save a few *hundred* dollars in operating costs, but may *generate thousands* of dollars in extra production. People are more likely to respond more actively to large, fat numbers, and the notion of 'saving' usually undersells the true value of products, services and ideas. It is how the saving, be it time or money, is invested that yields the real benefits for the customer.

Competitive advantage may be customer-perceived distinctive competences such as superior value or lower costs for industrial customers and increased market share or enhanced profitability for reseller customers. It may be all of these separately or collectively. The aim of relationship management is to organize integrated actions that produce *sustainable* advantages over competitors who may overperform at higher cost or underperform by not specifically meeting customer needs.

Suppliers must understand fully some of the pitfalls of going for the value-driven option. These include:

- creating differences that buyers do not value
- pricing in excess of values delivered
- failure to understand the real cost of differentiation (and not building it into the price)
- looking only to the 'core product' as the basis of differentiation and ignoring intangible aspects of service and support.

This latter point is especially important. With familiarity, the customer becomes accustomed to the special levels of service that you provide and may lose appreciation of the privileges that the relationship as a preferred customer imparts. The supplier must continue to reinforce in the customer's mind the costs and benefits of the less visible aspects of their relationship and to regularly resell the competitive advantage.

Creating value-driven strategy means achieving value superiority by serving customers' needs better than competitors do. Five issues have to be addressed.

1 Who is the customer? (We have to understand the customer's decision-making processes and identify exactly who in the customer's organization we have to convince of the value of our products/services.)

2   What values are the decision-makers seeking?

3   Will these customers perceive these values and be prepared to pay a premium for them?

4   Can we deliver these values better than our competition?

5   How can we enhance our position and achieve more meaningful value superiority?

Customer-perceived value consists of benefits that increase gross profit by

■ improving performance

■ increasing sales

■ reducing operating costs

■ reducing working capital needs

■ reducing risk

or reduce the investment cost of your product over its life cycle by

■ lowering purchase prices

■ lowering installation and set-up costs

■ lowering maintenance costs

■ lowering financing costs

■ lowering disposal costs.

How to develop competitive advantages

Advantages can be developed by either competitor-based thinking or by customer-based thinking. Competitor-based strategy is geared to superior quality, innovative technology, broader distribution, wider product ranges, superior technical service and better reputation and image. Customer-based strategy is geared to customer problem-solving which may include improved reliability, lower operating costs, faster response, one-stop shopping or quality assurance. The difference is how you measure the advantage – against the yardstick of competitor performance or against the benchmark of current customer productivity.

There are four steps to brainstorming competitive advantage:

1 identify alternative advantage positions;

2 screen the options; are they
   - meaningful; will the customer perceive the advantage?
   - credible; will the customer *believe* the advantage (given our past performance and reputation)?
   - unique, relative to the competition?
   - contributing to our long-term objectives?

3 select the option, making sure the organization understands and commits to delivering the advantage;

4 design implementation programmes and identify the key success factors critical to achievement of the perceived competitive advantage.

In the final analysis, success is determined by how clearly the customer can define how we differ from the competitor; the simple words that complete the phrase 'you are the supplier who …'.

Texas Instruments and Hewlett Packard are good examples of companies with strategic profiles at almost opposite ends of the spectrum. Texas Instruments was founded on the principle of gaining competitive advantage in large standard markets based on a long production run–low-cost position; their targets are high volume and low price with cost-driven experience curve manufacturing. Their finances are aggressively resourced and extended. Their people are competitive and motivated by individual incentives.

In contrast Hewlett Packard focuses on selected small markets based on unique, high-value products which are designed for performance. They are financially conservative with no debt. The team concept is of prime importance and is reflected in the format of their bonus schemes. Hewlett Packard's growth has been controlled, whereas Texas Instrument's early rapid growth was based upon the total belief in 'motoring down the experience curve', that is, pursuing a research and development programme to turn assumptions about high-volume economies of scale into a reality.

> Is it market share that helps profit or profitability that helps
> to promote market share?

Well-documented research such as Profit Impact on Marketing Strategy (PIMS) has established a strong correlation of market share with return on investment (ROI) although nobody is quite sure whether it is market share that helps profit or profitability that helps to promote market share.

Motivating your organization

Whether cost-driven or value-driven, gaining and sustaining competitive advantage perceived and responded to by your key customers is not a mechanistic process. Attitudes make for positive relationships and the personal dynamics of your organization can make or break the frail web of trust and co-operation that is a supplier partnership.

Everybody in your organization must be customer-driven; even those people who never come into contact with the actual customer must orient their thinking to understand that, whatever function they are involved in, they do actually have *customers*. The janitor has customers, the finance department has customers – they are *internal* customers, but they are still customers. If these customers are shabbily treated, they may pass their negative reactions on to the external customers – the real customers of the business. Everybody in the business is part of the customer chain and one dramatic jolt can reverberate down the line with unfortunate results.

The organization can only deliver the level of customer satisfaction that company morale permits.

So, how can the people in the organization be motivated to 'delight' the customer? Some of the things that contribute to a competitive service edge are:

- involvement of employees in decision making, delegation of responsibility and recognition of individual initiative;
- broader job descriptions that give employees understanding of the context of their job and the impact and value of their work on other work areas;
- cutting out management layers and increasing interaction between workers and management and workers with each other;
- task forces on key issues and quality or productivity projects;

- more sensitive recognition of employee status, and profit-sharing motivation;

- effective informal communication and information dissemination;

- customer satisfaction measurement and wider input to employee performance reviews (why not ask the customers what they think of your employees?).

All these factors will contribute to customer-driven attitudes and may help to explain why morale differs from one company to another.

An article in *Management International* (April 1991) diagnosed a perhaps even more fundamental malaise. It suggested that the contrast between a relatively lacklustre UK (at that time) and some more buoyant European economies might have something to do with the fact that, for example, the average German company distributes more than 75 per cent of the added-value it creates to its employees in the form of wages whereas the average UK company with a comparative figure of 60 per cent comes bottom of the European league. 'Value' or 'added-value' is wage costs plus profits before interest and depreciation. In the UK, the average investor share of value created is almost three times that in Germany.

> The surprised reaction of the directors at these self-evident working problems serves to highlight the management myopia in which many companies still operate.

Graef S. Crystal, an American compensation consultant, asserts that American chief executives in the last 20 years have increased their pay by 400 per cent in real terms, whilst workers' pay has stagnated (*In Search of Excess: The Overcompensation of American Executives*, WWNorton & Co.). American executives earn 160 times more than the average worker while their German counterparts earn 21 times more. In Japan the figure is a mere 16 times more than the average worker. Japanese chief executive officers average $300 000 per year in contrast with the *average* American equivalent's phenomenal $2.8 million. In many cases, this figure is *not* performance-related and may be classified not only as excessive but also undeserved. In addition, perhaps the huge amount of such remuneration puts the average chief executive out of touch with the working environment and how the average worker lives.

A recent TV series in the UK featured an experiment in which a number of chief executives spent a week working on the 'shop floor' of their various enterprises. One such individual, a charming man with an IT background from a major national removal company, discovered that a significant percentage of the workforce was still regarded as temporary casual labour, even after ten years of service. Other revelations he made to a wide-eyed board of directors included time wastage due to lack of mobile telephones in the trucks, the unsuitability of cheap hand trolleys for moving furniture and the inability of the centralized customer sales centre to cope with enquiry traffic. The surprised reaction of the directors at these self-evident working problems serves to highlight the management myopia in which many companies still operate. With this 'half-man, half-desk' management style, perhaps we can only expect the level of motivation, service and commitment from employees that we deserve!

Sadly, this morale-eroding discrimination between the aims of owners, chief executives and employees also can generate pressure for instant results and short-term returns – whereas the pay-off for building relationships through effective relationship management tends to be on a longer-term agenda.

SUMMARY

Marketing is only now maturing into a fully integrated function that is beginning to make customer-first theories really happen. Customer relationship management is at the forefront of this integration because it is creating stronger bonds with selected customers and this puts new emphasis on the need to achieve competitive advantage and distinctive competence in the perceptions of the customers. Purchasers, too, are introducing techniques to be selective about their suppliers in order to optimize the use of resources and create collaborative synergy for mutual benefit. Selection of preferred suppliers may be based on an evaluation of their financial and technical significance to the customer. For relationship management to work effectively, both parties – supplier and customer – need a mutual interest in collaboration and investment.

Relationship-building strategies can only be effective where there are tangible, sustained and relevant advantages over competition. These advantages are derived from cost leadership and/or distinctive competences which create added-value for the customer. The closer the working relationship, the more the supplier can reinforce the competitive advantage. A creative relationship in which the supplier is continuously reviewing the augmented product may be the main distinctive competence in situations where the product is essentially a commodity.

But most importantly, a competitive service edge depends upon a motivated workforce. Motivation goes hand-in-hand with involvement and customer management teams are the most effective means yet devised for involving workers at all levels in all functions at the sharp end of the business.

How much do you really know about your customers?

SELF EVALUATION

Before moving on to the next chapter, consider what sort of business is the best fit with your company? How significant is the contribution made by these customer relationship factors to the achievement of your company objectives?

Scale 1 = low importance, 5 = high importance	1	2	3	4	5
1 volume or revenue potential					
2 profit potential					
3 profit timescale					
4 potential customer growth (their business)					
5 long term supply probability					
6 relevant seasonal variation of demand (or lack of variation)					
7 standard products (for economies of scale)					
8 long production run batch orders					
9 wide range of relevant products used					
10 customer's market reputation and image (for referral business)					
11 customer's business attitude					
12 logistics of supply (uncomplicated distribution needs)					
13 need for support resources (technical, time, finance)					
14 geographical spread of customer (matching your operations)					
15 customer's financial strength and speed of payment					
16 strength of the competition for your customer's business					
17 Other factors					

WHAT IS A KEY CUSTOMER?

What gives a customer particular importance to your business? For most suppliers, the significant factor is that the customer contributes, or has the potential to contribute, sizeable revenue or profit. If this is the only basis for identifying the customers into which time and resources are to be invested, it might appear that the selection and targeting of customers is self-evident. And for some suppliers this is indeed so, for the infrastructure of their industries will dictate their priorities. Any mass-production food supplier in the UK has to target the top five supermarket chains if the company has any aspirations to market share. Aeroplane builders have limited, clearly defined outlets for their products. In some countries of the world, medical and pharmaceutical companies will have only a major customer, such as the National Health Service (NHS) in the UK, for their products. Yet, even within these industries, there is a degree of choice determined by probability of success. There will be different synergies with each grocery buyer; each airline has a different timescale for re-equipping and there is a great variety in size and influence of different hospitals and general practices in the NHS.

Your purpose is to define the type of business that you need to achieve your corporate objectives and the customers where such business is available. Your corporate objectives will embrace not only revenue and profit but also the direction of your business; new markets; new technologies; geographic expansion; new products and survival. You are seeking to exert a measure of control over your customer base. Start by asking yourself the questions:

■ what changes in your customer base have taken place over the last five years?

■ were the changes planned?

■ how does *your* rate of business growth compare with the growth rate of your customers?

■ do you control your business or does your business control you?

Key customer management is about volume, revenue and profit but goes further than large or major customer management in that it embraces all aspects of corporate planning, growth and survival.

Each key customer is, in effect, a market segment. We have to develop a process to evaluate objectively our actual and potential customer portfolio using the same principles as we use for market segmentation. This evaluation process is based on the *attractiveness* of a customer, or contract, and a realistic assessment of our probability of success with that customer, or contract, determined by our *current relationship status* with that customer

The criteria by which we are going to measure the *attractiveness* of our customers and our *current relationship status* with the customer must be agreed. These two measurements will be used as the basis of a matrix which will display our customer portfolio, actual and potential, and from which we will agree the broad strategy for each main customer and how our resources will be allocated to best effect.

This is the broad principle of customer strategic planning although there will be variances for different types of business (there are examples in the Exhibits to this chapter). The criteria you agree are specific to your business and each actual or potential customer is measured against those criteria.

Ongoing successful relationships will need greater operational flexibility and investment in new products, maybe even in new organizations and business skills. The implications of these changes make it mandatory to put some careful strategic thinking into the selection of those potential customers with whom such relationships are to be developed.

HOW DO YOU PRIORITIZE KEY CUSTOMERS?

In assessing what type of business is attractive, the objective is to find a match between your business strengths, or potential business strengths, and the specific customers who have needs and values that can be satisfied by your business strengths. Key customers are not always mass-market, national or even global customers. They might be key customers because their policies have considerable influence on their respective industries or because they are recognized technical innovators, monitored and copied by their peers. In evaluating customer attractiveness, two categories of matching attributes may be considered – *demographics* and *psychographics*.

Demographics

These are the physical characteristics of the buying/selling environment. They are the tangible benefits of the relationship and relate particularly to the competitive advantages or strategic thrust demonstrated
by the supplier (such as price, performance, quality or brand strength).

The demographic focus will be strongly influenced by the potential
for sales, profits and growth as demonstrated by using Pareto analysis.
Vilfredo Pareto was an Italian economist at the end of the nineteenth
century who first developed Pareto's Law to describe the concentration
of wealth and income in Italy. Sometimes it is called the 80:20 rule and
may be summarized as: 80 per cent of the results arise from 20 per cent
of the possible causes. Thus, in many companies 80 per cent of the
revenue will come from 20 per cent of the customer base, 80 per cent of
the profit will derive from 20 per cent of the products, 80 per cent of the
problems are created by 20 per cent of the people, and so on.

In consumer advertising, the Pareto effect is recognized in product
usage and is referred to as 'the heavy half', i.e., a high percentage of
product is used by only half the total purchasers. A US study of
media and markets by Simmons Market Research Bureau identified
'the heavy half' effect in users of cola, beer, bourbon, soap and toilet
tissue, amongst others.

- Cola : users 67 per cent (light half 17 per cent; heavy half 83 per cent)

- Beer : users 41 per cent (light half 13 per cent; heavy half 87 per
  cent)

- Bourbon : users 20 per cent (light half 5 per cent; heavy half 95 per
  cent)

- Soap : users 94 per cent (light half 25 per cent; heavy half 75 per
  cent)

- Toilet tissue : users 95 per cent (light half 29 per cent; heavy half
  71 per cent)

A bemused reader might speculate on the toilet tissue data. Why
should one half of the consumers use so much more toilet tissue per
capita than the other half of the population? Separate sources of
research reveal not some disturbing evidence of bowel disorder
amongst 50 per cent of consumers, but a difference of methodology.

Apparently half of us fold toilet tissue to use it, whilst the remaining half are crumplers and thus use more than twice as much. I have no explanation for the 5% of non-users!

With this form of segmentation, advertisers will focus their promotion and effort on heavy-half users for cost-effectiveness. As key customer managers, we may have to identify the heavy half customers, or potential customers, in our industry, unless we are positioned as a niche player or have other corporate objectives.

For example, the tobacco companies have continued to support the many thousands of small, independent confectionery, tobacco and newsagents shops (CTNs) giving few, if any, additional discounts, bonuses or similar concessions to multiples. The multiples, although worthwhile, have never assumed a dominant position relative to the large volume going through the CTNs. The effect of ceasing to trade with any single multiple was not disastrous and the tobacco suppliers were able to impose relatively stringent terms and conditions on these large customers.

Psychographics

These are the values and attitudes shared by suppliers and customers. They are the more intangible aspects of a relationship such as negotiating style, co-operation on problems, helpfulness and response speed when things go wrong. Psychographics define individuals as well as companies and, by segmenting your customer universe in terms of values and attitudes, you are taking the first step in the relationship thinking that is the core concept of relationship management.

Psychographic factors contributed in a major way to how one US electrical equipment supplier delineated its target customers and organized its sales effort. More than 7000 actual or potential customers were classified into four categories:

1 loyal customers – who perceived the company's product as *much superior* to a competitor's product;

2 competitive customers – who perceived the company's product as *slightly superior* to a competitor's product;

3 switchable customers – who perceived a competitor's product as *slightly superior* to the company's products;

4 competitor loyal customers – who perceived a competitor as *much superior* to the company's product.

The country was divided into three sales regions and general advertising was cut back dramatically. One region continued with the old sales strategy but received its share of the saved resources. The other two regions cut back on overall sales call frequency and formed a key customer team operating at regional level and targeting the *competitive* and *switchable* customers.

In a year in which industry sales declined by 15 per cent, the company's success in gaining contracts endorsed the new strategy. The results for the two reorganized regions compared with the one region that stayed with the old system are shown in Table 3.1.

Table 3.1   Comparison of results of old and new sales strategies

Customer categories	New strategy	Old strategy
Overall market	+15%	–10%
Loyal customers	–3%	+3%
Competitive customers	+22%	–9%
Switchable customers	+12%	–18%
Competitor loyal customers	–4%	–4%

In an array of positive achievements, it may be all too easy to point out the small percentage loss in the 'loyal customer' classification. As in so many companies, the pressure is so often focused on *new* business and *new* customers. This is reflected not only in sales bulletin headlines (one never sees headlines about contracts being *renewed* for next year), but also in the structure of sales remuneration that rewards expansion but less frequently recognizes the maintenance of 'status quo' relationships with key customers. Complacency is the hidden cancer of relationship management.

Customer attractiveness

In terms of the demographic and psychographic implications, there are four key areas to consider when setting out your criteria for customer attractiveness:

- the customer's business
- the customer's products/services
- the competition for the customer's business
- the potential for mutual profitability

Customer's business

- *Volume*

  Is there enough volume? Is your business volume-driven? Is the volume to be shipped to one location or many? What is the product mix? Is it in one large order or is volume fragmented into many orders involving complex administration? How do the peaks and troughs of customer demand fit into your production capacity? Are the products involved standard or specials? Will the level or type of volume affect business with other key customers? Is the volume too big a commitment to one customer for your company?

- *Customer growth*

  Is the customer's rate of growth in line with their industry? How does the customer's rate of growth compare with other customers? Is the customer growing too fast for their financial stability or management resources? What are the implications of growth in terms of pressure on future margins in the relationship?

- *International potential*

  If *your* business is international, is there international compatibility between the businesses? Do your businesses operate in the same international markets? Are the customer's decision centres located internationally where you can cost-effectively serve them? Are the customer's product and service specifications similar in different markets?

- *Seasonality and trade cycles*

  Is there seasonality built into the customer's demand – month-to-month, year-to-year? What external factors are likely to affect your customer's business – currency, legislation, raw material availability, competition, politics?

■ *Relations with suppliers*
What are the customer's attitudes to suppliers – win-win, win-lose? Is there evidence of loyalty by the customer? Does the customer appreciate loyalty? What quality expectations and systems does the customer have? To what extent will the customer want to be involved with your methods and procedures?

■ *Organization fit*
What are the relative sizes of the two companies? Is the customer too large, too small, too complex or just not your style? Is there an aggravation factor dealing with this customer?

■ *Image*
Is there any 'image' spin-off from being a supplier to this customer? Will there be referral opportunities?

Customer's products/services

■ *The product life cycle*
At what life cycle stage is the customer's product and how is this likely to affect purchasing policies and pricing expectations, present and future? At what stage is your product life cycle and what are the implications for your pricing expectations?

■ *Product complexity*
Can the customer cope with the complexity of your product? What are the educational and training costs of introducing your product?

■ *Added-value potential*
Does your product create added-value for your customer's business? Is the added-value sufficient to give you scope for premium pricing?

■ *Technology*
Can the key customer use and value your special expertise and the technology of your product? Will the relationship permit enhancement and development of your technology? Will you benefit from the customer's experience?

- *Differentiation*
  Will the key customer perceive your product or service as different from others?

- *Exclusivity*
  Will you be the sole supplier in your field to this customer? How acceptable is sole-supplier status to the customer?

Competition for the customer's business

- *Concentration*
  How many serious players are there competing for this key customer business or contract? How well are existing suppliers entrenched?

- *Capacity and need*
  How well is the competitive capacity suited and available for this key customer business? To what extent does competition want or need the business?

- *Barriers to entry*
  How effectively are new players restricted from this business due to costs, stocks, regulations, training and so on?

- *Exit barriers*
  How difficult will it be to dislodge existing suppliers?

- *Price sensitivity*
  How easily could the share of the business be influenced by future price changes?

- *Influence sensitivity*
  How easily could the share of the business be influenced by quality, service, reliability and other factors?

- *Vertical integration*
  How significant is the risk that the customer might develop own resources to provide your product or service in the future?

Potential for mutual profitability

- *Customer's profitability*
  Does this key customer make a healthy profit? What is the trend in share-price, cashflow and credit standing?

- *Customer's cost structure*

  Does the cost infrastructure of this customer favour you as a supplier? How significant in terms of cost is your product or service to this customer? What is the relationship of fixed and variable costs? How much debt is the customer financing and what are the implications of changing interest rates and inflation?

- *Scope for improvement*

  Can you improve the performance, profitability or efficiency of this customer's business? If so, how significantly? Have you access to information about performance? What are their current financial and management ratios?

- *Effect on your gross margins*

  Will this key customer improve your average gross margins? How soon will you see this improvement? Will this business have positive financial impact on critical areas of your business (e.g. problem products, underperforming locations)?

- *Resources*

  How much extra resource commitment will be necessary to secure this business? Are these resources readily available? Will your resource allocation to other customers be negatively affected?

OTHER IMPLICATIONS IN EVALUATING ATTRACTIVENESS

The pursuit of market share and the product life cycle concept might significantly affect how you measure attractiveness and your key customer strategy. So much has been written over the past 40 years by heavyweight marketers on these subjects that some of the basic ideas have been obscured and distorted. Market share has become a god in its own right and become detached from its context, without which it becomes meaningless. It might be argued that the life cycles for many products are now so short that the evolving stages are too brief to have any real significance. However, let us reiterate the basic tenets, with particular regard for the implications for customer relationship management.

Market share

The awareness of the importance of market share probably started in the 1930s when the newly emerging science of time and motion study became linked with the new industry of aircraft building in the US. The realization that every time the experience of building an aircraft was repeated the task was more efficiently and cost-effectively done gave rise to the idea of the experience curve. The improvement in productivity was even quantified. Every time the accumulated volume of experience doubles, the unit cost should decrease by between 15 per cent and 25 per cent. For example, if you had built 100 motorcycles and your 100th machine costs you $1000 to manufacture, your 200th machine should cost you $800 (1000 – 20 per cent), your 400th machine should cost you $640 ($800 – 20 per cent) and your 800th machine should cost you $512, or 20 per cent less than your 400th cycle.

It will be evident that, because doubling your previous accumulated experience becomes progressively more difficult to do, the reduction in unit cost is harder to achieve. Graphically depicted, the experience curve shows steep and dramatic cost reductions in the early stages but the curve flattens out as increased economies of scale become more difficult to achieve.

Herein lies the first caveat. Reducing unit cost will only happen if it is *made* to happen. It does not happen automatically. Theoretically, the company with the largest accumulated experience should enjoy the lowest unit cost and be in a position to defend itself against any lesser aggressor by virtue of being the lowest-cost producer, but high market-share companies sometimes become complacent and do not achieve the economies of scale that generate the incomes that can be reinvested in promotion or product development.

> When the market has matured and total demand has ceased to grow, your competitor cannot grow market share without stealing it from you.

At the time when British Oxygen enjoyed a virtual monopoly of industrial gas supplies in the UK, it should not have been viable for an American competitor to enter the British market. But they did and they succeeded because British Oxygen had not driven down their costs in line with the scale of their operation. Air Products not only succeeded because of the inefficiencies of their competitor, but also because they mounted a selective key customer campaign, cherry-picking their target customers and leaving British Oxygen with a host of geographically dispersed outlets with lower volumes and higher distribution costs. The past 20 years has seen the gradual break-up of British Oxygen, the component parts of which will possibly end up in the hands of their former French and, ironically, American rivals.

The idea of market share is that volume means lower unit costs, which permits investment in lower prices, product development or extra promotion which, in turn, builds market share. This is particularly important in the early stages of market growth where the economies of scale are more dramatic, but the real pay-off is when the market has matured and total demand has ceased to grow. Your competitor cannot grow his market share without stealing from you. As market leader with the lowest production costs, your position should be highly defensible. Indeed, your cost edge should enable you to influence, if not control, market pricing and reap the real harvest of your product investment. The race is over and you have crossed the line first.

The trick is to achieve economies of scale with flexibility of production.

But, in the twenty-first century, are these simplistic notions still valid? Market share as an argument is still valid in persuading retailers to stock your brand or resellers to prefer your product. Economies of scale make sense in production terms but the customer now expects differentiation and customization. The trick is to achieve economies of scale with flexibility of production, that is, to produce standard components that can be assembled in a permutation of different ways.

Ford have succeeded for years in producing a considerable permutation of models with three or four basic body shells. Dauphin, a Lancashire-based international office furniture manufacturer, have made substantial inroads into the market with an office chair whose five components – castors, adjustable stem, seat, arms and backrest – each come in a limited number of choices, that assemble together in a modular fashion to create a chair unique to individual distributors or even customers.

In many industries, leapfrog technology has devalued the experience curve and the advantages of production scale are, not infrequently, counterbalanced by the consequent relative slowness in adapting quickly to change. Philips lost much of their presence in the domestic television market by their inability to respond to styling changes that resulted from the introduction of the flat screen television. Kodak resolutely stuck to its film base while the world moved to computer images. Shower manufacturer Mira declined to take up an offer of an innovative thermostatic valve from its inventor, who consequently set up Aqualisa and gained a major market share.

Size *does* matter in cost-driven industries, but it is not *absolute* size but size relative to the competition that is critical.

Frequently small is not only beautiful but also flexible. Size *does* matter in cost-driven industries, but it is not *absolute* size but size relative to the competition that is critical. A marginal size advantage is unlikely to generate the cost differences that are fundamental to the market-share argument.

Further weaknesses of the market-share concept lie in how the market is defined and the fact that major players in a market may belong to a conglomerate operating in multiple markets with financial resources to buy up short- and medium-term advantage and sustain price wars.

Life cycles

The life cycle concept suggests that products and markets have a demand life cycle, the stages of which influence strategy and tactics, especially in matters of pricing and profitability. The cycle is usually a flat S-shape (although several other shapes have been recognized) and consists of four distinct stages – introduction, growth, maturity and decline. In managing key customers, an understanding of the implications of these stages for their businesses and the likely effect on their purchasing policies and relationships is essential.

During the *introduction* stage of a product, a business is likely to have slow growth and minimal, or even negative, profits. As a key customer, this customer is likely to make demands on suppliers for technical modifications, speculative tooling investment and anything that will reduce the short-term financial burden. This might include jointly financed promotion or technical development, extended credit terms, consignment stocks, sale-or-return arrangements and so on. The pricing policy of the key customer in the marketplace will affect the financial strain – penetration pricing policies being more demanding than price-skimming tactics.

The *growth* stage is marked by a rapid sales surge and increasing profits that may be ploughed back to finance the growth and fight off the competition attracted by the growth dynamics of the market. The key customer may reduce its market prices, improve the product or enter a wider range of market segments and distribution channels.

Any supportive actions by suppliers in these areas may well be rewarded when the customer's product successfully enters the *maturity* stage when sales growth slows down but profits begin to stabilize. The company will seek new innovative strategies to renew sales growth, including product and marketing mix modifications. By this time, the supplier's product and service should be locked into the customer's specification and the supplier should be enjoying an appropriate share of the profits.

Finally, the customer's product enters the *decline* stage, in which little can be done to halt the deterioration of sales and profits. The customer and supplier have to identify the truly weak products and for each one develop an appropriate strategy of continuation, focusing on milking or phasing out a weak product in a way that minimizes the loss to both parties.

All four stages have implications for suppliers:

- the *introduction* stage is a risk stage, when the supplier has to decide on the probability of success and the resources that have to be invested;

- the *growth* stage calls for decisions on capacity commitment and extension, as well as careful volume and price calculations;

- participation in the *maturity* stage profit harvest will depend upon the indispensability of the supplier's product to the customer and on resisting the temptation to abuse that dependence in the interests of future co-operation on new products;

- the pain of continuing the supply of a less-profitable product during the *decline* stage may have to be traded off against the prospect of further collaborations on new products within a proven, well-established relationship.

Life-cycle analysis has applications for people as well as products. A new business may be started by an *innovator*, who single-handedly takes the business through the introduction stage. When the business moves into the growth stage, there are too many decisions to be made too quickly by one person and, after a major crisis, the management of the business may devolve to a number of task forces or functional managers led by a *co-ordinator*. As the business enters its maturity stage, the need may be for an *administrator* to prepare the company for profit-optimization. The onset of the decline stage may call for an *undertaker* to bury the enterprise with minimum consequences. People may then be moved into other projects designed to extend the company or product life.

If a business is targeted as a key customer whilst it is in the introduction stage, the relationship may be based upon working with a single autocratic individual entrepreneur. The key customer manager must foresee the growth stage when the autocratic entrepreneur will be deposed and will be sensibly building up a network of contacts with the future functional decision makers. From the onset of maturity, the future of the key customer is likely to be more in the hands of the financial managers and an effective customer manager will be laying plans for that change of authority long before the event.

All companies are part of an intricately balanced supply chain and the key customer manager must have some real appreciation of the implications of key customers' market position in the chain in terms of market share and life cycles of both products and people.

MEASURING THE CURRENT RELATIONSHIP STATUS WITH KEY CUSTOMERS

However attractive a customer may be, an investment decision can only be made after considering how realistic the chances are that a key customer partnership can be achieved. It might be quite unrealistic to expect to have an open, constructive relationship with a customer wholly owned by your competitor. For example, Procter & Gamble are active in the bakery and catering industry where several major customers are owned by Unilever – a decidedly limiting factor on penetration plans.

Measurement of your current relationship status with a customer will be both quantitative and qualitative, using criteria such as:

- your current share of the customer's business
- your share relevant to your main competitor's share
- the trend in your share over the last three years
- the extent to which your customer is locked into your product
- the customer's perception of your technical strength
- the customer's perception of your service
- the customer's perception of your price competitiveness
- the age of your relationship
- the breadth of your contact base
- the customer's attitude to your company.

It is possible that some items will appear on both your attractiveness and current relationship status criteria lists. For example, a significant share of the customer's business or a wide contact base might enhance attractiveness and also indicate a good relationship status.

CALCULATING ATTRACTIVENESS AND RELATIONSHIP STATUS SCORES

Step 1

The first step in this process is to agree two lists of criteria – one to measure attractiveness and the second to measure your current relationship status. Each list should be limited to ten criteria (unless the business is exceptionally complicated).

Step 2

The second step is to weight the criteria on each list on an agreed scale according to relative degree of importance. This is best done by group consensus, embracing all functions in the business. Several weighting methods might be used:

- the weighting of each criterion to be agreed separately on a scale, for example, 1–5
- the weighting to be spread across the ten factors adding up to a total of 25 (or some agreed number)
- weighting of the criteria in ranking order by using paired comparisons.

Although this last method is more statistically valid, in reality it is the discussion and exchange of ideas which is the real benefit of the process. Although each criterion should be differentiated, it should not be allowed a disproportionate weighting that will distort the overall score.

Step 3

Each individual customer is rated against the weighted criteria on each list using, perhaps, a 0–4 rating scale. A rating of 4 indicates a factor that fully meets the ideal requirements for the supplier. For example, rating 4 on all 10 factors on the attractiveness evaluation therefore represents the highest level of customer attractiveness possible for the supplier. For each criterion there needs to be a clear definition of what each rating on the agreed scale means. For example, the volume criteria might specify ranges of product volume, such as 0 = less than 50 tons, 1 = 51 to 99 tons, 2 = 100 to 199 tons, and so on.

Step 4

The fourth step is to multiply the rating (0–4) for each factor by its weighting (1–5) to produce a weighted score for that factor. By adding all ten weighted factor scores on the attractiveness list for each contract or key customer, an index of attractiveness is calculated. The higher the index of attractiveness, the better the fit between the interests of both the supplier and the customer. In the example in Table 3.2 the total weightings add up to 25 with a maximum rating of 4 on each factor, and the maximum total score will be 100. The same applies to the current relationship status evaluation.

Table 3.2   The attractiveness and current relationship status evaluation

Attractiveness of customer

Criteria	Weighting (1–5)	Customer A		Customer B	
		Rating (0–4)	Weighted score	Rating (0–4)	Weighted score
Sales potential	5	3	15	1	5
Current sales volume	2	1	2	2	4
Growth of demand	2	4	8	0	0
Profit margin	4	3	12	1	4
Market image	1	4	4	1	1
Long-term supply	3	3	9	1	3
Exclusivity of supply	2	2	4	3	6
Financial strength	2	4	8	2	4
Technology orientation	2	4	8	1	2
Logistics	2	3	6	2	4
TOTAL	25		76		33

Relationship status with customer

Criteria	Weighting (1–5)	Customer A		Customer B	
		Rating (0–4)	Weighted score	Rating (0–4)	Weighted score
Share of customer's purchases	5	1	5	3	15
Relative share/largest competitor	3	1	3	4	12
Share trend	2	1	2	3	6
Bredth of contact base	4	1	4	4	16
Age of relationship	3	3	9	4	12
Price competitiveness*	3	2	6	3	9
Quality compatitiveness*	2	2	4	2	4
Your image (brand) strength*	1	2	2	3	3
Your technical strength*	2	4	8	3	6
TOTAL	**25**		**43%**		**83%**

*as perceived by the customer

Table 3.2 shows the evaluations for customer A and customer B. We have a very average relationship strength position with customer A, who has a high attractiveness rating. In contrast, our relationship strength position with customer B, who has a relatively low attractiveness score, is impressively strong. What should be our strategy for these two customers in the future? That will depend on other relevant priorities in our customer portfolio and the availability of resources. By plotting the attractiveness and relationship status scores for, perhaps, our top 20 actual or potential customers or contracts on the nine-cell customer strategy grid below we can sort out the levels of priorities in our key customer database and appropriate strategies.

THE NINE-CELL CUSTOMER STRATEGY GRID

The vertical axis in Fig. 3.1 represents the customer's attractiveness, the criteria for which are based on such factors as volume, growth, competition, profitability and product fit, as described earlier. Each individual customer is rated against each weighted criterion resulting in a classification of high, medium or low attractiveness for that specific customer.

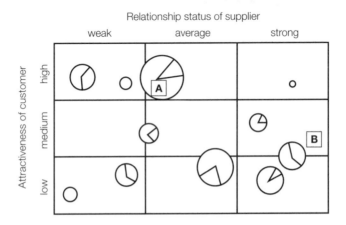

Figure 3.1   The nine-cell customer strategy grid

The horizontal axis in Fig. 3.2 represents your company's current relationship status or ability to compete for that customer's business. Each customer has certain success requirements that must be matched by your, the supplier's, required competences. Your relationship status is very much geared to the customer's perception of your relevant core competences and is a weighted rating of such factors as your current share of the business (relative to competition), price competitiveness, product quality, knowledge of the customer's business, technical strength and the intensity of the current relationship.

The way to find out about your customers' perceptions is to ask them.

The score for each factor must consider the relevance of that relationship status to the customer and its uniqueness relative to your main competitor. Some of these criteria are quantifiable (volume, share of business) but some are subjective and should be scored through the customer's eyes. For example, you may believe your technical strength is second to none but what we are rating is your *customer's perception* of your technical strength. As discussed in a later chapter, the way to find out about your customers' perceptions is to ask them, and this part of the evaluation process makes an excellent agenda for a regular formal dialogue with them. Your overall relationship status with the customer may be classified as strong, average or weak.

A number of customers are plotted on the strategy screen in Fig. 3.2. The size of each circle correlates with the *potential* of the customer and the wedge in each circle indicates your current share of their business. Alternatively your share may be indicated by colour codes. The bubble chart facility on a computer spreadsheet can display data in this way (Fig. 3.2) or specialized software is available.

Let us concentrate on customers A and B as detailed in Fig. 3.2 and shown on the strategy grids in Fig. 3.1. Although we have a sizeable share of business with the less attractive customer B, there appears to be three times more potential with customer A with whom we have a weaker current relationship status.

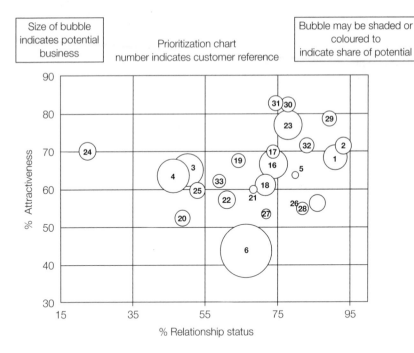

Figure 3.2 The nine-cell customer strategy grid (spreadsheet bubble chart)

In principle, it is difficult to improve a customer's attractiveness unless you are prepared to change the direction of your business completely in order to acquire new core competences. It is easier to improve your position with the customer by capitalizing on your relationship status. In the example shown in Fig. 3.1 the strategy might be to target customer A for customer development and resource investment, while putting the relationship with customer B on hold with the objective of maintaining business without any increase in resource allocation.

HOW DO YOU DEVELOP STRATEGIES TO INCREASE KEY CUSTOMER BUSINESS?

There are four generic strategies for key customers:

1 target for *development*

2 *defend* against competition

3   *maintain* with minimum resource

4   *withdraw*.

The *development* strategy will be used for selected customers who have a high attractiveness factor with good prospects for greater penetration. The *defend* strategy is designed to safeguard existing key customers from competitive inroads, particularly where potential growth may be limited. Both these strategies will absorb resources but the selected customers are likely to be crucial to the achievement of company objectives, both in the short and long term.

Maintenance with minimum resource is a strategy for customers with whom good business is enjoyed despite the fact that they may not really be a good fit with your attractiveness criteria or core competences. The policy will be to ensure that resource allocation is limited and this might mean substituting telesales for direct personal sales calls and relying more on mailshots or exhibitions for communication of information to the customer.

Withdrawing is an appropriate strategy where the customer is patently using more valuable resources than is likely to be justified, now or at any time in the future, by the business. An example of this might be a low-margin technical service contract that can only be scheduled at night in a location where it is almost impossible to recruit night-working engineers.

Of course, customers falling into these last two strategic classifications are unlikely to be key customers. However, there is always a limit on resources and the number of customers who can be selected for development. The nine-cell customer strategy grid shown in Fig. 3.3 can help us to sort out the broad strategic approach to each customer and allocate resources appropriately but how your customer portfolio is spread across the grid is as important as the individual positions. The supplier who has strong relationship status with many highly attractive customers may be allocating most resources to defensive strategies whereas the supplier with few such customers will be focusing on developing stronger relationships with less well-positioned customers.

Relationship status of supplier

		weak	average	strong
Attractiveness of customer	high	Maintain selectively	Develop	Develop Defend
	medium	Maintain minimally	Defend Maintain	Develop
	low	Withdraw	Maintain minimally	Defend selectively

Figure 3.3   Strategic options for key customers

WHAT CAN YOU DO TO DEVELOP POSITIVE KEY CUSTOMER RELATIONSHIPS?

In key customer management, the objective is to develop strong relationships with attractive customers and continuously strive to move the current relationship status towards the ultimate strategic partnership implicit in the top right-hand corner of the strategy grid in Fig. 3.3.

Many supplier and customer relationships move through the same patterns as the family cycle – courtship and proposal, wedding and honeymoon, marriage and complacency that, regrettably, might end up in breakdown and divorce.

In the early stages of courtship the would-be supplier is only one of many suitors, some already well established. Although there is little interdependence between the two parties, there is high sensitivity to each other's behaviour and even a little excitement and novelty value in the new relationship. Perhaps the first date (or first order) develops into a 'going steady' where both parties grow less interested in seeking other relationships and begin to appreciate the advantages of the new liaison. The proposal embodies much hope and expectation before, eventually, formal wedding vows are exchanged. Joint business development is pursued in the blissful honeymoon period where both parties invest great effort into ensuring the success of the marriage.

This cycle is explored more fully in a later chapter but suffice it to say here that the task of the key customer manager is to steer the relationship sensitively through the early stages and to keep the marriage alive once it has been consummated. The state of each customer relationship must be monitored and plans made to develop to the next stage of commitment or to protect the current position.

RELATIONSHIP BONDING

Each stage of the relationship development must be consolidated by a proactive, planned process of bonding, with the objective of strengthening the supplier–customer alliance and impeding competitive penetration.

There are four ways to create lasting relationship bonding:

- develop personal trust
- create entry barriers
- reinforce exit barriers
- initiate joint venture projects contributing to the achievement of your customer's objectives.

The strength of the bonding is measured by the *share* of the customer's business you have, together with the aggregate effect of these four types of bonding. Having selected the prospective partner, the aim is to develop the relationship from being an *ordinary supplier* to becoming:

- a *preferred supplier* within a specific range
- a *partner* addressing specific supply areas
- a *strategic partner* addressing the marketplace and total business for mutual benefit.

Relationship bonding

- *Developing trust*
  - regular factory visits at all levels
  - social activities and entertainment
  - high-frequency contacts

- supporting special events for the customer
- ensuring promises are kept
- open communication
- sharing mutual problems
- giving warning of future problems
- involvement by top management
- being flexible and empathetic

■ *Creating entry barriers*
- low competitive pricing
- superior products and applications
- electronic links
- network of relationships
- pricing based on overall business
- joint long-term planning
- joint innovation teams

■ *Reinforcing exit barriers*
- making the customer dependent on technical support
- agreeing overriders and retrospective rebates
- loaning equipment (e.g., computer systems)
- agreeing formal long-term contracts
- giving financial support (leasing, etc.)
- encouraging inter-company trading
- forming customer clubs (as airlines have done)
- utilizing consignment stocks
- incorporating unique component design and tooling
- capitalizing on family or cultural ties
- giving specialized training support
- moving into shared premises

■ *Joint venture projects*
- assigning staff to the customer
- creating joint project teams
- collaborating in joint business ventures
- pooling research and development facilities and staff
- working with the customer in market research
- a shared customer database

Customer evaluation system examples

Evaluation system a is a typical example of attractiveness and relationship status criteria together with weightings and rating definitions agreed by a multifunction team in a manufacturing company supplying components to industry.

Customer evaluation system A

Customer attractiveness evaluation criteria: industrial manufacturer

Factor	Weight	Rating	Interpretation
a Value potential	9	0	Less than £250k
		1	£251k to £500k
		2	£501k to £999k
		3	£1million plus
b Margin potential	8	0	Less than 20%
		1	20–25%
		2	25–30%
		3	30% plus
c Long-term supply	6	0	Avoids commitments always
		1	Does not enter long-term commitments
		2	Will commit up to 12 months
		3	Will commit to longer than 12 months
d Customer's business growth	5	0	Decline
		1	Static
		2	Average growth
		3	Significant growth
e Probability of developing more business	7	0	None
		1	Low
		2	Medium
		3	High
f Potential increase in absolute share of business	7	0	None
		1	Up to 10%
		2	11–20%
		3	20% plus
g Marketplace reputation	4	0	Poor reputation
		1	Have below average reputation

Factor	Weight	Rating	Interpretation
		2	Considered to be average
		3	Above average reputation and respect
h Financial strength	7	0	Insecure/slow payment
		1	Insecure/average payment
		2	Secure/slow to average payment
		3	Secure/fast payment
i Business attitude	5	0	Aggressive with suppliers
		1	Cautious with suppliers – no commitment
		2	Collaborative
		3	Positive partnership with suppliers
j Logistics	8	0	Highly specialized non-standard
		1	Complex
		2	Medium
		3	Standard (optimizes production resources)
k Support resource needs (mainly time)	7	0	Continual support in all aspects
		1	Frequent input needed
		2	Occasional support needed
		3	Self-sufficient customer
l Scope of Customer	5	0	Local
		1	National (mainly one country)
		2	International (Europe)
		3	Global
Total score (max. 234)			

Customer evaluation system A

Customer relationship status criteria: industrial manufacturer

Factor	Weight	Rating	Interpretation
a Our share of customer's total purchases	10	0	None
		1	Less than 15%
		3	15% to 50%
			50% plus
b Our share of customer's purchases relative to the largest competitor	8	0	No business/very small share/minor supplier
		1	Our share less than largest competitor
		2	Our share about equal to largest competitor
		3	Our share more than largest competitor
c Trend in our share of customer's purchases over last 3 years	5	0	Declining
		1	Static
		2	Increasing by an annual average of less than 5%
		3	Increasing by an annual average of more than 5%
d To what extent is the customer 'locked' in', committed or contracted?	4	0	No commitment
		1	Low commitment level
		2	Medium commitment level
		3	High commitment level
e Customer perception of our technical strength	6	0	Competitors are better
		1	No significant advantage over competitors
		2	A little better than competitors
		3	Significant advantage over competitors
f Customer perception of our service (availability, response)	8	0	Not as good as competition
		1	Slightly worse than competition
		2	We are same as competition
		3	We are better than competition
g Customer perception of our price competitiveness	5	0	Much higher than competition (+10%)
		1	We are slightly higher than competition (1–10%)
		2	We are same as competition
		3	We are lower than competition

Factor	Weight	Rating	Interpretation
h Age of relationship	5	0	No business yet
		1	Less than 12 months trading
		2	1 year to 5 years trading
		3	More than 5 years trading
i Customer contract base	5	0	No contracts
		1	Buyer contact only
		2	Buyer and technical contact
		3	Broad range of customer contacts
j Attitudes of contacts to us	5	0	Negative
		1	Friendly but neutral
		2	Friendly and involved
		3	Strongly positive
Total score (max. 186)			

Customer evaluation system b shows how a major international wines and spirits company approaches the evaluation of customer outlets in order to prioritize promotional investment. To some extent, with fast-moving consumer goods the key outlets for these products are self-evident. However, strategic planning involves considerable investment of promotional money and merchandising effort which demands careful consideration and prioritization for which the nine-cell grid approach is useful. Attractiveness is usually strongly related to location and types of consumer traffic – in other words, the 'image' of the customer. Relationship status assessment is replaced by evaluation of growth potential and business development opportunities, although attitudes are still a factor to be considered.

Customer evaluation system B

Customer image evaluation: fast-moving consumer goods

Factor	Low description value	0	2	4	6	8	10	High description value
Location	Suburban or downmarket, declining part of town							In key downtown or upmarket development location
	Off main street; little passing trade; you only go if you know it's there							Located on main road, close to major intersection; high traffic flow
	Known only to locals; low development importance							Wide catchment area for customers; high development importance
	Same old customers; little change in customer base							Customer base dynamic; high tourist traffic
Influential customers	Regular customers; few walk-in new customers							High walk-in traffic of potential customers for our products
	Local customers with set drinking habits and patterns							Customers set trends for premium product consumption (government/political/rich/famous)
	Low spend per customer, down-market trade							High spending per customer; signs of wealth; elite customers
Distribution priority	Single outlet; not part of group, family or affiliation							Multi-outlet group or shared ownership with other key outlets
	Important only for local reasons							Need to be there for wider visibility
	Not influential outlet for brand growth and trial							Key strategic distribution outlet; family or political group association
Management	Records of sales/consumption not kept and information not shared							Computerized records efficiently kept and information shared
	Payment is slow to us or wholesaler							Strong evidence of financial stability
	Management does not closely monitor staff activities							Staff are motivated and enthusiastic
	Decisions based on favours done/received not on good practice							Decision making is transparent; can be influenced by business logic.
	Staff not loyal: high staff turnover							Consistent, loyal quality staff
	No future planning; day-to-day mentality							Business plan evident showing objectives and strategies
Decoration and equipment	Tired furnishings and floor covers; exterior poorly maintained							Exterior exciting/inviting; change and innovation responsive
	Damaged equipment is not replaced or upgraded							Equipment is updated/leading edge

Factor	Low description value	0	2	4	6	8	10	High description value
	Unfashionable compared to leading outlets							Leader in new layouts and promotions
	Lack of discipline/poor image in staff behaviour and appearance							Staff supportive of special activities and customer service
	Lack of investment/money in image							Good regular investment in image
Segment importance	Not a leader in a premium segment							Leader/influencer premium products
	Sells mainly standard or 'house brand' products							Sells high-profit products; good premium brand image
Promotion opportunity	No promotion activity evident							High level of promotion activity
	Promotions poorly run							Well-organized effective promotions
	Mismatch between product promotions and customer base							Promotions are well targeted to customer base
	Promotion agreements not fulfilled							Promotion agreements fulfilled

Total image score
(Max. 270)

Average image score %

Customer growth potential evaluation: fast-moving consumer goods

Factor	Low description value	0	2	4	6	8	10	High description value
Outlet growth potential	Type of business in decline							Type of business is growing fast
	Area/region in decline							Area/region prospering
	Passing traffic in decline or future changes will not help trade							Positive improvements in road and pedestrian traffic will help trade
Our sales/share increase opportunity	We already have 70%+ of business; further growth unlikely							Low share of business currently; good opportunities to increase share
	Customer's sales in our focus categories are declining							Customer's sales in our focus categories are increasing
	Our share of customer's sales is above market share							Our share of customer's sales is below market share
Physical expansion by customer	Physical expansion not possible at current premises							Customer has space to increase business capacity/extra rooms
	Customer has no plans to expand							Customer plans to move to bigger or better premises
	Customer has no plans to open extra outlets							Customer plans to open additional outlets
Customer's attitude to our company	Has strong relationship with competition; past disagreement?							Has good history/relationship with our company
	Has little knowledge or experience of our company							Has good knowledge, experience and dealings with our company
	Very subjective, opinionated or apathetic in business decisions							Is open-minded and receptive to good business logic
	Has no loyalty/interest in building partnerships with any supplier							Is interested in building partnership with preferred supplier
Business practice	Does not benchmark current operation with key competitors							Customer travels extensively benchmarking best practices
	Close-minded; does not try new ideas; resistant to change							Tries new ideas; learns from competitors and suppliers
	Manager/owner has no formal business qualifications							Manager/owner has business qualification
Competitor aggression	Competitor overspending with customer							Competitor underspending with customer
	Competitor highly perceived by customer							Competitor not perceived highly by customer
	Competitor is contracted to dominate customer's business							Competitors underestimate customer potential; low activity level

Factor	Low description value	0	2	4	6	8	10	High description value
Family and political affiliations	No family or political affiliations known							Known affiliations supporting business positively
	Associated with disruptive or radical elements in society							Positive affiliations likely to assist expansion of current operations
History of owner, manager and key employees	Past involvement with any business failures							History of past business success
	No experience in this business							Positive experience in this business
	Key employees – no experience/ bad records in this business							Key employees known to be good operators
Staff conditions and training	Pay and conditions below average							Pay and conditions above average
	No training given to new staff							New staff fully trained
	Negative attitude to regular training and motivation of staff							Regular training and motivation is given to staff
Total growth score (Max. 270)				Average growth score %				

Each major outlet is assessed for image and growth using up to eight criteria, each of which has several sub-criteria on a scale of 0–10. The resulting total percentage for image and growth potential is plotted on a nine-cell strategy grid as shown previously in this chapter. No direct criteria weighting is used but importance is indicated by the number of sub-criteria.

Customer evaluation system c illustrates the method a major international contractor uses to analyze tendering priorities and to monitor how the relationship is developing during the bidding process.

Customer evaluation system C

Contract evaluation system: international construction company

High-value capital contracts demand substantial investment of resources in preparing bids and nursing pre-contract relationships. Meanwhile, budgets have to be prepared and forecasts made that, of necessity, must be made on a more concrete basis than the subjective assessment of the manager co-ordinating these activities. A major international contractor uses the analysis below not only to evaluate tendering priorities but also to monitor how the relationship is developing during the bidding process. Fifteen aspects of the contract are weighted and continuously evaluated at all stages of negotiation.

Criteria	Weight	Ratings
Level of contact	2	(–2) who is the decision maker?
		(2) one contact at technical level
		(4) several technical-level contacts
		(6) contact at two levels including commercial
		(8) more than two levels including commercial
		(10) senior management and technical contact at all levels
Decision process	4	(0) decision to be approved by parent company
		(2) decision by parent company: agreed in principle
		(4) we have recommender with limited influence
		(6) we have chief recommender only
		(8) our contact makes decision with others
		(10) our contact makes decision alone
Accessibility	4	(2) very difficult to contact
		(4) maximum one contact per month
		(6) maximum one contact per fortnight
		(8) maximum one contact per week including commercial
		(10) any time, any level
Basis of decision	4	(–10) unknown
		(2) not at all sure
		(4) some factors still to establish
		(6) established but not agreed
		(8) established and agreed
		(10) established, agreed and influenced in our favour

▷

Criteria	Weight	Ratings
Budget	3	(−10) unknown (2) neither planning nor pending (4) planned (6) approval pending (8) approved (10) signed
Our price vs. competition	1	(−20) way above all competition (2) no comparison available (4) we are more expensive than some (6) equal or unimportant (8) we are less expensive
Timing of proposal relative to competition	2	(2) unknown (4) competition submitted after us (5) ours still pending (6) ours and competition made together (8) we proposed last (10) ours the only proposal
Timing of proposal relative	3	(−5) two months before decision (2) decision date slipping (4) decision date unknown (6) one month before decision (8) two weeks before decision (10) shortly before final decision
Prospect's opinion of our proposal	2	(−5) no idea (2) unsuitable (4) incomplete (6) adequate (8) satisfactory (10) outstanding
When do we get the order?	4	(−5) later (2) in three months (4) in two months (6) in four weeks (8) next week (10) decision made – awaiting confirmation
Prospect status	4	(−10) uses us but unhappy (2) uses one competitor happily (4) uses several competitors

		(6) uses competition but unhappy
		(8) first-time user
		(10) our client and happy
Our experience in this type of work	2	(−5) none
		(2) not our usual field
		(4) done it once before
		(6) done it a few times but not recently
		(8) current similar work
		(10) our bread and butter
Development required	2	(−5) not known
		(2) completely new development; need to learn
		(4) extensive additional work required
		(6) 50% fit; additional work straightforward
		(8) minor modifications and some additions
		(10) none; current specification fits like a glove
Attitude to us	2	(2) negative
		(4) mixed bias for and against
		(5) not clear
		(6) neutral
		(8) positive
		(10) fully confident at all levels
Confidence confirmed by reference	4	(−10) no reference requested
		(−10) reference not to be taken up
		(2) no reference visit yet
		(4) reference visit made
		(6) reference visit made and visited us
		(8) visit made to reference, us and third parties
		(10) senior management met with our senior management

Based on the total ratings adjusted by weightings, the probabilities of success are estimated as follows:

- 245 points = 25 per cent probability of success
- 260 points = 40 per cent probability of success
- 275 points = 55 per cent probability of success
- 290 points = 70 per cent probability of success
- 335 points = 85 per cent probability of success

Customer evaluation system d applies to all salespeople, whether or not they are involved with key customers, demonstrating how they should develop profiles of ideal customers as part of the process of evaluating their priorities.

Customer evaluation system: ideal customer profiles

All salespeople, whether or not they are involved with key customers, should develop profiles of ideal customers as part of the process of deciding their priorities. One important benefit of applying some analysis to identifying the sort of business you want is that, at the same time, you identify the business that you do *not* want. Selling is a people-focused activity and, as a salesperson, it is all too easy to get seduced by the friendly customer with whom one spends more time than the amount of business available justifies. It is tempting to get too consumed by a fascinating technical problem that does not have a worthwhile sales pay-off. As salespeople, we learn by our experiences, but our experiences must be applied in a systematic way.

Step 1

List your best current and past customers (not prospects). Concentrate on those from whom you have got the most personal satisfaction – not just volume of orders. Use your gut feelings and at this stage try not to analyze the criteria for your choice. Aim to list your ten best customers in order of the extent of this 'feel good' factor, writing your favourite first, next best second and so on. Stop there.

Step 2

List your current and past worst customers. Again, concentrate on those experiences that have been losing experiences, for either you or the customer. Focus on feelings rather than orders. Start with the worst and list them in the order of the extent of the 'feel bad' factor, until you have listed ten.

Step 3

List the characteristics of your best customers – focus on psychographics such as collaborative attitudes, innovation, loyalty, appreciation of value-added features and so on more than 'creditworthiness' or 'has money to buy' or 'needs my product', which we must assume are basic requirements for all customers.

Step 4

Now list the characteristics of your worst customers – focusing this time on the negative characteristics such as 'slowness in decision making' or 'inflexibility in negotiation' or 'unwillingness to disclose information'; concentrate on psychographics.

Step 5

Using your best customer characteristics and your worst customer characteristics lists, distil the five characteristics that you consider most significant. In assessing the worst characteristics list, transfer the character-istic's opposite to the best characteristics list. For example, if 'slowness in decision making' is listed as a *worst* characteristic, write 'has clear decision-making unit and specified procedures' in your best characteristics list.

Step 6

Add five demographic characteristics of best customers (such as volume potential, profit potential, standard specifications) and rate your current best customers against each of the five psychographic and five demographic characteristics on a 0–10 rating scale (you can weight these factors if necessary). In this way, the fit of each customer or contract will be measured as a percentage of your ideal customer maximum score of 100.

Using the profiles generated

These figures are, of course, only rough guides and serve to encourage some objec-tivity in evaluating your potential key customers and contracts. All business relationships are unique and, as relationship management embraces a portfolio approach to the customer base, there will be some targeted customers who will fall short of the ideal customer benchmarks, particularly on demographics, in the shorter term.

However, the systematic approach on psycho-graphics will give some tangible measure of the *probability* of being able to achieve a preferred supplier relationship with a given customer. The discipline of having such a system signals your strengths and weaknesses in a possible relationship and will help in the preparation of a sales strategy and tactics.

Of course, it is tempting to abuse the system by using it to avoid *difficult* customers. For this reason, and to make judgements less subjective, the more people contributing to the evaluation system the better. The team approach to key customer evaluation is not only likely to be more objective, but also more creative.

SUMMARY

Relationship management can be likened to the family cycle of courtship, proposal, wedding, honeymoon and marriage. Much of the success of the relationship will depend upon the initial selection of a partner. Strategic customer alliances imply considerable commitment of resources but with great prizes if the relationships are successful. The key customer manager is instrumental in choosing partners and deciding strategies in order to enhance the partnership and maintain a happy marriage.

A structured approach to the prioritization of customers is essential to determine how resources should be allocated and all functions of the business should be involved in the process. The prioritization approach should scan the breadth of the customer base in order to appraise the relative importance of specific customers. Prioritization is based, usually, on establishing criteria for measuring the relative attractiveness of a customer in terms of mutual relationship advantages and realistically assessing whether your current relationship status would be improved by resource investment in that customer. In addition, the process of establishing these criteria is an excellent opportunity to develop motivated commitment and collaborative synergy in your organization between personnel and between departments.

4

How much do you really know about creating an effective KCRM organization?

SELF EVALUATION

In the matrix shown below, each of the fruits – apple, orange, banana, cherries, pear – has a numerical value. Vertically, the values of the four fruits in each column add up to the totals indicated at the bottom of the matrix. Horizontally, the four fruits in each row add up to the total indicated at the right-hand side. The total value of the four fruits in the bottom horizontal line is not calculated. What is it? You have 20 seconds to state your answer …

apple + orange + orange + orange = 62

banana + apple + pear + cherries = 59

cherries + pear + pear + orange = 55

cherries + apple + banana + banana = ?

= 57   = 55   = 65   = 66

DOING THE RIGHT THINGS BEFORE DOING THINGS RIGHT

Enthusiasm and skills are necessary for successful development of key customer business, but they can only work if they are applied in the right direction. To do things right you start by making sure that you are doing the right things.

The fruit puzzle at the start of this chapter illustrates the point about not getting so lost in detail that the strategy gets obscured. In any group, less than ten per cent of the participants will come up with the right answer; most people will try to work out algebraic equations for the value of each apple or pear or whatever. The more enlightened will realize, simply, that the cross-total of the four horizontal numbers must equal the downward total of the three vertical numbers plus the mystery number. Subtract one from the other and, eureka, the answer is 67.

> You need to develop a 'helicopter' mind, which is constantly in touch with day-to-day customer dealing, yet is capable of rising above it all regularly.

It is all too easy to get bogged down with the details – the cut and thrust of doing business daily with customers. You need to develop a 'helicopter' mind, which is constantly in touch with day-to-day customer dealing, yet is capable of rising above it all regularly to ensure that your general direction is on course; that the people you are talking to are the people you should be talking to; that the situation is being monitored continuously for new opportunities.

ANALYZING THE CUSTOMER MIX

Most of us tend to work with our heads full of apples, pears and oranges and sometimes lose sight of what we are trying to do. Customer relationship management is one concept which helps us to maintain a focus on our priorities. Identifying key customers is not difficult in some businesses because the customers are self-evident. Offshore drilling contractors know exactly who their customers are going to be; packaged food companies suggest that in the foreseeable future there will be only ten major purchasing agencies for most of the retail supermarkets in Europe: it has been predicted that eventually there will be only five automobile manufacturers left in the entire world.

However, for most companies, the customer base is, perhaps, a little less polarized. Even when, as in pharmaceuticals in the UK where there appears to be only one customer – the National Health Service – there are many different sub-customers, each of which will contribute in varying degrees to the success of your business.

A methodology for the evaluation of potential key customers has already been described: it is now necessary to analyze your overall customer mix – present and future – in order to determine how best to use your sales and customer support resources to implement your customer management strategy, as well as maintaining planned levels of general business. There are seven steps in the process.

Step 1: prepare a Pareto analysis

The Pareto analysis (see page 67 for a detailed explanation) is compiled by listing all customers in decreasing order of sales and plotting the cumulative sales related to the number of customers as shown in Table 4.1.

> The Kanthal Heating Corporation identified that with 10 per cent of their customers they were losing 125 per cent of their profit!

The Pareto distribution shows that the top ten (classification A) customers currently account for £3.2m or 64 per cent of total sales. The next 20 classification B customers add a further £1.1m or 22 per cent of total sales. The 20 classification C customers add only another 8 per cent to sales, and classification D customers represent half the customer base but account for only 6 per cent of total sales. Some companies have found that total profits actually *decline* as their customer base grows beyond an optimum Pareto point (see Chapter 6, Fig. 6.2). One such US company, the Kanthal Heating Corporation, identified that 20 per cent of their customers contributed 225 per cent of their profit; with 70 per cent of their customers they broke even and with 10 per cent of their customers they were losing 125 per cent of their profit!

Table 4.1   Pareto list – cumulative turnover against number of customers

Account number	Annual sales (£000)	Cumulative annual sales ($000)	Percentage of total sales
1 classification A ▼	520	520	
2	450	970	
3	400	1370	
4	300	1750	
5	300	2050	
6	250	2300	
7	240	2540	
8	230	2770	
9	220	2990	
10	210	3200	64%
11 classified B ▼	150	3350	
12	110	3460	
13	70	3530	
14	70	3600	
15	65	3665	
16	60	3735	
17	60	3785	
18	58	3843	
19	52	3895	
20	50	3945	
21	45	3990	
22	43	4033	
23	40	4073	
24	39	4112	
25	38	4150	
26	38	4188	
27	34	4222	
28	31	4253	
29	25	4278	
30	22	4300	86%
31–50 classification C ▼	400	4700	94%
51–100 classification D ▼	300	£5000	100%

If all customers were the same size in terms of sales, then the straight line in Fig. 4.1 would result. The steeper the ascent of the actual line, the greater will be the concentration of sales to a few large customers. The Pareto analysis becomes even more significant if it is possible to use profit data in place of sales data.

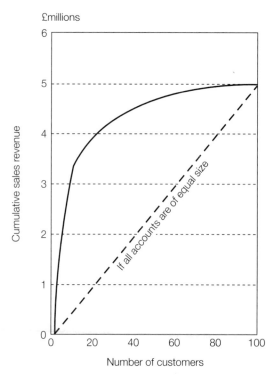

Figure 4.1   The Pareto distribution curve

Step 2: project future sales for top customers

Take the top ten customers (or as many customers as contribute 50 per cent of your sales) and try to make an individual projection of yearly sales for each customer for the next *three* years. Then calculate the percentage of total company sales contributed by each individual customer, both currently and at the end of your year 3 forecast. Calculate the percentage of *total company sales* generated from your classification A list currently and at the end of your year 3 projection.

Step 3: project future sales for development customers

List any additional customers or potential customers that have been identified as *target development customers* in your evaluation but which do not appear in your classification A list. Make an individual projection of yearly sales for each customer over the next *three* years and calculate the percentage of *total company sales* contributed by all your development customers, both currently and at the end of your year 3 projection.

Step 4: project future sales for general business

As in step 2, make a three-year forecast of sales to customers in classifications B, C and D. Depending upon the numbers of customers involved, the projection can be made either by individual customer or by each classification.

General business customers should be divided into two categories:

1   customers who have existing or potential business which can justify direct sales calls;

2   customers where there is not enough business to justify individual sales calls but where collectively there is enough business to warrant other forms of sales coverage, such as distributors, direct mail, telesales.

The degree of attention you will be prepared to give these classifications of customer will depend upon the shape of your Pareto curve. You may choose to group them by industrial sector or geographical area, or even in sub-categories B, C, D, according to volumes of business and different sales-call frequencies.

Step 5: estimate resource requirements

For your development customer list, estimate the extra resource requirement that development entails – for example, six *extra* sales calls per year per customer. This will be over and above the normal routine calling frequency.

For your classification A customers estimate resource requirements for each individual customer for each of the three years projected. Resource requirement will be quantified in terms of:

- minimum number of sales calls needed to achieve forecast level of business;

- minimum number of technical support calls needed for projected levels of business (if relevant);

- minimum number of deliveries needed for projected levels of business (if relevant).

For example, if you estimate that your top sales customer will sustain the same volume of business for each of the next three years and that, on average, a weekly sales call will be necessary, then your sales call workload will be 50 calls per year for three years. If you envisage a decline in business or an increase in business, you may see fit to reduce or increase the frequency of calling, thus amending your total annual sales calls on that customer in years 2 and 3.

The 'standard' call

When assessing sales call workloads, it may be useful to think in terms of a 'standard' call of average time duration. If, for some key customers, your experience indicates that a typical call would involve sales interviews with several people or regular lengthy technical discussions and that the time spent with that customer would be above average, it may be more realistic to quantify the workload for that customer in terms of a multiple of 'standard calls'. For example, if you can do an average of four sales calls a day in your industry but a sales call to one particular key customer always takes about half a day, you might quantify one physical sales call as two 'standard' calls in this situation.

In quantifying the total sales resource needed over a three-year period, you might find that the extra resource needed as your development customers grow might be balanced by some of your current top customers falling away (through circumstances beyond your control, of course).

Depending on your type of business, this workload analysis may be extended to technical support calls. In this case, there might be considerable fluctuation in technical service requirements. The introduction of some new product might involve a high level of technical support training or teething problems which might diminish as the customer acquires experience of the application.

If your distributions are highly sensitive due to the physical size of the product, number of deliveries or distances involved, you might see fit to introduce a delivery resource calculation including such factors as not only product units per delivery drop, but also number of drops, drop points and distances involved.

These qualifications serve not only to determine the size and nature of resources needed for the sales plan, but provide an essential basis for monitoring the profitability of your activities and negotiating with key customers in the full understanding of the cost implications of the alliances that you are setting up with preferred customers.

In establishing your resource requirement, try to be objective and not be influenced by current assumptions about people and money. Plan for the job to be done properly; consider constraints at a later stage.

Step 6: calculate total sales workload resource available and check against requirements

Calculate the total sales (and technical) resource available by multiplying the qualified people available by the number of 'standard' sales calls (refer to step 5) that can be realistically made in a working year. For most businesses, a working year will be 220 working days after deducting (say) 104 weekend days, 25 days for national holidays and vacations, 10 training and sickness days and, perhaps, 6 days for departmental meetings.

Therefore, five salespeople doing four standard sales calls per day for 220 working days per year will represent a 4400 sales-call resource. Of course, geography might be a factor to consider in calculating available resource in any one specific area. A rural representative might be expected to make fewer calls per day than a metropolitan salesperson. However, it could be argued that the distance disadvantage of the rural representative has, nowadays, been more than offset by the expansion of motorways and the parking problems and congestion of the city.

Having calculated the sales-call resource workload required in step 5 you now have four figures to juggle with:

1   Your key customer workload resource need (KCR)

2   Your development customer extra workload resource need (DCR)

3   Your general business resource need (GBR)

4   Your available resource workload (AR).

If your AR is less than you need for key customers, development customers and general business, either you increase the resource by extra recruitment or you modify your requirements by cutting down the number of customers you service or by reducing the frequency of sales calls.

GBR will be, by definition, the first area of review for elimination or reduction of sales calls. The task is to find a way to allocate your resources with the right priorities to the jobs that have to be done. Beware the temptation to compromise by cutting down on the frequency of calling on key customers. If your analysis has been done carefully and realistically, you *need* that resource!

Armed with the data and justification that you have prepared, strong representation should be made to your senior management for the strengthening of resources. If, after all this, you have to compromise, explore the probability of reducing your key customer list *before* you consider a general reduction in call rate. Your sales achievement is less likely to be eroded if you limit your targets and perform well than if you try to cover everything and compromise on the quality of calls.

As a general principle, your available resource workload (after deducting DCR) should be allocated between the different classifications of customer (A, B, C, D and so on) proportionately to the revenue or profit generated by each classification. For example, if your class A customers contribute 50 per cent of your sales, then half your available resource should be allocated to them.

Step 7: allocating the resources

Once the overall balance between *needed* and *available* resources is agreed, the task now is to allocate those resources in a workable key customer (including development customers) and general business organization structure. There are three options:

1   a decentralized customer management structure – where responsibility for identified key customers is delegated to the general business salesforce who report to a local area sales manager;

2   a centralized customer management structure – where key customers are handled totally separately from general business by a specialized team, sometimes geographically located, but reporting centrally to a national customer manager;

3   an integrated customer management structure – where key customer responsibility remains with the general salesforce but is centrally co-ordinated by a national key customer manager.

The workable option, or permutation of options, will vary considerably according to the type and size of your business and the markets in which you operate but, when evaluating which kind of organization is appropriate, four factors should be considered:

■   *skills and maturity* – you may have enough people to resource a key customer team, but are they skilful and mature enough to do the job? Can you import the necessary skills and, if so, what would be the effect on existing team members?

■   *geography and costs* – by carefully allocating key customer jobs to skilled and mature people, what effect will there be on travel and time efficiency costs to both the key customer team and the general business team?; will the extra travel involved actually reduce your overall resource of standard sales calls available (AR)?

■   *local contacts* – sometimes strength of local contact can outweigh shortcomings in skill and maturity, so will a central key customer team waste your competitive advantage in this area at a local level?

■   *motivation* - will the motivation of a dynamic key customer team be offset by the demotivation of local resources who see the best business being creamed off? To what extent does the attitude of local service and technical support influence specific key customer business and how will the local personnel respond to organizational changes? What implications are there for local bonus and commission systems? Are there some positive motivation opportunities through delegating authority and improving status at local level?

Exhibit 4a

Customer management structure: the Apex Component Company coverage plan

The data from Table 4.2 is used in this key customer coverage plan. These figures are derived from a real company but have been modified and disguised for the purposes of this example.

Table 4.2 Apex Component Company: three-year sales coverage plan

A Top ten customers coverage plan

Key customer	Yearly sales revenue £000					Percentage of total sales					Standard sales calls			
	Last Year	Forecast Year 1	Year 2	Year 3	Total	Last year	Forecast Year 1	Year 2	Year 3	Total	Last year	Forecast Year 1	Year 2	Year 3
1	520	540	550	560	1 650	10.4	9.8	9.2	8.0	8.9	142	142	142	142
2	450	490	510	530	1 530	9.0	8.9	8.5	7.6	8.3	130	130	142	142
3	400	440	480	520	1 440	8.0	8.0	8.0	7.4	7.8	120	120	130	142
4	380	380	380	380	1 140	7.6	6.9	6.3	5.4	6.2	120	120	120	120
5	300	250	200	200	650	6.0	4.6	3.3	2.9	3.5	108	108	96	96
6	250	240	230	220	690	5.0	4.4	3.8	3.1	3.7	96	96	96	96
7	240	250	260	270	780	4.8	4.5	4.3	3.8	4.2	96	108	108	108
8	230	250	270	300	820	4.6	4.5	4.5	4.3	4.4	96	108	108	108
9	220	220	240	250	710	4.4	4.0	4.0	3.6	3.8	96	96	96	96
10	210	230	250	270		4.2	4.2	4.2	3.9	4.1	96	96	108	108
Top 10 customers	3200	3290	3370	3500	10 160	64%	60%	56%	51%	56%	1100	1124	1146	1158
Total sales (£000)	5000	5500	6000	6800	18 300	100%								

B General business coverage plan

Customer classification	Yearly sales revenue £000					Percentage of total sales					Standard sales calls			
		Forecast					Forecast					Forecast		
	Last year	Year 1	Year 2	Year 3	Total	Last year	Year 1	Year 2	Year 3	Total	Last year	Year 1	Year 2	Year 3
B 10	600	700	800	900	2400	12	13	13	13	13	200	200	200	200
C 20	400	500	515	670	1685	8	9	9	10	9	160	160	160	160
D 50	300	300	300	300	900	6	5	5	4	5	150	150	150	150
Total	1300	1500	1615	1870	4985	26	27	27	27	27	510	510	510	510

C Development customers coverage plan

Development customers	Yearly sales revenue £000					Percentage of total sales					Standard sales calls			
		Forecast					Forecast					Forecast		
	Last year	Year 1	Year 2	Year 3	Total	Last year	Year 1	Year 2	Year 3	Total	Last year	Year 1	Year 2	Year 3
1	70	100	160	210	470	1.4	1.8	2.7	3.1	2.6	18	48	72	96
2	65	90	120	180	390	1.3	1.6	2.0	2.6	2.1	18	24	48	72
3	60	90	120	160	360	1.2	1.6	2.0	2.4	2.0	18	24	48	72
4	58	80	110	150	340	1.2	1.5	1.8	2.3	1.9	18	24	48	72
5	52	70	100	140	310	1.0	1.3	1.7	2.1	1.7	18	18	48	48
6	45	60	90	140	290	0.9	1.1	1.5	2.1	1.6	12	18	24	48
7	40	70	100	150	330	0.8	1.3	1.7	2.3	1.8	12	18	48	72
8	38	50	80	120	250	0.8	0.9	1.3	1.8	1.4	12	18	24	48
9	38	60	85	110	255	0.8	1.1	1.4	1.6	1.4	12	18	24	48
10	34	40	50	70	160	0.7	0.7	0.8	1.0	0.9	12	12	18	18
Development customers	500	710	1015	1430	3 155	10%	13%	17%	21%	17%	150	222	402	594
Sales £000	5000	5500	6000	6800	18 300	100%								

D Overall three-year sales coverage plan summary

Customer classification	Yearly sales revenue £000					Percentage of total sales					Standard sales calls			
		Forecast					Forecast					Forecast		
	Last year	Year 1	Year 2	Year 3	Total	Last year	Year 1	Year 2	Year 3	Total	Last year	Year 1	Year 2	Year 3
TOP10	3200	3290	3370	3500	10 160	64	60	56	52	56	1100	1124	1146	1158
DEV 10	500	710	1015	1430	3 155	10	13	17	21	17	150	222	402	594
GEN 80	1300	1500	1615	1870	4 985	26	27	27	27	27	510	510	510	510
TOTAL	5000	5500	6000	6800	18 300	100%	100%	100%	100%	100%	1760	1856	2058	2262

Customer analysis

The Apex Component Company manufactures components of both a standard and customized nature. It has a customer base of 100 accounts, the top two of which are distributors who ship to many hundreds of smaller users. These users are not directly serviced by Apex on a regular basis but occasionally need some technical advice, the request for which is channelled through the distributor. It will be seen that nearly 20 per cent of current sales are through two distributors and 64 per cent of total sales currently come from the top ten customers.

The sales forecasts are expressed in current money values and do not include any assumptions about inflation. Sales are expected to increase by 36 per cent from £5m to £6.8m in three years. However, sales to key customers will increase by only 9.4 per cent in this period and the percentage of total business that will come from the top ten will reduce from the current 64 per cent to 51 per cent over the three years.

This is not entirely unwelcome at Apex, because they plan to increase their key customer base and would like to slightly reduce their dependence on their top two distributors. This does not mean that the distributor relationship will be any less committed, indeed they forecast nearly 18 per cent more business from their number two customer, but they have, to some extent, reached saturation point in penetration with many of their top ten customers.

As a means of extending their key customer base, ten classification B customers have been selected for specific development, based on criteria that go beyond merely sales revenue potential. These ten development customers have been listed and reclassified as development customers. Currently they contribute only £0.5m (10 per cent of annual sales revenue) but, with specific attention, it is expected that this figure could almost treble in three years to £1.4m.

More than half of the total forecast sales growth in the next three years will come from these ten development customers. At that time, it is anticipated that the top ten customers plus the development ten will be contributing 73 per cent of Apex's total sales.

In summary, Apex plan to increase their total sales by 36 per cent in the next three years, the major part of this increase being achieved by developing ten selected target customers, while also maintaining normal growth patterns for the current top ten customers. In addition, dependence on the top two distributors will decrease.

The coverage plan

Sales-call frequency varies from quarterly calls on some smaller direct customers to well over 100 calls per year on each of the top five customers. Particularly for large customers, the duration of a sales call can vary significantly from a one-hour stock check and top-up order, to a one-day technical meeting with an original equipment manufacturer to sort out specifications for a new product. For example, each of the distributors has a dedicated desk for the Apex salesperson, where it is expected that half a day a week is spent sorting out the more complex orders from the distributor's customers. Additionally, time is spent out in the field with the distributor's salespeople for the purposes of sales training and product education.

Careful appraisal of necessary sales-call frequency has been made for each of the top ten customers and calculated in terms of standard calls. For example, one full training day in the field with a distributor salesperson would count as four standard sales calls because, in an average Apex working day, a salesperson would make four sales visits.

A call pattern on a key customer might involve weekly visits on storekeeper contacts (one standard call), with monthly calls on the purchasing manager (an extra standard call) and quarterly meetings with the general manager (an extra standard call). In a year this would add up to 52 store calls + 12 purchasing calls + 4 general manager calls = 68 standard calls. However, this does not mean that the calculation of standard calls correlates with the number of the customer's people to be seen. Each situation will vary and will be evaluated on consideration of the time involved. This could be complicated by the complexity of contact locations and accessibility to customer personnel as and when it fits in with the salesperson's schedule.

Over the years, Apex has identified a correlation between call frequency needs and size of customer and uses this as a broad guideline for resource planning, as shown in Table 4.3.

Table 4.3 Apex: correlation between customer size and call frequency

Sales £000 per year	Standard calls per year
fewer than 10	3
10–20	6
20–50	12
50–75	18
75–100	24
100–150	48
150–200	72
200–250	96
250–350	108
350–450	120
450–500	130
500+	142

Applying these guidelines to last year's data in Table 4.2, it may be noted that 1100 standard calls, or 62 per cent of available resources (AR), were made on the top ten customers, who contributed 64 per cent of revenue. The ten newly selected development customers who, to date, account for 10 per cent of revenue have absorbed about 9 per cent of available resource. Of available resource, 29 per cent was allocated to general business customers, who pulled in 26 per cent of revenue. In broad terms, Apex looks as though, up to now, it has had its resource allocation about right.

But what of the future? What changes may have to be considered in the allocation of available resources to achieve the forecasts and objectives? Clearly, as so much is expected from the ten selected development customers, some extra investment of resource will be necessary.

On a strictly year-for-year basis and, using the same call frequency guidelines, next year (Year 1) will need a 5.5 per cent increase of available resource to 1856 standard calls. The following year (Year 2) will need a further 11 per cent increase in available resource to 2058 standard calls. Even these calculations assume no increase in general business coverage, so where do we get the extra available resource that by Year 3 will mean an extra 502 standard calls per year?

There are four options:

1 *reduce general business sales calls*: general business is forecast to maintain a regular 27 per cent of Apex business, which is still a meaningful percentage of the total revenue. Reducing the current modest allocated resource of 510 calls per year would almost certainly be unwise; the 98 per cent cut in coverage necessary to generate 502 extra key and development customer calls would be totally unacceptable. It might be possible to step up indirect sales coverage through telesales and direct mail to offset some smaller cuts in sales coverage for general business customers;

2 *reduce call frequency on top ten customers*: a possibility but, if you have appraised the need realistically in the first place, this is a second-best option;

3 *reduce the number of development customers*: another possibility but your development customers represent 52 per cent of the forecast growth and cutting out two or three will only marginally save on the resource needed;

4 *increase the sales team*: the current available resource is four salespeople, each capable of 440 standard calls per year, that is, a total available sales resource of 1760 sales calls per year. Using the same individual resource figure, by year 3 the resource needed will be 2262 sales calls per year, or five salespeople.

The figures disguise a potential hazard in the fact that the resource plan is *reactive*, that is, the resource is increased as sales increase. The purpose of the plan is to have the resource in order to achieve the sales increase, not the other way round. In the Apex case, the resources should be calculated on the basis of the next year's forecast, that is, an available resource of 2058 sales calls should be in place for year 1, calculated on the basis of forecast sales for year 2.

The relevance of this forward planning will depend upon the nature of the business and the length of the sales cycle. How quickly will the customer's business respond to increased frequency (and depth) of sales call?

In practice, reviews of coverage should be continuous. Key customer business monitoring should allow trends to be quickly and easily identified. Moving annual totals (MATs) are, perhaps, the simplest and easiest device with which to do this – a month-by-month running cumulative total of the previous 12 months. Not only do MATs provide a continuous picture from which adjustment of allocated resources can take place, but they can also provide a useful mechanism for bonus system payments.

Depending upon the type of business you operate, a similar planned approach to the allocation of resources can be worked out for technical support engineers or the cost implications of distributing your products. Workload is the key and, if your company is much bigger than Apex, the method is still valid and probably even more essential, because your available resource will be much bigger.

SALES COVERAGE EXERCISE

The importance of sales coverage organized on the basis of workload has been emphasized. Now try this short exercise.

Your customer database has been analyzed and each customer has been classified A, B, C or D as an indication of the importance of that customer to the maintenance of current business and the achievement of corporate objectives.

	No. of customers	Total revenue
Classification A	50	£4m
Classification B	100	£4m
Classification C	150	£3m
Classification D	200	£2m
Totals	500	£13m

You have *five* sales representatives who average *four standard sales visits* per day in a five-day working week. In practice this means that each representative does about 880 standard sales visits per year.

In classifications A and B, 20 customers have been identified as *target development customers* and it has been estimated that this development will entail an *extra* five standard sales visits on each of these customers over and above the routine visits over the next 12 months. In addition, each sales representative is expected to make 80 sales visits on prospective new customers who are not currently on the database.

The task

Calculate the overall annual coverage plan for your sales team, ensuring that their efforts are directed appropriately for the business. What should be the call frequency for each classification of customer?

Note: A standard sales call represents an average call which takes a quarter of the working day. For some large, complex customers, a sales representative might spend half a day, or *two* standard calls, on each visit. For example, a major customer, although only *visited* 12 times a year, may be rated as a 24 calls-per-year customer because each visit lasts half a day.

(The solution to this test is detailed at the end of this chapter.)

In a small company there is a tendency for everybody, whatever their function, to get involved with customers, while in a large company the ivory tower syndrome can be broken down by co-opting senior management to key customer teams. Part of this co-opting process is to commit such managers as a resource allocation, so that the financial controller makes 40 standard calls per year and the general manager makes 60 standard calls per year. In this way, the reactive attitudes of senior management – being available for customer liaison 'as required' – is converted into a pro-active plan to develop the web of customer contacts at all levels, which is at the heart of the concept of key customer relationship management.

Exhibit 4b

Customer management structure: The Xerox company

The permutations and possibilities are infinite but an example of customer relationship management working at its best is demonstrated by a closer examination of how Xerox operates in Belgium. They have a three-tier structure – a key customer organization, a general sales organization and distributors. Their key customer organization consists of five key customer teams each handling up to 12 customers at any one time. The teams specialize by type of customer and are multifunctional in that all senior managers are co-opted to one or other team (usually as members, not co-ordinators).

The general sales organization is structured along traditional geographic lines with area and regional sales managers. Salespeople deal with all product lines and, for geographic or contact reasons, may be seconded as part-time members of one of the key customer teams to develop their experience and maturity.

The third layer of the sales organization (distributors) deals with a myriad of small customers, who collectively add up to a worthwhile sector of the market but are so fragmented and dispersed as to make direct sales coverage not cost-effective. Distributors have exclusive territories and are managed by two sales managers.

Such an organizational structure splendidly addresses the old problem in sales organizations of career progression: what do you do with the able salesperson who needs the motivation of promotion and status? The theoretical sales promotion ladder in Xerox has many rungs. The trainee salesperson might start as a relief or back-up representative before getting a specific sales territory. From there, they would progress to being a full member of a key customer team after some part-time assignments. An experienced key customer team member might return to the general sales team as an area manager. The next promotion is back to a key customer team as a manager (or co-ordinator), returning eventually to general sales as a regional manager or distributor sales manager. In this way, the salesperson has the opportunity to demonstrate leadership and teamworking skills at an escalating level of responsibility. Those with people-management skills might go on to sales director or general management positions. The salesperson with particular aptitude for selling, rather than for people management, might be promoted to more sales-oriented jobs such as distributor sales manager.

A more complex exhibit concerning the organization of a multi-product pharmaceutical company may be explored on the **www.business-minds.com/KCRM** website.

HOW DO YOU PLAN INTERNAL RESOURCES?

The planning and setting up of internal support services, whether a general sales office or one dedicated to key customer business, demands similar levels of analysis and calculation of resources needed in order to respond quickly and positively to customer situations. The first stage is to list the customer-impinging tasks undertaken by internal staff, from the receptionist to the secretary to the general manager. This checklist should be framed in such a way as to make it a tool for calculating the internal resources needed as the business grows and for monitoring the quality or service given. An example checklist follows:

Internal resource calculation

Tasks	Monitoring criteria
■ *Orders*:	how long does it take to process an average order? how many orders are there per key customer per year?
■ *Telephone contacts inward*:	how many incoming telephone calls are being handled by reception? when are the peaks and troughs of traffic flow? how many times does the phone ring before being answered? how long do customers wait before being connected? what is the length of an 'average' phone call?
■ *Telephone contacts outward*:	how many outgoing telephone calls are there per order/customer/day/week/month? what is the average duration of customer

calls? when are the peaks and troughs of outgoing telephone traffic?

■ *Liaison with technical and other departments:* how many instances of such liaison are there per order/ customer/day/ week/month? what is the average duration? when are the peaks and troughs?

■ *Preparing quotations:* what is the average time to prepare a quotation; how many quotations are there per customer/day/ week/month?

■ *Correspondence and memos:* how many written contacts are there per customer/day/week/ month? what is the average time to prepare one item?

■ *Getting information:* how much time is taken for this activity per customer/day/week/ month/order?

■ *Updating customer records:* how much time is taken for this activity per customer/day/week/ month?

■ *Contacts per salesperson:* how much time is taken for this activity per salesperson/manager/ day/week/month?

■ *Preparation of presentation material:* how much time is taken for this activity per customer/sales-person/presentation?

■ *Showroom visits:* how many visits are made per day/week/ month? what is the average duration of visits and number of work hours taken to do this?

- *Exhibition work*: how many exhibitions are there per week/ month/year? what is the average duration and number of work hours involved?

- *Telesales calls*: how many calls are there per day/week/month? what is the number of customers to be covered and the planned call frequency?

- *Departmental meetings and training*: how many meetings are there per year? how long are the meetings? how much time is spent with salespeople in the field on customer familiarization visits?

- *Reports*: how many internal reports are there per month? how much time is taken to prepare each report?

The main purpose of this analysis is to assess the resources necessary to maintain the highest level of service to customers, particularly key customers. These activities may be divided into two categories – *fixed* and *variable*.

- *Fixed*

  This refers to those activities that take a specific fixed amount of time irrespective of the number of customers, orders or salespeople involved. Reports, departmental meetings and training will take, almost certainly, a set, predictable number of hours or days per year.

- *Variable*

  Almost all other activities can be related to numbers of customers, orders or volume of business. The more the workload of these activities can be correlated to the number and size of customers, the more the internal resource can be planned to meet the service levels demanded, and the more easily can bottom-line profitability be determined for key customer activity.

Some activities, such as field sales supervision, exhibition work or showroom visits, may be semi-variable in that there may not be a direct correlation with changes in business volume. In these cases, the workload might change in *steps*: for example, business might grow to a point where the company chooses to take part in three exhibitions a year instead of two, thereby increasing this activity by 50 per cent overnight. The company might appoint a fifth sales-person, thus stepping up the need for daily contacts by 25 per cent instantly. It might be more realistic to treat these activities as fixed.

If possible, an analysis of the variable workload should be established customer by customer for key and development customers. For example, in the Apex Component Company exhibit, the forecast sales to the number one top customer in year 1 is £540 000. The internal sales resource workload necessary to service this single customer is highlighted in Table 4.4. which also attempts to quantify the total internal sales office workload.

Estimating the workload for each of the key customers and development customers, together with general business as a whole, gives a total workload of 13 950 person-hours per year, which correlates directly with numbers of orders and numbers of customers. Adding other department activities gives a total internal sales administration workload for the department of 18 865 person-hours in a year.

If the average number of working days (220) translates into 1708 hours, a total of 11 people are needed to fulfil the internal sales administration workload. As the *variable* workload directly related to volume of business has been established as 13 950 hours, or 74 per cent of the total department resource, it is possible to estimate the departmental workload in year 3. An estimated 36 per cent increase in business would increase the variable workload by 5022 hours, or the equivalent of three more people.

Of course, these calculations take little account of the peaks and troughs of not just seasonal but daily business. For example, there could be heavy telephone traffic in the early morning and mid-to-late afternoon, which could cause delays in answering or a queue building up on the switchboard. The efficient handling of incoming telephone calls is a key success factor in any sales office, but is absolutely vital in a key customer organization. A disproportionate

Table 4.4 Sales administration workload calculation

Sales administration workload for Number 1 customer

£540k @equation: average value £2400=225 orders @ 1hr/order	= 225 hrs/year
60% of orders involve 1/2 hr inter-dept liaison	= 68 hrs/year
20 out/in telephone calls per week @ ¼ hr each	= 50 hrs/year
30 special quotations per year @ 4 hours	= 120 hrs/year
50 items of in/out correspondence per year @ 1 hour	= 50 hrs/year
Getting special information and updating records (est.)	= 50 hrs/year
Total internal resource needed for No. 1 customer	= 763 hrs/year

Sales administration workload for internal sales office

Total administration workload for top ten customers	= 6 300 hrs/year
Total administration workload for development customers	= 3 400 hrs/year
Total general business workload	= 4 250 hrs/year
Total administration resource need	= 13 950 hrs/year

plus

Telesales operation

80 customers contacted weekly (½ hr call duration)	= 2 000 hrs/year

Contact work with/on behalf of salespeople

5 salespeople; 1 hour per day per salesperson	= 1 250 hrs/year

Preparation of presentation material

50 major presentations per year @ 4 hours per event	= 200 hrs/year

Exhibit work

3 major exhibitions per year – preparation and travel	= 168 hrs/year
– stand administration	= 72 hrs/year

Reports and memos

3 departmental reports weekly @ 2 hrs per report	= 3000 hrs/year
25 departmental memos weekly @ ½ hour per memo	= 625 hrs/year

Reports and memos

3 departmental reports weekly @ 2 hrs per report	= 300 hrs/year
25 departmental memos weekly @ ½ hour per memo	= 625 hrs/year

Showroom visits

100 per year @ 3 hours	= 300 hrs/year

Total resource needed for internal sales office	**= 18 865 hrs/year**

part of the customer's perception of a supplier is based on their experience with telecommunications. For this reason:

- don't be afraid to over-staff your reception facility;

- stipulate to everybody in the office that no incoming call must exceed four rings before being answered – and anybody can answer;

- get into the habit of phoning your own office twice a week for the express purpose of monitoring the time it takes for a call to be answered.

The Apex Component company has a limited range of regular customers but if your company has thousands of customers, then the analysis and calculation of workload should be done by customer groups or classifications, based upon averages for that group or type of customer. If your business is capital goods-based or project-based, then substitute 'contracts' or 'projects' for 'customers'.

Customer management is about the allocation and investment of resources towards targeted areas with significant leverage in order to have a dramatic impact on your business. Resources do not come cheap and you will never have enough. Instinctive arguments only work with chief executives if they are backed by hard analysis and justification. It may seem pedantic, but this level of sometimes painstaking detail goes with the job of customer management.

HOW CAN YOU IMPROVE YOUR SALES FORECASTING?

Putting numbers onto future company sales and profit is hazardous, even though the swings and roundabouts theory can balance out specific inaccuracies. Forecasting sales to a particular key customer may not have the cushion of overall statistical smoothing but should, at least, be based on a trusting and open disclosure of mutual expectations.

Each customer is unique, but it is important to differentiate between three types of seller and buyer situations: repeat end-user sales, sales to distributors and contract or capital goods sales.

Repeat end-users

You have to forecast potential changes in the customer's business overall and your share of the business. Seven steps are involved and these are:

1 tabulate past figures of customer *total usage* of your type of product from *all suppliers*;

2 tabulate *your* past sales figures to this customer;

3 calculate *your share* of the customer's business over recent years;

4 estimate changes in the customer's *total future business*;

5 estimate changes in *your share* of the customer's total business;

6 translate these estimates into *numerical forecasts*;

7 consult with and check out forecasts and mutual *expectations* with the customer.

Sales to distributors

The method of forecasting is the same as for repeat end-user sales but with additional emphasis on evaluating the likely changes in your distributor's *final user market* and their share of it.

Contract or capital goods sales

Capital goods purchases are characterized by long lead times, high values and irregular orders. The two main issues in forecasting are *probability* and *timing*. There are five steps to such forecasts:

1 divide the year into four quarters or periods appropriate to your business;

2 estimate the likely sales value of the contracts under consideration;

3 estimate the probability of getting the contract in the form of a percentage;

4 estimate the probability of securing the contract in a particular period by skewing 100 per cent across the periods in which it could possibly land;

5 calculate the forecast value per quarter by multiplying your probability estimate by the timing estimate and anticipated contract value.

Provided that there are ten or more contracts under review, this forecasting method will give a reasonably accurate idea of likely order input per quarter. See Table 4.5 for an illustration of this.

Table 4.5   A method for forecasting contract sales

	Estimated Value £000	Contract probability	Timing probability				£000 value			
			Q1	Q2	Q3	Q4	Q1	Q2	Q3	Q4
Contract A	200	75%	20%	60%	20%	–	30	90	30	–
Contract B	200	20%	50%	50%	–	–	20	20	–	–
Contract C	400	50%	–	10%	50%	40%	–	20	100	80
			Sales forecast per quarter (£000)				50	130	130	80

In a complex multi-product company, the task of assembling and manipulating data may represent 80 per cent of the forecaster's task. This is one activity where software can contribute significantly in taking the burden. Spreadsheets are invaluable but such user-friendly programs as Prophecy have real added-value.

HOW DO CUSTOMER TEAMS WORK?

In considering organizational change, too often we fall into the trap of focusing on our own constraints and conveniences. In a customer-driven environment, we have to organize ourselves in the most efficient way to service and meet the needs of the customer.

Our internal difficulties, such as changing the commission scheme, altering lines of command and revising our control systems are secondary to the prime need of tailoring ourselves to the customer's environment. If our customers are the other side of the world, we have to adjust our communication times to match their clocks: if our customers speak little English, we have to translate our product labels and operating manuals.

In the same way, changing our sales organization structure to embrace customer relationship management principles may give us the opportunity to reconsider the traditional functional approach to company structure. If we are relationship building with selected key customers, we need co-ordinated performance at all points of inter-company contact – service, distribution, production and accounts.

Team members and their responsibilities

Any reorganization of customer management presents a splendid opportunity to break down traditional formal interfunctional barriers by introducing the concept of the *customer team*. The customer team is multifunctional and led by a key customer co-ordinator. The members of the team may be drawn from the following areas or departments:

- *regional sales* if the customer has widespread geographical locations or international operations;
- *customer service* if there are specific service complications and emergencies with major implications for the customers' operations;
- *technical* if there are possibilities of special product applications;
- *training* if there is a significant education element to ensure the customer gets the full benefit of your product;
- *product experts* if there are highly specialized products involved;
- *internal sales* if there is a high incidence of direct customer–supplier communication by telephone and fax;
- *distribution* if the schedule of deliveries is complicated and exceptional degrees of flexibility and response are paramount;
- *advertising* if creative merchandising and promotion are major aspects of the customer relationship;
- *production* if product availability, inventory or fluctuations in demand are sensitive areas of the customer relationship;
- *finance* if there are significant financial implications in negotiations, such as leasing, capital investment or taxation;
- *senior management* if high-level company politics are a significant relationship factor.

Customer teams may handle a limited number of key customers, grouped, perhaps, by industry. For example, the *financial services* key customer group may specialize in banks, building societies and insurance companies; the *service company* key customer group might include car-rental companies, airlines and travel agents in their portfolio. In this way, a key customer group is well-placed for specialized development of new products, services and applications to suit the specific needs of the customers they deal with.

In very large businesses with high-volume customers, a supplier might have a customer team dedicated to one customer. In the US, Procter & Gamble has a customer team for Wal-Mart. In Belgium, Xerox has one team working full-time on the European Union organization in Brussels.

Businesses with smaller resources may have to be content with a key customer team which is less dedicated, in a technical sense, and embraces a variety of key customers. Frequently in such cases the members of the customer team have a variety of roles. Each member of the team may co-ordinate a handful of customers themselves but act as a team member for other customers who are co-ordinated by other members of the team. Of course, in companies with a limited number of staff it may be impractical for, say, a highly specialized technician to serve on *every* customer team. In such circumstances, it may be advisable to have *core* customer team members with *affiliate* members who are kept informed but do not attend team meetings. The principle of affiliate members should be extended as far across the organizational structure as possible; ideally, every employee should be an affiliate of at least one customer team. In this way, staff are motivated and an enterprise discovers hidden talents and becomes less dependent on specific individuals.

If, in extreme cases, the concept of customer teams is unworkable then the effort must be made to focus the agenda of management meetings on specific key customers rather than on functional reporting or time-based subjects.

SUMMARY

Marketing has been described as the allocation of resources. The use of resources in key customer management is critical. The key customer manager is making a conscious investment of people and money into selected customer alliances. This needs a customer coverage plan with the starting point being the assessment of workload requirements and the resources available.

All good business starts with activity. Sound forecasting methods will also play a part in optimizing the use of resources. Ensure that your organization is a mirror of how your key customers' decision systems work. This will usually mean creating customer teams for your largest customers because of the complexity of the sales, technical and administrative contacts. When these teams are effective they create synergy. Synergy – when the whole is greater than the sum of the parts – might be described as the prime outcome of leadership in an organization.

EXERCISE: SALES COVERAGE TEST – POSSIBLE SOLUTION

Data

	Number of customers	Total revenue	Call frequency per year		Total routine visits per year
Classification A	50	£4m	24		1200
Classification B	100	£4m	12		1200
Classification C	150	£3m	6		900
Classification D	200	£2m	3		600
Total customers	500	£13m		routine visits	3900
				+ development	100
				+ prospecting	400
				= total workload	4400

Method

1 Calculate total available resource (calls per year for five sales representatives)

2 Deduct development workload = net available resource

3 Deduct prospecting visits = net resource for routine visits

4 Based on revenue, divide available resource by classification

5 Divide available resource per classification by number of customers = calls per year

6 Adjust, if advisable, from classification A downwards

7 Balance the planned coverage with available resource (increase if viable)

How much do you really *know* about planning your business?

SELF EVALUATION

Check out the following statements about your organization; the issues and implications are discussed in Chapter 5.

Tick your answers as appropriate; ? = not sure.

	NO	?	YES

How would you describe your market supply chain?
- *a fragmented market with many competitors of equal size*
- *low market growth precipitating fights for market share*
- *undifferentiated products that allow buyers to change suppliers*
- *high fixed costs or product perishability encouraging price wars*
- *high level of demand and supply fluctuations*
- *high exit barriers that keep companies competing with low profit*

What are the main entry barriers to new competitors or substitute products?
- *economies of scale*
- *product differentiation: strong brand names and customer loyalty*
- *capital resource requirements*
- *cost disadvantages: due to inexperience, locations, technology*
- *access to distribution channels*
- *government policy, licence requirements and so on*

Does your key customers' purchasing power reflect the fact that
- *they are volume purchasers in heavy, fixed-cost industries?*
- *the products they buy are undifferentiated?*
- *the products they buy are a significant part of their overall costs?*
- *the products they buy do not affect their product quality?*
- *their companies are struggling with losses or low profits?*

	NO	?	YES

Do you think you need a business plan because
- *your key customers absorb a major part of available resources?*
- *your key customers impact significantly on corporate objectives?*
- *senior management needs to be convinced about your strategy?*

Does your current business planning process adequately cover
- *market analysis?*
- *environmental analysis?*
- *competitor analysis?*
- *base-line projections if no changes are made?*
- *key results areas?*
- *key performance factors?*
- *possible constraints on performance?*
- *strengths and opportunities?*
- *weaknesses and threats?*
- *strategic options?*

Looking at your company organization structure:
- *has the work been grouped into units of corresponding activities?*
- *is the organization too flat or does it have too many levels?*
- *are all specific vital functions covered – external and internal?*
- *does everybody know exactly what is expected of them?*
- *has the workload been evaluated and resourced?*
- *do individuals have the skill and ability to perform their tasks?*

What are your main strategic issues?
- *which and how many key customers are you targeting for growth?*

	NO	?	YES

– which products are you seeking to emphasize and
develop?

– what is the minimum acceptable and expected growth in
business?

– what must be the minimum acceptable and expected
profitability?

– what price and quality policy must be pursued with key
customers?

THE KEY CUSTOMER MANAGER AS ADVISER AND COUNSELLOR

In basic selling, when you are dealing with a multiplicity of
customers, the scope of discussions with individual customers may
be fairly limited: what are their needs relative to your product's
features and benefits? how does your offer differ from your
competitors'? how can your customer's resistance to change be
overcome? Key customer management, by definition, is dealing with
a *few* customers who have or will have a significant impact on your
survival. Key customer management is about knowledge of those
customers – knowledge in *depth*.

Customer managers must have the ability to discuss at any level
almost any business topic, both with their customer's people and
their own people – finance with financiers, marketing with
marketers, materials requirement planning with production
engineers, or whatever. It is not necessary to be an expert in all these
areas, but it is essential to know the language, to know the questions
to ask and to know enough to understand the customer's questions.
Customer managers are trying to orchestrate the many relationship
influences in the customer's organization structure and, at the same
time, gain the approval and commitment of all the players in their
own company team. To this end the key customer managers must be
part of their own company's business planning process and ideally
play significant roles in their customers' business plan preparation.

An appreciation of how a *business plan* is drawn up is mandatory, starting with an understanding of how the *value chain* in which the company and the key customer are involved works.

SUPPORTING THE VALUE CHAIN IN YOUR BUSINESS

Every business is part of an added-value chain: it buys something, does something to it and sells it on at a higher price. The difference between the price it pays and the price at which it sells is added-value. Hopefully, the added-value is more than the cost of doing what has to be done.

Any chain is only as strong as the weakest link and it is in everybody's interest to maintain the strength of the chain and to keep the members of the chain equipped to compete yet be profitable. The key customer manager will regard the customer as the *next* link in the added-value chain but will have to have enough vision to assess the threats and opportunities further down the chain with the customer's customer, or even his customer's customer's customer.

No matter how beneficial your product may be, if your *customers* cannot sell *their* products, you are in trouble. Occasionally customer managers might have to take a backward glance at their own supply sources in order to ensure that they can maintain a competitive position in the chain but, for the most part, their efforts will be directed

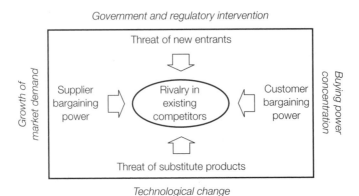

Figure 5.1   Forces influencing the value chain

forward down the chain, closely watching the competitive forces that will affect the health and prosperity of their customers' business.

There are five factors that may have impact on the strength of a customer's business.

1 *Competition within your key customer's own industry*: the intensity of marketplace competition that your customer experiences might be particularly strong due to:

- a fragmented market where there are many competitors of equal size;
- low market growth, precipitating fights for market share between ambitious competitors;
- undifferentiated products that permit buyers to change suppliers readily and with minimum switching costs;
- high fixed costs or perishability of the product, which encourages price wars when demand slackens;
- a high level of demand and supply fluctuations due to large incrementations of capacity leading to periods of over-capacity in the industry;
- high exit barriers that keep companies competing with low, or even negative, returns on investment.

2 *Threat of new entrants*: the ease with which your customer's business can be threatened by new competitors will depend upon the entry barriers present and the reaction that new entrants can expect from existing competitors – the entry barrier being one of six types:

- economies of scale: the new entrant has to come in on a large scale or to accept a cost disadvantage (assuming the incumbents are optimizing their efficiency) in terms of production, research, service, marketing, distribution, financing and sales-force utilization, for example in the petrochemicals and consumer electronics industries;
- product differentiation: particularly evident in the strength of brand names and customer loyalty. This forces entrants to spend heavily on advertising which is, perhaps, the most important entry barrier in the cosmetics, over-the-counter drugs and investment banking industries;

- capital resource requirements: the need to invest big money in order to compete, particularly if that investment is non-recoverable, such as up-front advertising or research and development;

- general cost disadvantages: entrenched companies have cost advantages in experience, locations, proprietary technology or access to raw materials, such as in the aircraft building industry;

- access to distribution channels: the fewer the wholesale or retail channels and the more the existing competitors have them tied up, the tougher the entry into that industry will be, for example in the soft drink industry;

- government policy: licence requirements, regulations and controls on such aspects as pollution standards and safety can limit or even foreclose entry, for instance to television franchises and telecommunications.

So entrants might well be deterred if incumbents have, on earlier occasions, been unwelcoming to newcomers or have substantial defensive resources measured in terms of cash, borrowing power, productive capacity or strong influence with distribution channels or major customers. Thriving industries with high attractiveness for new entrants will be jealously and fearlessly protected by the incumbents and any customer manager who is seduced into supplying a newcomer to an industry must expect a disproportionate backlash in business with existing customers.

3 *Threat of substitute products or services*: such products impact in two ways:

- in extreme cases they can wipe out the existing business with breakthrough technology, for example, wordprocessors vs. typewriters, video vs. instant movie film, digital photography vs. traditional film;

- by placing a ceiling on prices that can be charged, substitute products limit the potential of an industry and unless the product can be differentiated significantly, the industry will suffer in earnings and perhaps growth. For example, fibreglass prices were limited by many cheaper insulation substitutes such as cellulose and styrofoam

4 *Powerful buyers*: the customers of your key customer may have, to varying degrees, the power to force down prices and demand higher quality or more service from your key customer, as well as playing competitors off against each other, and will be particularly powerful if:

- they are volume purchasers in heavy, fixed-cost industries;
- the products they buy are undifferentiated;
- the products they buy represent a significant fraction of *their* overall product costs;
- the quality of the products they buy does not affect the quality of their own products;
- their companies are struggling with losses or low profits.

5 *Powerful suppliers*: suppliers can exert pressure on an industry by raising prices or reducing quality, possibly squeezing profitability out of an industry unable to recover cost increases in its own prices, so they can (but might be unwise to do so) exert their power when:

- they have a relative monopoly on supplies;
- they have a strongly differentiated product with high switching costs for the customer;
- they pose a threat of integrating forward into the customer's business;
- the customer is not particularly important to the supplier in terms of size or profit.

As advisers and counsellors, key customer managers have to demonstrate awareness of the business pressures on their customers and display in dealings with them an empathy that, in the longer term, will ensure the survival and growth of their own business.

WHY DO YOU NEED A BUSINESS PLAN?

Consideration of the implications of this value chain will recur frequently in planning key customer business. Planning is not a specific, isolated task; it is an integrated, all-encompassing process of managing the future. It is the art – but not the science – of making decisions based upon knowledge, trends and assumptions. The planning system should answer four questions:

1 *Where do we stand?* – internal and external analysis;

2 *Where do we want to go?* – mission, policies, objectives, planning gaps;

3 *How are we going to achieve this?* – strategies, action programmes, action plans;

4 *How can we monitor progress?* – review and control.

As a customer manager, you will either be directly responsible for key customers or manage a team of customer co-ordinators and must be a key player in the preparation of your overall company or divisional business plan. The format of the corporate business plan will be appropriate to the size and nature of your company and the diversity of markets into which you sell your products or services. The creation of a business plan is a both a top-down and a bottom-up process; directors and senior managers will determine overall company direction and objectives that, in turn, will influence strongly the criteria used to prioritize your key customers and activities. The key customer management must determine the resources needed and forecast results which will, in turn, shape the options available in the business plan. Most of this strategic thinking will stem from specific development plans for each individual key customer prepared by the person co-ordinating that business.

> Planning is the art – but not the science –
> of making decisions based upon knowledge,
> trends and assumptions.

At least, that is how it *should* work. Sadly, and only too often, companies suffer from 'spreadsheet-itis' – where careful planning is discarded when the profit figure in the bottom right-hand cell of the spreadsheet does not match up to the demands of the board and the numbers get manipulated to produce the desired result. The business plan's effectiveness depends upon the commitment to credibility in its preparation and the way in which it is used as a management tool.

The planning horizon should stretch perhaps no more than three years ahead, but even this may be too long for some high-technology companies. However, three years is probably an appropriate period of time to measure the effectiveness of any key customer operation that is primarily concerned with the investment of resources into long-term relationships with preferred customers.

HOW DO YOU STRUCTURE A COMPANY BUSINESS PLAN?

The business plan is made up of two major sections:

- situation analysis
- the action plan

A summary of the business plan documentation is shown in Table 5.1.

Completing the situation analysis

Market analysis

A *short* description of the markets served by your company and their business activities:

- what are the activities? how is the operation divided up? what are your product lines? what is your geographical distribution? what are your service departments? what markets are served? what types of customer? and so on;
- describe each activity:
  - major product lines
  - market sectors; volume, trend, share, competition in those market sectors
  - market share and position, quality, price, service, extent of product range, distribution
  - strengths and weaknesses in your market sectors
  - the distribution channels for your products

- turnover and gross profit from these activities
- number of people involved in these activities; production, sales, and so on
- relative importance to your customers of your product and service in terms of finance, technology, brand or supply.

Table 5.1   Summary of company business plan documentation

The company business plan	
Situation analysis	**Action plan**
1 Market analysis	1 Mission statement
2 Environmental analysis	2 Policies
3 Competitor analysis	3 Objectives and planning gaps
4 Position analysis	4 Overall strategies to fill planning gaps
5 Base-line projection	5 Action plans and action programmes
6 Key result areas for achievement of objectives	6 Adjustment of action plans and planning gaps
7 Key performance factors	7 Review and control
8 Constraints on performance	
9 Strengths (internal) and opportunities (external)	
10 Weaknesses (internal) and threats (external)	
11 Strategic options for profitable growth	
12 Organization structure	
13 Current strategic emphasis	
14 Major strategic issues	

Environmental analysis

Environmental factors are those forces over which an organization has little or no control but that do, however, affect the operation of the organization. Changes in environmental factors can bring major opportunities if recognized. They may also constitute a threat, making it necessary to make changes in products or in the way in which the organization operates. By recognizing the political, technological and socio-economic changes which, in your opinion, have an effect on your business, you can determine their probable effect and prepare offensive or defensive plans, either to make the most of the available opportunity or to minimise the influence of the perceived threat.

Include only those environmental factors which, in your opinion:

■ will have a major influence on factors which are relevant to your business;

■ are likely to take effect in the planning period.

Table 5.2   Examples of environmental impact and response

Factor	Impact	Response
Economic factor		
Continuous inflation of 6% to 7% per year	Rising costs; some consumer resistance to price rises	Tighter internal cost controls; fixed price policy; review of product design
Technological factor		
Gradual replacement of steel with plastic in leading product	Lower weight; probably cheaper; easy to transport; increased support competitiveness	Watch technological development; old stocks kept low; export specification changes to product

Competitor analysis

An accurate analysis of the competition is essential if planning is to be effective. This analysis will indicate the characteristics and activities that competitors have developed which have led to success or failure. This information can be used for the formulation of realistic objectives and for working out counter-strategies and plans.

Typically there will be only a limited number of competitors for each product with whom you compete directly and with whom you are best acquainted. Make this competitor analysis for each major product line. Try to adopt a quantitative approach. For example, evaluate each competitor as perceived by your customers on a scale of 1 to 10 (worst = 1 and excellent = 10). Indicate the share of business held by each competitor and evaluate your own company in the same way. Subsequently determine which characteristics, in your opinion, describe your top two competitors. At this stage you are making a more general assessment but, as part of your key customer development planning, you will be setting up customer-specific performance reviews for each individual key customer which will be more detailed.

Base-line projection

Project the results for the planning period on the basis of an *unchanged* operation.

This is the trend under current circumstances if the policy remains unchanged. *No* account is taken of plans for the future. Later on in the planning system you will formulate objectives for the planned period. These will improve your base-line projection because, on the basis of the strategies and the plans of action you formulate, you are going to develop your strong points, exploit potential opportunities, minimize your weak points and operate more effectively.

The base-line is, therefore, a projection for when policies remain unchanged.

First, construct a *base-line* per product at *constant* prices.

Second, take the following into consideration:

■ the expected *percentage price rise* per year

■ the estimated *percentage of overall market growth* per year

■ any other *external* factors that will affect the data, such as currency shifts or raw material shortages.

Make a base-line projection for turnover, gross profits or volume as appropriate. This will give you a kind of risk-analysis: that is, where will the company stand if it keeps on doing business the same way it has been doing.

Key results areas for achievement of company objectives

■ Areas of responsibility where performance makes a significant impact on the achievement of business objectives, either positively or negatively

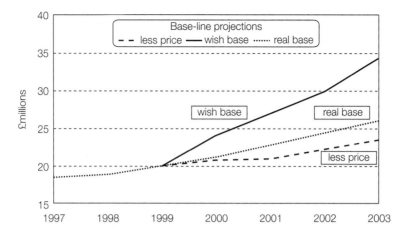

Figure 5.2   Base-line projection and 'wish' objectives

■ Areas of responsibility where performance could produce bottlenecks or breakthroughs for others

Key result areas are the most important present or future information
standards by which management can evaluate and check the results
achieved. Key result areas must be capable of being measured objectively and are, therefore, absolute data, ratios or percentages. Some
of these norms will also appear in the objectives that will be formulated later.

The importance to planning this part of the analysis is the recognition and introduction into the planning system of key criteria for
measuring and controlling the various activities. For example:

■ average percentage gross profit to be 27 per cent minimum;

■ average sales per key customer to be at least £1.5 million in year
   2000, increasing to £2.25 million in year 2003;

■ debtor balance no higher than 45 days;

■ drop-in total sales costs as a percentage from 22.8 per cent in year
   2000, to 19.9 per cent in year 2003.

Key performance factors

These are the activities relating to key results areas that your organization must carry out effectively in order to maintain business in the
first place and to achieve target objectives in the second place.

Orientate your planning towards those activities and make sure that you take them into account when drawing up your action plans. Examples of such activities might be:

- maintaining essential knowledge for all sales personnel through at least three days of product training per year;
- protecting your reputation for good quality by maintaining product rejection below two per cent of total output;
- responding to and acting upon 98 per cent of service calls within 24 hours of receipt;
- supplying prototypes of new packaging to key customers within three weeks on initiation of new project.

Constraints on performance

These are certain obstacles that may, under the existing circumstances, set limits with respect to the percentage of revenue growth you can achieve in sales, profitability or both. Examples might include:

- a shrinking market for the most important product lines
- government importation limits or price restrictions on your products
- two larger competitors dominating the market
- excess of industrial capacity, leading to severe price competition
- insufficient means to finance growth
- limited opportunities for growth through a lack of product development.

Such limitations are related to or arise from weaknesses or problems. However, they are not necessarily identical to them. Often these constraints are external factors.

With the aid of the market, environmental and competitor analyses and an audit of constraints on performance, now consider your strengths and weaknesses. Do this from two points of view:

1 *the intrinsic analysis of your company* – an analysis of what goes on *inside* your company, designating these internal factors as *strengths* and *weaknesses*;

2   *the extrinsic analysis of your company* – an analysis of what goes on *outside* the company, namely the way in which the company operates in the environment and its position in comparison to its competitors. For the purpose of differentiation, external factors are designated *opportunities* and *threats.*

Strengths and opportunities

Strengths are characteristics within your organization that increase its effectiveness. Opportunities are those aspects outside your organization with regard to relationships, products, services or activities that, by means of further development, expansion or improvement of operating methods, offer major prospects of profitable growth.

The importance of this analysis is that the identified strengths and opportunities can be used as a basis for plans of action for the further exploitation of these strengths and opportunities. It is, moreover, sensible to distinguish between the strengths that will be further exploited during the planning period and those which will not be further exploited. In principle opportunities should *always* be further exploited, at some point.

Weaknesses and threats

Weaknesses are characteristics *within* your organization that hinder its effectiveness. Threats are those factors *outside* your organization that form a major obstacle to profitable growth. Here, too, it makes sense to distinguish between those factors that *can* be acted upon within the planning period and those that *cannot.*

Strategic options for profitable growth

Every enterprise sells a permutation of products to a variety of customers. When seeking profitable growth, there are four strategic options to consider:

- penetration: increasing the sales of *existing* products to *existing* customers

- expansion: expanding the *number of customers* to whom you sell *existing* products

- development: developing *new products* to sell to your *existing* customers

- diversification: developing *new products* for sale to *new customers.*

What are the possibilities? Quantify what things might be done to improve your operating methods, which new customers can be targeted, which new products could be sold to existing and to new customers. Perhaps the best way of defining all the potentials for profitable growth is in a brainstorming session – stimulating everybody to come up with creative ideas. However, in general terms, the cost of creating new relationships makes the new products for existing customers option the most attractive for many suppliers. This viewpoint is also reflected in advertising, where the true value of established brand names is now much exploited in launching new products such as Virgin financial services and Mars ice cream bars.

Organization structure

This is the arrangement of responsibilities and authority among individuals in order to maximize the effort to achieve the objectives of the organization. The organization structure is a tool that should enhance the effort to achieve those objectives that result from planning. The effectiveness with which the team executes its plan can be directly affected by the way in which it identifies, evaluates and groups the work to be performed in the pursuit of its objectives. A review and critique of the organization structure can provide a basis for future organization design in the light of new objectives and programmes. Assess the organization from different points of view, for example:

- has the work been grouped in manageable units of corresponding activities?

- is the organization too flat or does it have too many levels?

- are all specific vital functions covered – external and internal?

- does everybody know exactly what is expected of them?

- has the workload been evaluated and can it be fulfilled with the available resource?

- to what extent do individuals have the skill and ability to perform their allocated tasks?

Current strategic emphasis

This is a summary of your *current* strategies for achieving your *base-line projection*. When determining your current strategic emphasis, take the following points into consideration.

- What were the objectives when the current strategy was formulated?

- How relevant are those objectives to the current situation?

- What has been the overall strategy (general course of action) in the past three to five years? For example:
  - on what factors has the emphasis been laid – on products (which?), markets, cost control, growth in turnover, profitability, volume?
  - in which areas (functional or geographic) have staff, time and money been concentrated?
  - what are the base-line wish objectives for these areas?

Later on in the business plan, you will formulate objectives. At the moment, however, state briefly how you intend to achieve the desired base-line.

Major strategic issues

During the entire planning process, various strategic issues keep appearing. It is important that agreement is achieved about these issues before you carry on with further planning. Vital decisions will have to be taken that determine the future of your enterprise. *You are now beginning the decision-making process.* Decisions must be made partly on the basis of the possible growth options you have already explored, so state your major strategic issues. For example:

- which and how many key customers are you going to target for growth?

- which products are you seeking to emphasize and develop?
- what is the minimum acceptable and expected growth in business?
- what must be the minimum acceptable and expected profitability?
- what price and quality policy must the enterprise pursue with key customers?

Some of these strategic issues will be encountered later in the policies, objectives and strategies yet to be formulated. Throughout this process the situation analysis should be reviewed continuously.

Formulating the action plan

The mission statement

This is a statement of the activities you wish to develop and overall position you wish to achieve during the planned period. The mission statement reflects most of your strengths and your opinion about those areas in which you will develop your efforts. It may include the following aspects:

- products
- markets or customers
- volumes or resources
- geographical coverage
- costs
- profit
- performance standards (quality, delivery and so on).

A mission statement is the keystone of your planning structure. It does three things:

1 it highlights *deviation* when planning, strategies that fall outside of the activities not being accepted;

2 it gives a *direction* to your plans in that, because you have reached agreement about the orientation of the activities you wish to develop, wasteful effort can be prevented;

3 it generates *commitment* – it is essential that all members of the team are committed to the *same* mission and that everyone applies their efforts in the same direction.

Perhaps most importantly a mission statement will define, by exclusion, the business that you do *not* want.

There is a relationship between the mission and the strategic plan. When the strategic plan is being drawn up and periodically revised, the mission may be adjusted. The nature of the activities may change, though more frequently the mission may be enlarged or reduced in scope. This can be caused by the following:

■ from the internal situation analysis (strengths, weaknesses) you may find that certain efforts are being misdirected;

■ from the external situation analysis it may appear that, in the existing mission, certain opportunities are not being exploited to their fullest extent or even that they no longer, or ever did, exist;

■ the desired objectives may require strategies that are excluded by the mission, so either the objectives or the mission must be adapted; for example, a growth objective may depend on the development of a new product, but the mission excludes specific product-development strategies.

You should compress your mission into one or two paragraphs. It is the first chapter of your strategic plan for the planning period and it should answer the basic planning question: 'Where do we want to go?'

Key customer policies

Policies are general statements or agreements that give direction to thinking, decision making and management actions for achieving company objectives. We are chiefly concerned with policies that influence decisions in strategic planning. Policies are not about daily operational decisions and procedures unless these decisions are so critical that they have a major influence on the progress of the plan.

There are, in the main, three types.

1 Restrictive policies, which prevent certain strategies. For example:

- we do not sell directly to the end-user;
- we do not sell to the government;
- we do not sell any products under own-label or badged brands.

2 Limiting policies, which usually set limits for people involved in planning. For example:
- not more than 20 per cent of our turnover will come from a single exclusive distributor;
- one purchaser will not account for more than 30 per cent of the revenue;
- contract decisions involving revenue of more than £1 million plus will require board approval.

If possible these limiting policies should be quantified and, therefore, will set clearly defined, observable limits.

3 Guiding policies, which give a certain direction to those involved in planning. For example, growth must be realized more by product penetration and customer expansion than by product development.

Policies, particularly limiting policies, set parameters that may not be exceeded without some sort of administrative signal. For example, if you formulate a policy of the type 'no more than 20 per cent of the turnover will come from a single distributor', all orders exceeding 20 per cent will be rejected unless special approval is given. The structure of policies is of a strategic nature because it hinders or stimulates certain strategic actions. The policies themselves are, however, not strategies but agreements that indicate a direction or set limits that must be observed when strategic decisions about the use of available means are taken. Policies are important to planning because a properly structured set of policies will:

- help you to define your mission properly;
- save you from taking the same decisions again and again;
- ensure that no plans are developed that will not be accepted by management;
- ensure that objectively observable limits are set that cannot be exceeded without management action;

- establish a mandate for the manager that defines limits of authority and action.

Objectives and planning gaps

Once you have formulated your mission and your policies, the objectives must be drawn up. Objectives should be:

- from the heart (in the first place); a 'wish objective' rather than the result of calculation
- measurable
- applied to all operational aspects of management
- prioritized in terms of urgency and importance
- challenging, but logical and attainable.

Formulate your wish objective for turnover, gross profit, percentage market share, number of people and, if possible, net profit. There may be other objectives (which cannot be directly expressed in financial terms) that you wish to achieve and that result in strategies and actions, for example:

- taking all possible measures in order to obtain high-quality personnel
- increasing trust and goodwill with the customer
- improving job satisfaction for employees.

As can be seen in Fig. 5.2 earlier, there are wish planning gaps for each year:

The wish objectives are	£m	24.0	27.0	30.0	34.0
The real base-line is	£m	21.4	22.9	24.5	26.2
So the wish planning gap is	£m	2.6	4.1	5.5	7.8

The management of the enterprise is, therefore, charged with two crucial tasks:

1 to achieve the base-line (business as usual);

2 to fill the gap by innovation and change.

Strategies

Planning gaps are filled by strategies that are expressed in action programmes.

Strategies are statements about the *general trend* the company will follow in order to achieve its objectives. Strategies are quite broad: the specifics of who, what, where, when and to what effect are agreed in the action plans. For example, to make an analogy with travel:

- the *objectives* give the place and time of arrival;
- the *strategy* gives the means of transport (car, train, aeroplane, and so on) and the overall route;
- the *action plans* specify the timetables, connections and state exactly what the route is to be (when, where, and so on).

The strategies state in which activities the company will place its resources. External activities will use strategic terminologies such as 'penetration', 'expansion', 'development' or 'diversification'. For internal activities the words 'training' and 'improving' are likely to recur.

List and number your strategies and state the priority of each strategy: A = urgent; B = essential; C = desirable. Examples of strategies that could be organized in this way are:

A (1) to expand the key customer base by 40 per cent
   (2) to increase penetration in the top ten customers by 10 per cent
B (3) to develop the top ten customers by broadening the range of products
   (4) to initiate joint research and development projects with the top ten customers
C (5) to develop and train internal sales resources
   (6) to improve electronic communication systems
   (7) to improve accessibility to customer database

In compiling a strategy checklist ask:
- do the strategies make optimal use of the available opportunities?
- do the strategies exploit your strengths enough?
- are the strategies based on the perceived growth strategies (strategic options)?

- are the strategies in accordance with capacities and means?
- are the strategies too risky?
- are the strategies compatible with the stated objectives?
- can it clearly be seen from the strategies where the majority of efforts will be aimed in order to achieve the objectives?

Action plans and action programmes

Action plans are the means by which your strategies are implemented. The careful choice and preparation of action plans is, therefore, extremely important to the success of the strategic plan. The action plan sets out the major company endeavours with regards to the use of *time, people* and *money* in order to achieve the stated objectives. It specifies *what* will be done, *when* it will be done, *who* will do it, *what* it will cost and *what* it will achieve.

Action programmes consist of a number of action plans that have the same aim. They are deduced from the total situation analysis which is a search for a way in which possible growth strategies can be executed, strengths can be exploited, weaknesses can be minimized, competitors can be defeated, and the existing product, market and relationship situation can be improved.

A strategic plan may be divided into a number of action programmes under classifications such as sales, marketing, finance, organization changes, and so on, and, as we have seen, each action programme usually consists of several action plans.

Draw up action plans only for those things that will change during the planning period. No action plan has to be drawn up for all those things that have already been done to achieve the base-line, unless you wish to improve or alter something.

The following are some guidelines for drawing up an action plan.

- Identify each action plan with a title and a number.
- Identify which overall objective this action plan refers to.
- Identify the specific objective of each action plan – why is it being carried out?
- Identify who bears the general responsibility for the plan concerned (this person may, of course, delegate).

- State, preferably in chronological order, which steps must be carried out in order to execute the plan.

- State who is responsible for each step and when this step must be carried out.

- Do not give too many details in each of the steps, but do specify each step for executing and controlling the action plan.

- Review all steps in order to make sure that there are no overlaps and no steps have been forgotten.

- The steps must be orientated towards results – use verbs to describe each step and avoid too many plans that do nothing except evaluate.

- Quantify the extra financial resources that are required, including the additional capital requirement and the additional expenses that the plan creates (therefore, do not include the costs of existing personnel and other costs that have already been budgeted). A more or less fixed percentage of general costs is often mentioned when increasing turnover, so this is an additional cost and the change to that percentage should be calculated. If extra personnel must be engaged, this too must be indicated and quantified.

- Quantify the expected financial results, including turnover, gross profit (percentage and absolute), net profit and return on capital employed (if possible).

- Non-financial results may also exist and these should be identified.

- Define the suppositions that you have made in the preparation of the plan.

- Assign a priority to each action plan.

Strategic planning is not a system of bookkeeping, but a totally integrated process for managing the future.

Adjustment of action plans and planning gaps

The penultimate step in the planning system is the adjustment of the action plans to take account of the planning gaps. In theory the objectives of the action plans should be sufficient to fill them. What should be done, though, when the planning gap is not filled? Frequently the immediate reaction is to lower wish objectives but this is premature if the following questions have not yet been examined:

- are all the people within your organization capable, talented and creative enough to make new suggestions?

- are your personnel well motivated: are they sufficiently interested and prepared to make new suggestions?

- should the market definition be adapted: does the current market definition offer sufficient potential to achieve the stated objectives?

- do the stated policies and internal organization set too many limits for the perceived opportunities to be optimally exploited?

Only when you are convinced that everything has been tried in order to fill the gap between your wish objective and the base-line with action plans, and the gap is *still* not filled, are you justified in lowering the wish objectives to create practically achievable objectives.

Finalize your definite overall key customer objectives for the planned period with regard to:

- turnover
- gross profit and percentage
- net profit
- capital employed
- return on capital employed
- number of employees
- geographical distribution
- share of the available business
- new products and existing product penetration.

Review and control

The last step of the strategic planning is control. Every action plan should include a schedule for progress evaluation, a chronological plan and estimated costs. Every action plan must be checked individually in order to make sure that no changes have to be made to it or alternative action plans started. The degree of supervision exercised will depend on the relevant experience, maturity and confidence of the people implementing the action plan. Diagnose problems on the basis of facts *and* feelings. Omitting either one of these aspects distorts perspective and is potentially disastrous.

SUMMARY

The job of customer management demands entrepreneurial skills both within your own business and that of your customers. It is essential to have an understanding of your customers' markets and finances and be able to put together a total business plan for your company's key customer initiative. With all functions of the business are competing for resources, you will need an appreciation of the broad issues and priorities to develop a collaborative and synergistic approach to resource allocation.

6

Do you *really* know how profitable your key customers are?

SELF EVALUATION

The quarterly costs of an industrial company are shown below. In the example, there are two direct fixed costs (purchases and salaries) and one indirect fixed cost (rent) that have been allocated across four functions – the salesforce, technical support, distribution and sales administration. Salaries and purchases (which includes travel expenses, stationery, fuel, lighting, heating and exhibitions) are as charged, but rent is allocated on the basis of space occupied. After deliberation, it has been decided that the most realistic method for allocating these functional costs to individual customer profitability statements is as follows:

1 salesforce: as a cost per actual sales visit
2 technical support: as a cost per actual field service day
3 distribution: as a cost per unit of volume despatched
4 sales administration: as a cost per order processed.

	Total £	Salesforce £	Technical £	Distribution £	Administration £
Salaries	86 000	40 000	20 000	20 000	6 000
Purchases	51 000	20 000	5 000	25 000	1 000
Rent	33 000	–	5 000	25 000	3 000
Total	170 000	60 000	30 000	70 000	10 000
No. of sales visits		750			
No. of technical days			200		
Unit volume				70 000	
No. of orders					500
Cost per unit allocated to customer statement		£80 per call	£150 per call	£1 per unit	£20 per order

The company has an annual turnover of £4m of which 60 per cent comes from three key customers, the profitability statements for whom are shown below.

Quarter ending March 31st	Customer A	Customer B	Customer C	All customers
Sales	£300 000	£100 000	£200 000	£1 000 000
Discount	£90 000	£25 000	£80 000	£250 000
Manufacturing costs	£150 000	£50 000	£100 000	£500 000
Gross contribution	£60 000	£25 000	£20 000	£250 000
Salesforce (£80 per call)	£3 200	£2 400	£1 600	£60 000
Technical (£150 per day)	£4 500	£3 000	£4 500	£30 000
Distribution (£1 per unit)	£21 000	£7 000	£14 000	£70 000
Sales administration (£20 per order)	£600	£400	£40	£10 000
Total expenses	£29 300	£12 800	£20 140	£170 000
Trading profit	**£30 700**	**£12 200**	**£ (140)**	**£80 000**

What interpretation would you make of this data and, in particular, what would you do about the loss-making customer C? These issues are discussed later in this chapter.

COMPETING FOR RESOURCES

No matter how skilful the presentation technique, you must be able to justify the rationale of your case to those who allocate resources to you. Investment of resources is the central issue in most persuasion situations and, whether we are talking about time or people, the common denominator will be money. The cost of any problem must outweigh the price of any solution. That is why the quantification of the problem is so important in presentation both to customers and your own management. The size of the problem correlates directly with the motivation to do something about it.

The cost of any problem must outweigh the price of any solution.

The performance of the key customer manager will depend on being able to get resources and allocate them profitably, so the job demands a real understanding of how money works, both in the manager's own business and in the customers' businesses. Not only do key customer managers have to project the likely results of their actions in terms of profit, but they have also to demonstrate the financial effectiveness of the investment after the event in order to maintain credibility and secure further allocations of resources.

The company profit and loss account measures the profitability of the total business but, because it represents all the component parts of the business, it may not show how profitable each of the parts are nor highlight areas for potential action.

Major customers will be responsible for generating, or failing to generate, a significant part of the profit. If a key customer manager is to increase the profit earned from large customers and control the effort invested in them, it is necessary to understand the profit mechanism that operates. The more we seek to customize our products and services, the more essential this becomes.

Most managers will get a regular operating statement showing the revenues and costs their departments have incurred; usually, suppliers will also generate profit and loss accounts by *product*. In many companies, however, the spectacular omission is a profit and loss account for each *key customer*. In this new era of marketing, when we are investing in building relationships on a selected, prefer-ential basis, measuring our performance with each customer is a first priority. However, the fact that precise numbers appear on a piece of paper does not always mean that they represent an accurate picture of the relationship. For profitability measurement to be of real value, management must be aware of the assumptions made in their calcu-lations and the limitations of such data. Accounting is not a finite activity; the allocation of costs and credits is a discussion that key customer managers must be able to understand and, if necessary, argue about.

Because margins are tighter with large customers, suppliers may sometimes question the profitability of such business. Research in a global electrical component manufacturer, however, suggests that the reduced unit cost of dealing with volume customers more than compensated for reduced unit contribution, as shown in Fig. 6.1.

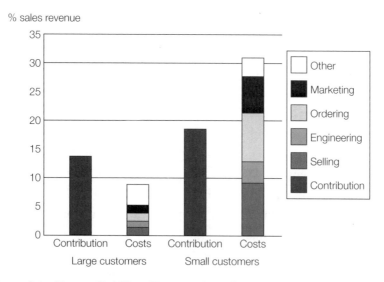

Figure 6.1   The profitability of large and small customers

Tracking customer turnover, volume sales, discounts and directly variable costs is not too difficult. The ambiguities arise in the method of allocation of less specific items such as salesforce, technical support, distribution and administration costs.

HOW TO CREATE A KEY CUSTOMER PROFITABILITY STATEMENT

Let us recapitulate on some basic definitions of cost. *Variable costs* are those that vary in line with changing sales volume, such as raw materials, packaging and so on. *Fixed costs* are those that do not vary over a period of time with changing sales volume, such as management salaries, rents and, maybe, advertising. *Direct costs* are those that are directly attributable to a specific entity such as a product, department or customer. These can be fixed or variable. *Indirect costs* cannot be attributed to a specific entity. One final complication is that there are some costs that are *semi-fixed* (or semi-variable) which vary with changing volumes but not pro rata, for example warehousing, which might be increased in stages.

Many companies calculate overall profitability on the basis of *contribution*, which is simply net sales less direct variable costs and, in this way, avoid the complications of allocating semi-variable and fixed costs. In the delicate business of evaluating key customer relationships and strategies, it may be necessary to go at least one step further in the analysis of the details.

The exercise at the beginning of this chapter sets out a simplified version of the profitability statements for three key customers of an industrial company. The method of cost allocation will vary from company to company and will depend upon how the salesforce and technical support is organized, the size and weight of the product, the method of distribution and the nature of administration involved in servicing the customer.

Interpretation of the customer profitability statements in the exercise

The profit and loss accounts for customers A, B and C reveal an interesting imbalance. Customer A, with 30 per cent of the company sales, generates nearly 40 per cent of the net trading profit. Customer C, on the other hand, with 20 per cent of the turnover, manages to turn in a small trading loss.

The company clearly has a high dependence on customer A, who is not given the same generous discount levels as customer C. If customer A used its power and demanded similar discounts, that would reduce the company overall trading profit by over 37 per cent at a stroke. Although smaller in volume, customer B's business looks very attractive, contributing more than 15 per cent of trading profit from only ten per cent of turnover.

Two customers – A and B – account for 40 per cent of sales and nearly 54 per cent of the net trading profit. It seems that the two priorities are to do something about the non-profitable customer C, and to reduce the company's dependence on customers A and B. Several alternatives are possible:

Drop customer C

This course of action assumes that £19 100 fixed overhead allocated to customer C will disappear if business with customer C is curtailed. In reality the net effect would be to increase the allocation to customers A and B.

Renegotiate with customer C

The reason for the apparent loss on customer C's business is the extraordinarily high discount that has been negotiated, presumably on the basis that customer C places few, but very large orders, despite the fact that the costs of selling, servicing and distributing to customer C are no different (pro rata) than for customers A and B.

The situation also represents a real danger to the relationship with customer A if the privileged level of discount given to customer C ever became known. Renegotiating with customer C is likely to be difficult as this customer obviously has an astute buyer and 40 per cent discount is an unfortunate precedent.

It may be possible to turn the situation around over a period of time by stripping down the product to basics and charging for all extras, including technical support. Another alternative is to examine new options on current distribution methods which call for multiple drops despite the fact that the volume has been grouped into just two orders.

Reduce dependence on customer A

This could be achieved by targeting customer B for development or increasing the key customer base with selected customers among those who make up the other 40 per cent of sales revenue. However, this may be a more long-term option and the immediate task is to 'lock in' customer A's business in terms of technical support and service levels to establish entry barriers for competition.

Customer profitability analysis provides a benchmark against which the cost structure of servicing specific customers can be compared and the main reasons for below-average performance identified. The reasons may include varying levels of discounts, disproportionately high demands on selling and technical resources, or variations between the length of credit taken, for example. Analysis of different customer cost structures can identify how effectively resources are being utilized. Customer A, for example, produces £66 of revenue for every £1 of technical support expenditure, compared with £44 for customer C and an overall company average of £33. This could mean that the technical engineer servicing customer A is more efficient or it could mean that not enough technical support is being invested in this important customer. Further analysis will determine the reality of the situation.

Similarly, other cost elements such as distribution, incentives, advertising, and so on, can be compared and action taken to improve the effectiveness of investment and expenditure in individual key customers. The profitability analysis provides a key input into the customer planning process by identifying the current profit position, determining future profit objectives and measuring the impact of new strategies and activities.

The number of factors to be used in pinpointing individual customer costs will depend on the monies involved and the work involved in tracking the figures. For some customers, it may be appropriate to monitor the profitability of different products in the product mix. In these cases, the costs and revenue under 'Customer contribution' should be identified by each individual product and described as product contribution to profit, financing and general overhead.

Some guidelines for setting up customer profitability statements in two different types of business are shown in the following exhibits, 6a and 6b.

Exhibit 6a

Profitability statement: fast-moving consumer goods

Gross sales value — invoiced sales at full list price

Less invoiced discount — normal standard discounts

= Net sales

Less manufacturing cost — ex-factory product manufacturing costs

Less distribution cost — cost of delivery to customer's premises

= Gross contribution

Less sales allowances — special discounts, rebates above normal

Less marketing allowances — special marketing events, joint promotion

Less consumer deals — one-time money-off and 'flashpack' deals

= Net contribution

Less direct sales cost* — direct selling costs, including management

Less fixed overheads* — all other fixed costs (general, administration)

= Trading profit

Less payment discount — prompt payment discount

Less debtor interest — financing cost for monthly statement balance

Less stock interest — financing cost for customer stock holding

= Profit after interest

* costs allocated to agreed formula

Profitability statement: industrial company

Gross sales value	– invoiced sales at full list price
Less invoiced discount	– normal standard discount
Less delivery charges	– when contract carrier is used
= Net sales	
Less cost of goods sold	– product manufacturing cost ex-factory
= Gross profit	
Less negotiated discount	– special discounts, etc., above normal
Less direct sales cost	– direct selling costs including management
Less installation costs	– cost of installation and specification modifications
Less product trial costs	– pre- and post-installation testing
Less customer training	– incurred by supplier and not invoiced
= Gross contribution	
Add invoiced service	– invoiced extras including spare parts
Less direct service costs	– as incurred or allocated
Less cost of spares	– as incurred
= Net contribution	
Less debtor interest	– financing cost for statement balance
Less stock interest	– financing cost for inventory or invoice delay
= Operating profit	
Less sales admin overheads*	– fixed sales costs allocated
Less service overheads*	– fixed service costs allocated
Less general overheads*	– general fixed costs allocated
= Net profit	

* costs allocated to agreed formula

THE HORIZONTAL COSTING SYSTEM

With suppliers and key customers moving towards more collaborative, 'open book' accounting relationships, a more sophisticated approach may be needed. The trend is towards activity-based costing (ABC), which can give a more accurate picture of customer profitability by measuring the processes involved in dealing with a key customer rather than the traditional functional analysis.

However, many suppliers are now operating in a *price-led* key customer relationship where they have to deliver to a price that enables their key customers to compete in their markets. Here it may be necessary to go one step beyond activity-based costing and analyze the value added by these activities. A methodology that focuses sharply on added-value and puts a real emphasis on removing cost from the supply chain is known as the 'horizontal' system.

A manager may be faced with a 30 per cent cut in payroll to meet a 30 per cent cost reduction target. Yet 30 per cent of the work done in the department adds no value to the customer. By cutting jobs, the manager puts the same workload on fewer people, causing lower morale, declining customer service, and ultimately lower profits. If the unnecessary work had been cut out first, productivity might have increased, profits raised, new investments permitted to bring in more customers – and perhaps, in the long run, jobs created, not cut.

> Do only work that adds value to the customer
> Work that does not add value to the customer
> is a waste of time and money.

Unfortunately, the company's accounting and information systems does not reveal the wasted work. In this age of global competitors and demanding customers, the battle for profits is a fierce one. The only way for you to be profitable is to keep costs down while still offering the value – in terms of speed, innovation, and quality – needed to satisfy your customers. To achieve those goals, there is one basic rule: *do only work that adds value to the customer.* Work that does not add value to the customer is a waste of time and money.

Yet most company accounting and information systems do not even measure customer value. Designed to report to top management and shareholders, they focus only on the results of work, such as revenues and profits. They do not examine whether that work adds any value. The management controls of traditional accounting systems leave managers groping in the dark.

Focusing on the customer instead, the 'horizontal' system looks behind the numbers and asks the right questions, so that managers can make the right decisions – decisions leading to satisfied customers, rewarded employees, and the transformation of the bottom line.

Work for the customer, not the boss

The traditional vertical organization structures divide work into functions and departments and then into jobs and tasks. Managers are at the top of the chain of command. Their role is to put people into the right tasks, and then to measure, control, and reward their performance. In contrast, the horizontal structure is based on the perspective of the customer. It consists of a small number of core business *processes*, for example product development (from concept to launch), production (from procurement to shipment), or customer service (from complaint to resolution). The information system in horizontal structures is not designed to help managers control, but instead to help managers and workers join together to satisfy the customer. As a result, the numbers in these structures do not flow from the top down or from the bottom up. Instead, they flow horizontally across the business.

Horizontal systems are based on the recognition that work is the primary cause of costs – and that the only work worth doing is that which satisfies customers. Thus, the basic questions asked by a horizontal system are simple. Does a piece of work add value for the customer? If it doesn't, why is it being done at all? And what are the causes of this unnecessary work?

Studies show that huge amounts of work in every type of organization add no value to the customer. Eliminating this work would drastically reduce organization costs and increase profits. To transform your bottom line, you need to create a horizontal structure that organizes your business around customers and key processes and is supported by information systems that measure the value of work.

Price-led costing

Traditionally, pricing techniques were simple: add up your costs, add your desired margin, and there's your price. This 'cost-plus' approach worked when producers could plan and sell what they produced at their chosen price. Today, aggressive competitors and discriminating consumers force the use of more sophisticated pricing techniques. You cannot just choose your price; customers choose the price and you must manage your costs accordingly. The key is to reduce costs while not reducing customer value.

A first step is to move from cost-led pricing to price-led costing. In other words, rather than setting prices based on costs, you must set costs based on desired prices. A popular technique of price-led costing, used by manufacturers in Japan, is called *target costing*. Japanese manufacturers typically start with a target cost based on the price the market is prepared to accept. Then they tell designers and engineers to meet it. They also work with suppliers to meet cost guidelines for parts.

The emphasis in target costing is to reduce costs at the design and development stage – before it hits the production stage. This avoids the typical struggle to reduce unit costs during the manufacturing stage. Companies no longer have to make unnecessarily high volume production runs, for example, just to lower the unit cost. Mercedes-Benz CEO, Helmut Werner, summarized the target-costing approach when he said: 'Mercedes now has to produce cars to match market-driven prices, not make the autos its engineers design at whatever the cost.'

Activity-based costing

Traditionally, product costs were calculated by charging unit costs to products – such as material or labour – and allocating other costs such as general overhead expenses. In contrast, activity-based costing (ABC) calculates the costs of the product based on the costs of activities needed to create that product. But the problem remains the same. Whether you calculate costs using traditional or activity-based methods, you are still using an internal cost-plus approach. The customer is still out of the loop.

Value analysis

Once you set overall target costs for products based on market prices, the next step is to meet those costs. Target costing uses value analysis processes such as 'functional analysis' to help reduce actual costs to target cost levels. Functional analysis examines the costs of each proposed function of a product – *and decides whether that function adds value to the customer.*

The customer value of each function determines the acceptable cost level allowed to create that function. The goal is to match costs with customer value. Functional analysis often requires a series of five to ten meetings during which internal and external advisers thrash out cost-reduction strategies. The goal is to reduce target costs and find ways for actual costs to meet these newly lowered targets while still meeting the needs of customers.

How horizontal systems work

If your company is losing money, you may decide you have to cut costs by cutting jobs. The problem is that your department or company may not be losing money. If you take a horizontal approach to your costs – that work is the primary cause of costs and only work that adds value should be done – you might find a completely different picture of your organization.

For example, in Table 6.1, example 1 examines the profits of four branches of an insurance company using traditional accounting methods. Head-office costs – the head-office resources used by the branches – are allocated based on the number of people in each branch. Thus if branch A has twice as many people as branch B, branch A is charged twice the head-office costs of branch B.

Example 2 measures costs using activity-based accounting methods that recognize that work is the primary cause of costs. Thus, instead of mathematically distributing costs based on head count, accountants analyze how each branch actually uses head-office resources. Because of this different approach, branch D, which makes less use of head-office resources than other branches, sees its profits increase dramatically. For branch C, the situation is reversed.

Table 6.1   Different methods of calculating profit

Example 1
Profits based on traditional accounting

Northern Region Profit Summary (£000s)	Total	Branch A	Branch B	Branch C	Branch D
Profit before head-office costs	9 600	3 000	3 600	1 800	1 200
Head-office costs	6 600	2 250	1 875	1 350	1 125
Net profit	3 000	750	1 725	450	75
Number of branch staff	880	300	250	180	150

Example 2
Profits calculated activity-based accounting methods

Northern Region Profit Summary (£000s)	Total	Branch A	Branch B	Branch C	Branch D
Profit before head-office costs	9 600	3 000	3 600	1 800	1 200
Head-office costs (activity basis)	6 600	2 640	1 320	1 980	660
Net profit (activity basis)	3 000	360	2 280	(180)	540

Example 3
Profits based on horizontal accounting methods

Northern Region Profit Summary (£000s)	Total	Branch A	Branch B	Branch C	Branch D
Profit before head-office costs	9 600	3 000	3 600	1 800	1 200
Less: Value-adding costs	3 366	1 056	792	990	528
Real profit before non-value adding costs	6 234	1 944	2 808	810	672

Activity-based systems present a more accurate picture of costs. One problem is that these methods are not part of the general financial information system of a company. Instead, they are used on an *ad hoc* basis for specific projects to provide information to managers. The key difference is that while activity-based methods recognize work as the cause of costs, they do not provide the information concerning the value of work for customers. Answering this question can significantly alter financial results and the management decisions that stem from those results.

Identifying value-adding and non value-adding costs

Unlike activity-based methods, horizontal systems analyze activities to identify value-adding and non value-adding costs. Assuming that non value-adding costs should be eliminated, horizontal systems calculate profitability on the basis of value-added costs only. Example 3, showing the horizontal system analysis, shows that all four branches of the insurance company are profitable. The company has cut costs without cutting jobs – just by eliminating non value-adding costs.

The horizontal approach is not a panacea. Downsizing will not suddenly disappear forever. Competitive pressures sometimes leave companies no choice but to make drastic cuts. But how they make those cuts may differ. By cutting jobs but not the workload, many companies find themselves on a downward spiral of fewer people doing more work, leading to lower morale, declining customer service, and eventually lower profits ... leading to more job cuts.

Horizontal organizations avoid this downward spiral. Before cutting the workforce, they cut the workload first by eliminating non value-adding work – leading to higher productivity, more profits, more investment to bring in more customers, maybe even more jobs. By exposing waste and highlighting value, horizontal systems provide more appropriate information about which departments, products, or customers are profitable.

Finding and retaining profitable customers

Research shows that the longer customers stay with your company, the more profitable they become. After initial marketing and set-up costs of acquiring customers have been incurred, customers begin to generate profits. The longer they remain loyal, the more familiar they become with your products, services, staff, and methods – and thus lower your costs for serving them.

Not all customers, however, are profitable. Activity-based systems analyze the resources used by different customers or groups of customers. The results are often surprising and disturbing. Using activity-based methods, managers often discover that small numbers of customers create most of the profits, while large numbers of customers are simply draining profits.

Figure 6.2 shows typical results from ABC studies. The top 5 per cent of profitable customers brought in 150 per cent of the profits. And while the first 50 per cent of customers continued to add to a company's profits, the remaining 50 per cent took profits away.

Activity-based methods help you identify unprofitable customers. Horizontal information systems tell you what to do about them. They identify the causes of costs, but also who is responsible for those costs. Eliminating work that doesn't add value to the customer can turn unprofitable customers into profitable ones.

But an organization is not necessarily to blame for all non value-added work. Each of your customers draws on your resources in different ways. Some are inexpensive to serve, and some are demanding. Some are willing to pay extra for good services, while others demand excellent services, fast delivery, and low prices. Customers can push you to engage in poor quality or irrelevant work, causing a drain on profits. For example, first-class passengers on

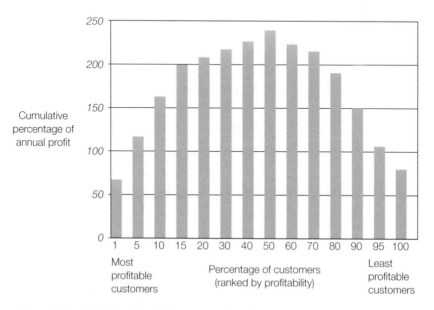

Figure 6.2   Relationship between number of customers and profitability

airlines are demanding and continuously revise their travel plans, which makes them unprofitable on short-haul flights.

By helping you identify *customer-driven* poor quality or irrelevant work – the non-value added work that customers force you to do – horizontal systems help you identify unprofitable customers. Knowing which customers are profitable and retaining them is key to your bottom line. Profitable customers become more profitable. Unprofitable customers continue to drain profits from your bottom line as long as they remain customers.

The aim of vertical accounting systems is to support top management information gathering. The aim of horizontal information systems is to support customer satisfaction. That is why horizontal accounting and information systems analyze work according to whether or not it adds value to the customer. To eliminate non value-added work you have to be able to identify and quantify it. You cannot make the right decisions if you do not have the right numbers. Here's how horizontal information systems can give you those right numbers.

The horizontal information systems process

To explain how the horizontal process works, let's take the hypothetical example of a salesman named Sam. In a horizontal system, the *time* of individual workers, or groups of workers, is recognized as the cause of costs. Therefore, horizontal systems take traditional costs and re-analyze them by activity time.

Sam's costs – including salary, travel expenses, and other costs – add up to £5000. Sam spends 40 per cent of his time selling. Thus his selling activity cost is 40 per cent of £5000, which equals £2000. Once you've calculated activity costs, you can analyze the value of each activity for the customer. This evaluation is done according to two criteria: relevance and quality.

Relevance

Doing work that is irrelevant to the customer clearly adds costs without adding value. Relevance, however, is not always a black or white calculation. Selling may be 100 per cent relevant to the

Table 6.2   Implementing a horizontal information system

Stage 1 - Analyzing costs by activity time

Traditional general ledger				Activity ledger		
Salary	4000	Re-analyzed by activity time →	Selling	5000 x 40%	2000
Social costs	300		Travelling	5000 x 20%	1000
Motor expenses	500		Reporting	5000 x 20%	1000
Telephone	200		Meetings	5000 x 20%	1000
Total cost	£5000		Total cost		£5000

Stage 2 – Calculating added-value costs based on relevance

Activity ledger		Relevance rating	Cost of irrelevance	Value-adding cost
Selling	2000	100%	–	2000
Travelling	1000	75%	250	750
Reporting	1000	50%	500	500
Meetings	1000	25%	750	250
Total cost	£5000	–	£1500	£3500

Stage 3 - Calculating the value-added work index (VAWI)

	Activity cost	NVA cost (quality)	NVA cost (relevance)	Net value-added work	Quality Index	Relevance index	VAWI
Selling	2000	1200	–	800	40%	100%	40%
Travelling	1000	–	250	750	100%	75%	75%
Reporting	1000	–	500	500	100%	50%	50%
Meetings	1000	–	750	250	100%	25%	25%
Total cost	£5000	£1200	£1500	£2300	76%	70%	46%

Stage 4 – Applying costs to products and customers

Traditional system		Horizontal system	
Gross profit	4000	Gross profit	4000
Less: selling costs	5000	Less: value-adding costs	2300
		Real profit	1700
		Less: cost of irrelevant work	1500
		Profit before quality costs	200
		Less: costs of poor quality work	1200
Loss	(£1000)	Accounting loss	(£1000)

customer. Reporting tasks, on the other hand, may be only 50 per cent relevant.

Working with Sam, managers have assigned 'relevance ratings' in percentages to each activity. These relevance ratings are then used to calculate the value-adding and non value-adding costs of the activity. For example, travelling is deemed only 75 per cent relevant to the customer. Since Sam's travel costs total £1000, the value-adding cost of travelling is £750. The non value-adding cost is £250.

Quality

Poor quality work also adds costs without adding value. For example, if Sam is forced to chase the factory to ensure that deliveries are completed, he is wasting time – and thus costs – because of the factory's poor quality work. Once again, percentages can be used to determine value-adding and non value-adding costs. Sam spent 60 per cent of his selling time on unnecessary work caused by poor quality. If his selling costs are £2000, 60 per cent of those costs – or £1200 – was non value-adding costs.

Once you've quantified the costs of work quality and relevance, you will have the data for a complete work-value analysis, known as the *value-adding work index*.

The value-adding work index (VAWI) measures specifically how much of the work done in your organization adds value to the customer. It is the central measurement of all horizontal information systems. The VAWI is calculated by combining the quality and relevance indices explained above.

The third chart in Table 6.2 shows how Sam's activity costs have been analyzed according to quality and relevance. As the chart shows, 46 per cent (or £2300) of his £5000 activity cost was spent on value-adding work.

This kind of report allows managers to work on locating and eliminating non value-added work. Steps can be taken, for example, to lower the non value-added costs due to problems of poor quality. Management could penalize the factory for poor deliveries – thus reducing the quality problems that added non value-added costs to Sam's selling costs.

Charging costs

Once you've identified value-adding and non value-adding costs, you can apply them to products and customers – and get an accurate picture of their profitability. For example, let's assume that Sam's numbers involved just one customer whose gross profit to the company was £4000. To determine the customer's profitability under traditional accounting measures, you would subtract Sam's £5000 costs from the customer's £4000 gross profit and find that the customer was unprofitable by £1000 (see Stage 4 in Table 6.2). If you charge only the value-adding costs of £2300 to the customer, however, you would show a net profit of £1700.

These figures show that the customer can be profitable – if you reduce internal non-value-adding work.

SUMMARY

In order to monitor total performance, it is important to be able to pinpoint the results of your resource investment in specific customers and, for this purpose, a customer profitability statement is a vital tool, not only to measure progress but also to justify the investment of additional resources in the future. Since accounting is not a precise science, an uncomplicated method for cost allocation should be agreed, but it should be a broad allocation process and enable the implications of negotiations to be fully realized and the progress of the customer relationship to be measured in 'bottom-line' terms. As target costing increasingly becomes an essential feature of supplier–customer relationships, more sophisticated profitability measurement systems, such as activity-based costing and horizontal value-added analysis will have to be adopted by suppliers.

7

Do you *really* have a business plan for each of your key customers?

SELF EVALUATION

Check out the following statements about your organization; the issues and implications are discussed in Chapter 7. Tick your answers as appropriate; ? = not sure.

	NO	?	YES
Do you have a business plan for each of your key customers?			
Do you know the primary business goals of each key customer?			
Is each of your sales goals linked to a specific business problem or valid business opportunity with each customer?			
Do you formally monitor the progress of each business initiative?			
Do you have access to the financial data of each key customer?			
Do you know who are the key customers of your key customers?			
Can you identify three strengths with each key customer?			
Can you identify one vulnerability that could jeopardize your plans?			
Have you set up bonding initiatives with key customers to ■ *build trust?* ■ *create exit barriers?* ■ *reinforce entry barriers?* ■ *establish joint customer projects?*			
Do you have regular formal performance reviews with your key customers?			
Do you have customer-specific competitor action plans?			
Do you have a planned referral programme to get new business?			
Do you identify individual roles in each customer's decision-making process?			
Have you a clear idea of individual attitudes of your key customers?			
Does your company have processes to pool customer information?			

USING INFORMATION TO CREATE A BUSINESS BUILDING PLAN

The sharing of information between buyers and sellers is one of the principal keys to a successful business relationship for both parties built on open, trusting attitudes. This is not just a question of demonstrating a positive outlook – the accessibility of information permits the exercise of creativity in finding acceptable solutions in difficult areas of the relationships. In the words of Harold Macmillan (British prime minister 1957–63), 'jaw, jaw is more constructive than war, war'.[1]

> Relationships are driven by feelings and intangible factors,
> without which everything could be sold by direct mail and
> most salespeople would be out of a job.

Companies put considerable effort into customer record systems and modern CRM software can collate, analyze, screen and mail-merge a plethora of hard facts about customers. What is more difficult to find is an equally user-friendly system that will store soft facts, that is, feelings. Relationships are driven by feelings and intangible factors, without which everything could be sold by direct mail and most salespeople would be out of a job.

Attitudes and reactions of customers tend to be recorded in a narrative style and, before long, we have accumulated for each of our customers a fat file of highly subjective comments about the attributes and foibles of our customers. Our early sales training may even have equipped us to look for the stereotypes – the silent type, the peppery colonel, and so on.

In customer management there can never be enough information – hard or soft – and it may be collected at all levels from many customer team members who interface with different functions in your customer's organization. What is needed is a *structured* system for hard and soft information, collated and *continuously updated* in a format that must be both *succinct* and *accessible* by all team members. This system is the basis of a development plan for each individual key customer (an example development plan for your own use is included at the end of this chapter).

---

[1] Canberra, 30 January 1958

The precise format of each document or chart in the development plan will depend upon the nature of the business, and the relevance of the content can only be decided by those who are involved in preparing and implementing the plan. Much of the information suggested – particularly the hard data – will be self-evident and may be already incorporated in your customer records, but some aspects of the plan may require clarification and guidance. All customer development plans should be prefaced by a one-page executive summary.

The executive summary

This is a short, narrative summary of the current position with this customer, updated regularly by the customer co-ordinator to enable top management to have access to an instant briefing if necessary.

Each key customer will have been selected by a system of evaluation against the attractiveness and relationship status criteria, as were described earlier, in Chapter 3. The result will be that each customer has some form of classification according to its priority to the supplier company. At its simplest this will be 'A', 'B' or 'C', or some index value of importance, but you might adopt a more descriptive method. Thus 'Aa' might indicate a high attractiveness and relationship status score and 'Cc' might mean a low score on both criteria. By definition, key customers would probably be in the 'A' category of attractiveness but might rank 'Aa', 'Ab' or 'Ac' according to their current relationship status rating. This classification should be indicated on the summary.

Another quick indicator of the health of the relationship with the key customer is to indicate in percentage terms:

- *your share of the customer's business* – a straight factual percentage;

- *your share of the customer's mind* – a judgemental percentage that is a measure of the customer's *awareness* of your products, your company and how you can fulfil their needs;

- *your share of the customer's heart* – this might well be the 'relationship status' calculation as described in an earlier chapter

(Chapter 3), or a judgemental percentage that is a measure of the strength of the relationship or the preference the customer has for doing business with you rather than some other company.

Companies that make steady gains in mind and heart shares should, inevitably, make gains in customer business, but other permutations can suggest some interesting interpretations:

- *high mind share and low heart share* – the customer agrees with the logic but does not like us, which means low business;

- *low mind share and high heart share* – the customer likes us but is not convinced that there are any advantages to our product or service;

- *high business, high mind share and low heart share* – the customer is buying because of a superior product but does not like us and is probably searching for an alternative supplier;

- *low business, high mind share and high heart share* – an inert customer who may have an undisclosed reason for not buying, or perhaps it is just that our sales skills need strengthening.

THE CUSTOMER DEVELOPMENT PLANNING PROCESS

The planning process is summarized in Fig. 7.1. Understanding of both the supplier's and the customer's overall corporate plans has already been emphasized in Chapter 5. The methodology for evaluation and prioritization was covered in Chapter 3. A typical template for a customer development plan is shown in Exhibit 7a at the end of this chapter but the extent and depth of the planning will vary with each customer situation. The plan might include some of the following suggested documentation.

Customer profile

This collates details of this specific customer and may include:

- company name, addresses, telephone and fax numbers, e-mail and website details

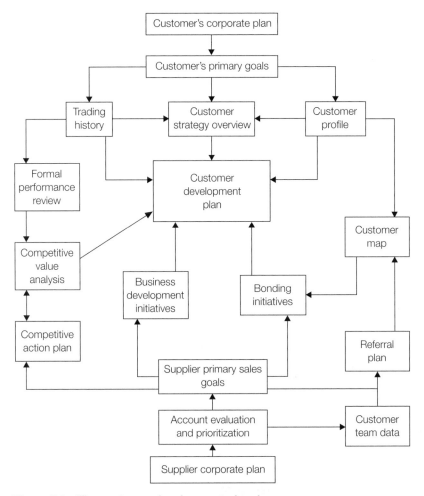

Figure 7.1 The customer development planning process

- affiliated companies, divisions or branches (indicating with how many you deal currently) and delivery locations
- size (employees, revenue, branches, and so on) and organization structure
- number of separate decision-making units and key customer people
- relevant information about their products and markets served
- their key customers
- payment terms
- information on processes, equipment, and so on.

This is straightforward factual information, which may have implications for the costs of servicing or the opportunity for sales referrals. Where the customer is an original equipment manufacturer or a value-added reseller and your product is being sold on down the value chain, there might be a strong emphasis on data about trends in your customer's markets.

Customer trading history

This is a history and forecast of trends relating to this customer. How far back the history goes will depend upon the relevance of this data to the present circumstances but two years' history and a two-year forecast, as well as current data, is a typical time span. It should include:

- their financial data (annual revenue and profit trends)
- customer's annual spend on your type of products with key product share analysis compared with at least two main competitors
- sales of your products or service to divisions or branches
- explanation of annual variances in their purchases and your sales
- key trends in their supplier relationships.

Customer's primary business goals

This is a listing of the specific customer's overall business goals (short term and long term) extracted from its corporate plan and covering areas of marketing, manufacturing, finance, expansion, product development, and so on, to which you, as a supplier, may be able to contribute.

Customer strategy overview

This is an assessment of current strategic relationships and plans:

- your strengths with this customer (identify three specifically);
- your vulnerabilities – what events could really jeopardize your position?

- your opportunities (short term and long term).

An opportunity (or problem) in the customer's current situation is usually a gap between current actual performance and expected performance, or a driving aspiration by the customer to improve existing methods, adopt new methods or expand into new activities. These should be seen to be addressed by your primary sales goals.

Your primary sales goals

Sales goals should be a clear statement of business objectives for the key customer within the planned period. They must be in line with the customer's goals and should be described in terms of *customer responses*, not supplier actions, using phrases such as 'the management committee will approve ...' or 'the customer will agree to purchase ...'. Goals are only realized when the customer agrees to something and to do this a customer should have a *valid business reason* which is linked to a *stated opportunity* in the customer strategy overview above. Some examples of this are:

- *primary goal*: to secure approval for product X from the purchasing committee, thereby increasing our total share of the business from 50 per cent to 75 per cent by period 12 with a 5 per cent average price increase overall from period 9;

- *valid business reason (linked to opportunity)*: customer is experiencing unsatisfactory levels of downtime in production and is aware that a reduction of downtime would have significant impact on unit production costs. Product X can extend production runs and reduce downtime by about 10 per cent.

Each sales goal must be broken down into a series of initiatives, or action plans, which fall into two categories:

- business development initiatives which are about products, applications, productivity improvements, merchandising, promotional campaigns and any activities where there are measurable results;

- bonding initiatives, which are less directly measurable activities, to develop or consolidate customer relationships (such as social events, special customer software, technical support and training).

Business development initiatives

These are the specific action plans drawn up for each primary sales goal. When there is a long sales cycle, intermediate progress objectives should be identified and sub-listed with time deadlines. The details might include:

- the objective of the initiative
- date initiated
- current supplier and current purchases value
- planned purchase value
- anticipated order date
- success probability percentage
- who is responsible.

This section might be supplemented with a running evaluation of the success of such initiatives with this customer over, maybe, the past two years or even by using moving annual totals showing:

- number of initiatives launched in past 12 months
- number of successful initiatives
- percentage rate of success
- failed initiative analysis – price? technical reasons? quality?
- value of extra business achieved for you
- added-value achieved for the customer.

Bonding initiatives

These are specific activities, described in Chapter 3, aimed at strengthening customer relationships and indicating who is responsible and time deadlines:

- building trust
- creating exit barriers
- reinforcing entry barriers
- joint customer projects.

Customer team data

This is a list of your personnel assigned to this specific customer, and other relevant data:

- main customer co-ordinator
- sales team members (and functions)
- external support team members (and functions)
- internal support team members (and functions)
- planned review dates for development plan (and actuals).

Ideally the customer team should be drawn from all relevant functions – sales, service, technical support, distribution, internal office administration. In addition, at least one senior management person should be seconded, particularly if there is a need for 'political' high-level contacts with the customer's senior management.

Alternatively, there might be a requirement for specialized expertise (financial, technical, and so on), which might be available within your supplier company or might justify importing external part-time resources (consultants, agencies, and so on). Perhaps the ideal customer team also includes customer staff as well.

Members of the customer team might be specific to this team or serve on other teams as well. The main customer co-ordinator may even work in other customer teams in a less prominent role. This will all depend on the size of the customer organization task and available resources; it may be appropriate to designate 'core' team members who would be involved in all team meetings and 'affiliate' members on a need-to-know basis. General salesforce personnel may also be seconded to the team, either because they are involved in the sales coverage plan for the customer or as part of their personal development. The actual existence of this defined team document is the first step in stimulating motivation by giving the team an official identity and purpose.

A system of review dates should be established on which all core members of the team will meet to evaluate, co-ordinate and agree overall progress on the action programme for the customer. These reviews are particularly important following the formal performance reviews with the customer but, in general terms, the frequency of these meetings will vary from weekly, when the activity plan has a high degree of urgency, to six-monthly, when the sales cycle is less intensive or when travel logistics are involved.

Formal performance review

The customer manager should make a formal appraisal of each key customer performance at prescribed intervals. Many companies commission an annual audit of their customer reactions and attitudes from an outside, independent research agency but a formal review meeting with the customer should be a routine activity at least every six months. This review process is discussed in more detail later in this chapter. The review should show:

- the driver list (criteria on which the customer evaluates suppliers);
- how the customer weights or ranks in importance the criteria;
- how the customer currently rates your performance (relative to competitive suppliers);
- the value analysis comparison (performance against price for you and your competitors);
- key points for action – by who, by when – as agreed with the customer.

Competitive action plan

This is a summary of the competitive penetration of this customer and a customer-specific proactive plan to beat your competition:

- competitors' products, services and contracts
- competitors' achieved price levels
- details of discounts or special terms given by competitors
- competitors' contract expiry or review dates

- customer's overall rating of main competitors (from review meeting or estimated)

- main competitors' strengths and weaknesses

- how do we neutralize competitors' strengths?

- how do we exploit competitors' weaknesses?

- what do we have to do to win business from competition?

- what could competition do to win business from us?

It is particularly important to identify dates when competitor contracts expire or come up for review. On a computer-based information system prior notice of such dates would be triggered automatically. The customer's attitudes to specific competitors will depend on information gained at the customer review meeting and may have to be estimated but sometimes the business, mind and heart share rating system described earlier may serve the purpose. The evaluation of competitors' strengths and weaknesses should reflect their business, mind and heart share scores.

Strategies to displace competitors should tie in with competitors' strengths and weaknesses, together with your company's strengths and weaknesses. All competition displacement strategies should be arrived at by:

- capitalizing on your strengths;

- minimizing the relevance of your weaknesses;

- minimizing the importance of your competition's strengths;

- exploiting your competition's weaknesses.

The referral plan

All customer development plans should incorporate a record of opportunities and initiatives for sales referrals to other departments or companies with responsibility nomination and identification of action required. For most industrial, service or professional enterprises, the most effective way of building up the customer base is by exploiting the strength of current customer relationships. Every customer manager should be charged with the task of generating at least five new business prospects per year from each of their key customers. Indirectly this is a measure of the closeness of the relationship with the customer.

These referrals may be suppliers to or customers of the customer: they could be trade friends, golfing partners or simply the 'firm next door'; they can be solicited from the general manager or the delivery-truck driver; they might be close contacts or just other companies that your contact knows about. Referrals lubricate the business and open the doors for new contacts; asking for referrals endorses the respect you have for your contact's experience and judgement and the continuous quest for new contacts projects your energetic, single-minded pursuit of new opportunities. However, in Europe we tend to be less energetic in chasing referrals than in the US and more conservative about asking customers for leads to other customers. Here are a few suggestions on the methodology of referral acquisition.

■ Ask for referrals with a specific *number* in mind: for example, 'John, I think you will agree that we are doing a good job for you and, as you now know all about us, may I ask you for the names of *five* companies or people who you think could benefit from what we do?';

■ Ask for referrals with a specific *name* in mind: for example, 'We would like to make a strong effort to do business with Hamptons: I'm aware that you know Lionel Hampton and, if possible, would like you to give me an introduction to him.' If appropriate, try to get a personal introduction from your customer; this will considerably enhance the quality of the lead;

■ Ask for advice on how your customer base could be extended: for example, 'You know the type of service we have: if you were me, who do you think would be the best companies around here who might benefit from our services?';

■ Trade prospects: constantly give your customers prospects for their business and expect some reciprocal action on their part;

■ Reward customers for good referrals with a meal, box of chocolates or tickets for the match, but beware, this reward should not be offered as an incentive. Give it as a post-referral token of appreciation to encourage them to do it again.

CUSTOMER MAPPING IDENTIFIES THE 'SOFT' INFORMATION

Customer mapping is a system for recording the less tangible aspects of customer relationships in a concise and constructive format. The day-to-day dealings between supplier and customer give rise to many personal interactions at all levels and in all functions. Office staff, distribution people, invoice clerks, and so on regularly interface with their counterparts and, perhaps subconsciously, absorb information and form opinions about them which, collectively, could be meaningful and stimulate fresh initiatives. This information might be more reliable than that gained from sales contacts, distorted as it may be by the rituals of negotiation behaviour. Unfortunately, it is rare to see this valuable intelligence collated methodically and in a format that can be used for proactive customer development.

The concept of customer mapping addresses this omission by condensing this 'soft' data in the form of seven concise charts, samples of which are provided in Tables 7.2–7.8:

- the decision-making process
- influencing sources
- internal relationships
- external relationships
- committee structure
- key events
- motivation analysis.

The decision-making process

This is the master chart in the mapping process (see Table 7.1). Its purpose is to identify:

- the participants in the decision-making process

- the degree of influence they have

- at what stages in the process they participate

- their roles in the decision-making process

- their attitudes to their jobs

- their attitudes towards us.

Customer management starts with knowing all the relevant players in the customer's organization, their roles, when they are likely to participate in decisions and their attitudes, both to us and to their job. All customer personnel likely to have any influence on the supplier decision-making process or relationship should be listed. In addition, any external influences such as consultants, technical advisors or non-executive directors should be recorded.

Assessments should be made about each participant in the decision-making process concerning their role, attitudes and whether they are friends or enemies.

Table 7.1 records assessments of each member of the decision-making unit regarding their role, attitude and the state of current relationships with us. In addition, timescales of the decision-making process and degree of individual influence – expressed as a percentage – are considered. Usually there is one such chart for each customer but in complex multi-product or contract situations you might have a different chart for each group of decision makers or project.

The members' roles in the decision-making unit

There are five role classifications used in the chart, each of which is designated by its initial letter in Table 7.1.

- *Evaluator*: this is the person whose major concern is the price-performance of your product – the bottom-line impact you can make on the organization – and, with direct access to funds, there is usually only one definite evaluator who can give the approval for your project. The bigger the financial numbers or risk, the higher in the organization the evaluator may be but it is not always the financial director or chief executive officer who plays

Table 7.1 The decision-making process

Customer: Apex Corporation

Objectives: To secure supply and installation contract for new warehouse computer system with customer-agreed satisfaction with installation by 1 January next year

Role	Job	Relations	Decision making unit	Deadlines	Identification (28/3) — of need or problem	Prioritization (17/4) — size and urgency	Specification (1/6) — preferred options	Consultation (12/6) — with potential suppliers	Approbation (22/8) — of supplier proposals	Evaluation (15/9) — shortlist of proposals	Negotiation (30/11) — with preferred suppliers	Implementation (31/12) — final decision and follow-up
DE	A	N	Southall									30%
E	P	N	West		20%	20%					20%	20%
S	R	B	Hinchcliffe		30%		20%	30%	20%	40%		
S	A	N	Unsworth		10%		20%			20%		10%
S	A	C	Ferguson		20%			20%	40%			20%
U	P	S	Parkinson		20%	20%			20%		20%	
U	R	E	Watson			10%			20%			20%
S	A	S	Jackson		20%	20%	20%			20%	20%	
U	R	N	Short				20%	10%	10%			
S	P	E	Grant		10%			20%		20%		
U	P	N	Barmby				40%					
					100%	100%	100%	100%	100%	100%	100%	100%

Assessment of DMU member's position

Note: percentages represent degree of individual influence on decision-making process

this role. The person who has the budget is the person you have to identify.

Difficult business conditions may move the evaluator upwards in the organization. In hard times, senior management start to count the paperclips. Ascertain the financial 'break points' of authority for individuals. It may be more cost-efficient if you can bring your price to just within the financial buying authority limit of a friendly contact than to have to start selling all over again to the next level of management.

- *User*: this role is filled by the person or people who will actually use the product or service. The user is primarily interested in the effect the product or service will have on the job that has to be done.

If you are selling aeroplanes, the pilots, maintenance teams and even cabin staff may have an input that affects the final decision. Companies such as Boeing have teams permanently circling the world making user-friendly presentations to the operational people who keep airlines flying on a day-to-day basis. Complex sales or customer relationships may involve many users who, though they may not have the authority of final approval, may have substantial powers of veto. Any salesperson selling lithographic plates to a printing works knows that it is the person on the machine who ultimately determines what is acceptable.

Because users are focused on how the product or service affects the job, it is important to recognize the effect of personal motivations on their judgement. Likes and dislikes are more likely to contribute to their preferences than logical facts and figures.

With retailers of consumer products, the user is most likely to be the person who is concerned with the logistics of handling the product – warehousing, space requirements, inventory, point-of-sale display materials, pricing details, and so on. The actual consumer is usually more the concern of the marketing strategy planners.

- *Screener*: sometimes referred to as the 'gatekeeper', it is the task of the screener to limit the field of suppliers; they do not decide who wins, but they decide who can play. Screeners make judgements about the measurable and quantifiable aspects of your product or service based upon how well it meets specifications, whether these be financial, technical, quality or legal.

Buyers can be screeners, ruling out vendors on the basis of price, delivery, specification or logistics. Credit managers can be also be screeners, vetoing new business on the basis of financial risk. Governments can be screeners, too, by enforcing anti-trust regulations to block merger deals. Screeners serve as gatekeepers in the business game.

Screeners may be difficult to identify because they may not be a strongly visible part of the buying process or because they can easily be confused with evaluators. They do not have the ultimate authority to decide for, but they may have considerable influence in deciding against. Their authority is limited because they may not be in a position to appreciate the total picture. The negative points they identify may be outweighed by positive factors elsewhere.

Of course, the judgement of the screener may be deemed final in matters such as safety, but, for the most part, the salesperson will attempt to provide screeners with the broader picture in order to temper any negative influences. In this way, a salesperson in a technical situation will often play two screeners, say a buyer and a technical engineer, against each other by telling each of them the reasons for the other being keen on the product or service. Sometimes the confusion between the roles is not deliberate. The well-meaning screener can believe that the decision is theirs, it having been delegated by the evaluator.

■ *Influencer*: this person can impact politically by using personal skills to lubricate (or otherwise) the corporate decision processes. Influence may exercised using powers of connection or coercion for reasons unconnected with the merits of the proposal.

■ *Decider*: sometimes known as the 'approver', this is the person who will have the ultimate decision and may not take part in the deliberations until the later stages after the other 'roles' have contributed to the debate. Although the decider is usually a senior figure in the decision-making unit, sometimes this role is played by lower status individuals based on, perhaps, some specialized knowledge or merely strength of personality.

In complex corporate decision making today, all these role classifications have to be filled. People may double up their roles, but there will usually be only one decider who, frequently, is also the evaluator. We have to cover all these roles, even though our natural tendency is to relate to those people with whom we are comfortable and avoid those who might show up our little ignorances about cashflows or electronic data processing. Nor must we make assumptions that relate these roles to job functions. We must probe our key customers and find out who, in reality, are the personalities fulfilling these roles – and, sometimes, it *does* come down to personality when decisions have to be made. When we are selling ideas, we have to prepare evaluator and user justifications, surpass the screener's specifications, enlist the support of the influencers and give our decider the confidence to make the commitment.

How all this is received will be influenced by the attitudes of the decision-making unit to the current business situation. People are motivated to act when there is a discrepancy between that person's perception of reality and the desired results. That discrepancy may be perceived as a *problem* or an *opportunity*:

- *problem perception* – a situation where actual performance is below expectations – provides the highest probability of sales success. It has been said that fear of loss is a greater motivation than desire for gain and, provided that the person is aware that there is a problem, the bigger the problem, the more urgently the solution options will be explored. You sell survival, not improved lifestyles. All the person wants is to get things back to normal. This does not necessarily mean that your solution will be accepted;

- *opportunity perception* is a situation where actual performance is meeting or, perhaps, exceeding expectations but the person can see opportunities for improved performance. This person is, by definition, ready to agree with any proposals to exploit this perceived opportunity but it does not necessarily mean that your solution will be the one that is accepted.

The most difficult situation to sell into is where actual performance is perceived as just about meeting expectations, no more, no less, and there is no perceived need unless you can demonstrate a discrepancy. People are scared of 'rocking the boat' and suggestions for change are perceived as a possible threat to a sensitive performance equilibrium. In this situation, it might be more diplomatic to play a waiting game until problems or opportunities are perceived as serious enough to necessitate action.

Assessment of attitudes

However the situation is perceived, each individual will have a different job attitude and response mode. Essentially, there are three different classifications of reactions: *active, passive* and *resistant* to change, each of which is designated by its initial letter in Table 7.1.

■ *Active* response mode indicates a person who responds quickly and is a stimulator of change. It has both positive and negative connotations, in that the relationship may always be in a state of change. This will present frequent opportunities for the non-supplier but sets a dynamic pace of change for the existing supplier. Active response modes applied to problem business situations (see above) may be perceived as nit-picking; when applied to opportunities, they may promote a somewhat unstable climate.

■ *Passive* response mode indicates inertia in the decision-making unit member with no visible signs of reaction to the situation. The person may be in sit-tight posture because expectations can be comfortably met and there seems to be no point in making life difficult. The person may either not perceive that there are problems or opportunities, or not rate them significant enough to do anything about them. There is also always the possibility that the person may not know what to do about them.

■ *Resistant* response mode may be rooted in a lack of perception that there is a significant problem or opportunity. It is, however, more likely that this resistance will stem from lack of confidence in the suggested solution or anxiety over the possibility of failure in implementation. The negative implications of change can loom large in evaluating the options and, quite often, resistance is due to the existence of too many options and anxiety that the right one may not be chosen.

Assessment of state of current relationships with us

When all these factors have been considered, we can make an overall assessment of the individual member's attitude towards us as a supplier or potential supplier.

There are five different classifications of attitude: champion, supporter, neutral, blocker and enemy, each of which is designated by its initial letter in Table 7.1.

- *Champion:* the ally or friend inside the customer organization, who will guide you though the decision-making process by giving you information and helping you to identify and manage the other members of the decision-making unit. The champion lubricates the selling process, not in any dishonest way, but by giving you feedback and warning you of mistakes and pitfalls.

  What are the motivations of champions? Champions help because they want you as a supplier, they prefer your product, they may have enjoyed a good experience with you in the past, they feel good about the relationship or, simply, it may be in their own interest that you succeed.

  In customer management, finding a champion who has credibility in your customer organization is imperative. However, sometimes that champion may be *outside* your customer's organization as an ex-employee or a well-established non-competitive supplier who has a thorough inside knowledge of the customer.

- *Supporter:* someone in your customer's organization who supports you or your products, although maybe not exclusively.

- *Neutral:* someone who neither supports or rejects you or your competitors. This may be because they do not have any real preferences or because they are unwilling to declare them.

- *Blocker:* someone who may have ulterior motives in blocking your proposals. These might be political, personal or simply because that person has different budget priorities.

■ *Enemy:* someone in your customer's organization who actively supports your competition, for whatever reasons, and positively rejects you or your products.

The significance of this support or rejection will, of course, depend upon the number of other decision-making unit members with positive or negative ratings, their role in the unit and to what extent this relationship can be improved by the customer team.

When considering strategies, it may help to identify 'friends' and 'enemies' in the unit by appropriate green and red markings on the chart.

Phases of the decision-making process

In addition to assessing roles, job attitudes and relationship status of unit members, Table 7.1 maps the relative influence of each member over the eight phases of the corporate decision-making process. The total influence at each phase is split by percentages over the number of individuals who make up the decision-making unit for that phase.

A customer's decision-making process when considering a change of supplier or evaluating which supplier should be awarded a particular contract may be analyzed as eight identifiable sequential steps or phases:

■ *identification* of the need or problem: the customer identifies a situation where there is a gap between *current* performance and *potential* performance, which can either be a *problem* – where performance is less than expectations – or an *opportunity* – where there is scope for improvement in current performance;

■ *prioritization and options*: the relative importance, size and urgency of the gap is assessed on the basis of financial and technical implications and possible courses of action are considered;

■ *specification*: preferred options are identified and specifications prepared;

- *consultation* with potential suppliers who are capable of meeting the specifications: specific proposals and bids are solicited;

- *evaluation*: proposals are discussed with potential suppliers and evaluated;

- *approbation*: some proposals are eliminated and a shortlist of potential suppliers is chosen for negotiation;

- *negotiation*: negotiations are conducted with the shortlisted suppliers;

- *implementation*: the supplier decision is made and contracts are finalized.

This process (sometimes called the sales cycle) might be completed in a single meeting with one person or spread over scores of meetings, take several years and involve hundreds of people in many locations. It depends upon whether you are selling paperclips or Boeing 747s.

In all buying or selling situations, the phases are essentially the same. There is, however, a universal truth: the earlier that the supplier is involved in the customer's decision-making process, the better. The key customer manager is not only collaborating with the customer in the preparation of the specifications, but should be productive in identifying the need even before the customer does. Becoming aware of the situation *only* when invited by a customer to submit proposals almost certainly means that it is already too late, and the intention is merely to use you as a benchmark for another preferred competitive supplier.

Careful consideration of who is involved in each of the phases in Table 7.1 is vital. You need to know not only *who* the players are, but also *when* they will participate in the game. Too often, decision-making unit members, who may have an important role in the overall decision-making process, might not appear until the later phases, by which time you might already have been screened out and, therefore, no longer be a supplier under consideration.

Influencing sources

Table 7.2 identifies the main sources (internal and external) of influencing information on individual members of the decision-making unit. In developing strategies and tactics to ensure that each member of our key customer decision-making unit achieves a personal win from our proposals, it may be useful to consider individual preferences about information sources. Where does the unit get the facts that assist it in decision making?

Sources will be numerous and varied, depending upon the industry in which you work but may include:

- demonstrations
- presentations
- exhibitions
- seminars
- scientific papers
- trade journals
- specialist magazines
- advertising
- other trade users
- direct mailshots
- internal reports
- competitors.

It may be useful to use a simple coding system, for example A = always, S = sometimes, N = never, to indicate an individual's relative preferences.

The purpose of this chart is to identify ways in which a more personalized approach might be made to a member of the decision-making unit. For example, if an individual has a history of *never* attending demonstrations, it would be counterproductive *and* diminish your credibility to arrange one for that person. If this individual is a well-known trade figure, it might be more appropriate for your product or system to be seen working on the site of somebody else in the same industry.

Table 7.2 Influencing sources

Customer Apex Corporation
Influence coverage plan

Role	Job	Relations	Decision-making unit	Demonstrations	Presentations	Exhibitions	Seminars	Trade press	Magazines	Advertising	Other trade users	Direct mail	Internal reports	Competitors	Consultants	Social
				Influencing sources												
DE	A	N	Southall		✓						✓					✗
E	P	N	West				✓				✗					
S	R	B	Hinchcliffe	✓			✗							✓		
S	A	N	Unsworth			✓										
S	A	C	Ferguson		✗									✓		
U	P	S	Parkinson					✗						✓		
U	R	E	Watson	✗				✓								✗
S	A	S	Jackson	✓												
U	R	N	Short						✓							
S	P	E	Grant											✓		✓
U	P	N	Barnby			✓				✗						✓

Assessment of DMU position

Internal relationships

This is the political analysis of the customer, and understanding the politics of the business is integral to successful customer partnerships. Table 7.3 maps, with cross-referenced ticks and crosses, the internal relationships within the decision-making unit, particularly how the members get on with each other.

Identifying good relationships between certain individuals may help you to spread favourable response if one of them is your supporter. When evaluating your project, it is important strategically to keep apart people who do not like each other. If one of the two 'enemies' likes what you are proposing, then, by definition, the other will reject your ideas. Your purpose is not to get caught in the crossfire. If necessary, arrange separate meetings or presentations for each of the antagonists.

External relationships

Key customer relationships frequently involve contacts between many departmental functions – sales, order processing, customer service, technical support, production, distribution, finance and, perhaps, senior management on a social or industry level. In addition, the customer might have strong external contacts with consultants, advisers, banks, trade associations, government agencies or mutual customers.

Such relationships are noted in Table 7.4 with the purpose of taking advantage of strong contacts in the allocation of customer development activities, or perhaps avoiding aggravating any personal conflicts that may have built up historically between individuals in supplier–customer transactions.

External relationships with other companies may provide opportunities, if they are also your customers, to use those companies as references or demonstration sites for your products. If they are non-customers, then they should be targeted as reference prospects.

Table 7.3 Internal relationships

Customer — Apex Corporation

Relationship plan

Internal relationships

Assessment of DMU position			Decision-making unit	Southall	West	Hinchcliffe	Unsworth	Ferguson	Parkinson	Watson	Jackson	Short	Grant	Barmby
Role	Job	Relations												
DE	A	N	Southall	■							✓		✓	
E	P	N	West		■				✓					✗
S	R	B	Hinchcliffe			■	✗					✗		
S	A	N	Unsworth		✓	✗	■							
S	A	C	Ferguson					■				✓		✓
U	P	S	Parkinson				✓		■	✓				
U	R	E	Watson							■				✓
S	A	S	Jackson		✓				✗		■			
U	R	N	Short			✗						■		
S	P	E	Grant					✓		✗			■	
U	P	N	Barmby					✓						■

Committee structure

In Table 7.5, relevant committees (for example, technical, purchasing, management) or working groups are identified and their members listed with assessments of individual influence and any apparent friendly or unfriendly attitudes towards you or your project.

The more formal approval elements of the decision-making unit are represented by such committees and, although decisions are endorsed by meetings of these groups, much of the selection and recommendation will have been pursued by individual members of the committee *before* the official gathering. Each member may have areas of expertise or experience which will determine the influence they have with their peers, and a potential supplier will have taken care to position proposals favourably with the more influential committee members before the meeting.

Table 7.5 maps the members of all the committees relevant to the supplier–customer relationship and attempts to assess the influence exercised by each committee member. Friends and enemies should be visually highlighted in order that strategic actions can be planned by the customer team.

Key events

Table 7.6 is similar to a critical path analysis plotting the deadlines for the receipt of *information*, preparation of *reports* and the dates of *approval meetings* in the decision-making process. Significant competitive activity is also recorded.

- *Information deadlines* are the target dates by which data or presentations or proposals have to be submitted by us to individual decision-making unit members.

- *Recommendation deadlines* are the target dates by which individual decision-making unit members must screen and prepare their recommendations to submit them to other unit members or committees.

- *Approval deadlines* are the target dates for meetings and committees to approve your proposals. These dates may, in turn, be predetermined by other events in the customer calendar

Table 7.4 External relationships

Customer	External contact plan
Apex Corporation	

Assessment of DMU position			Decision-making unit	Customer–supplier contacts								External contacts				
Role	Job	Relations		Office manager	Telesales executive	Marketing manager	Service manager	Service engineer	Chief executive	Financial controller	Production director	Banks	Government	Other customers	Competitor A	Competitor B
DE	A	N	Southall	X					✓					✓		
E	P	N	West							✓		✓				✓
S	R	B	Hinchcliffe			X					✓			✓		
S	A	N	Unsworth			✓										
S	A	C	Ferguson	✓		✓		✓			✓			✓		
U	P	S	Parkinson				X									
U	R	E	Watson				X						✓			
S	A	S	Jackson				X									
U	R	N	Short					✓								
S	P	E	Grant							X					✓	
U	P	N	Barmby		✓											

Table 7.5 Committee structure

Customer Apex Corporation — **Committee coverage plan**

Role	Job	Relations	Meeting Dates → Decision-making unit	17th Technical committee	12th Purchasing committee	1st & 15th Management committee	14th & 28th Quality group	15th Factory committee	Weekly Product development group	Weekly Project X task force	5th & 20th Productivity working group
DE	A	N	Southall			50%					
E	P	N	West		10%	20%			30%		10%
S	R	B	Hinchcliffe			10%		10%		30%	30%
S	A	N	Unsworth	20%			10%		20%	30%	
S	A	C	Ferguson	20%		20%		10%			20%
U	P	S	Parkinson	30%	30%		10%		20%		30%
U	R	E	Watson		30%		30%		10%	20%	
S	A	S	Jackson	20%			30%	20%			
U	R	N	Short		20%			20%		10%	
S	P	E	Grant				20%	20%	20%		10%
U	P	N	Barmby	10%	10%			20%		10%	
				100%	100%	100%	100%	100%	100%	100%	100%

Table 7.6 Key events and activities

Customer Apex Corporation

PROJECT Supply and installation of new computer system and inventory system for warehouse network

	Identification	Prioritization	Specification	Consultation	Evaluation	Approbation	Negotiation	Implementation
	of need or problem	*size and urgency*	*preferred options*	*with potential suppliers*	*of supplier proposals*	*shortlist of proposals*	*with preferred suppliers*	*final decision and follow-up*
Information deadlines	20/3 Jackson Report on Section Y	04/4 Watson Consultant Report due	25/5 Barmby specification report	3/6 Ferguson develops tender detail	1/8 Tender closer date	25/8 Shortlist issued	30/9 Detailed proposals submitted	1/12 Decision announced
Recommendation deadlines	24/3 Jackson/Unsworth consultation	15/4 Factory committee review	31/5 Short/Jackson report to management	10/6 West approves tender	20/8 Tenders evaluated and discussed	12/9 Shortlist recommendations	10/11 Negotiations complete	12/12 Implementation logistics finalized
Approval meeting deadlines	28/3 Quality group meeting	17/4 Technical committee meeting	1/6 Management committee meeting	12/6 Purchase committee approves	22/8 Presentation to purchase committee	15/9 Final shortlist agreed	30/11 Contract approved by management	31/12 Final installation approved
Actions by competitors	28/3 Competitors take Southall to lunch		28/5 Hinchcliffe does not go to competitor's seminar		30/7 Competitor's tender 10% less than expected!!!			

(starting a new operation or a restructuring of the organization, for example).

- *Actions by competition* are significant competitor-triggered events that could influence or change the timescales in the decision-making process.

Table 7.6 is particularly relevant where order dates are critical to manufacturing schedules. The dates of committee meetings, at which approval is given for projects to go ahead, are frequently predetermined six months ahead and, by backward planning from these dates, a set of key event deadlines can be pinpointed.

A failure to meet one of the key event deadlines is likely to put back the ultimate decision for at least a month to the next approval meeting. By mapping key events in this way, forecasts of orders can be much improved, resulting in greater efficiencies in stock control, work-in-progress and other critical manufacturing timetables.

Motivation analysis

Table 7.7 attempts to identify observed motivations and interests as seen in the individual behaviours of the customer's decision-making unit members. Input to this chart is a customer team effort and it is advised that no more than four behaviours should be identified for each individual decision-making unit member.

> The primary block to developing business is insensitivity to the people politics and feelings around you – your own and your customer's people.

Decisions may well be more influenced by emotion than logic – why else would salespeople be necessary? David Stafford-Clark, the famous psychiatrist, wrote, 'While intelligence provides a screen or filter for experience and the means of storing and assessing its results, the springs of action are essentially emotional ... and in the exercise of decision it is feeling that is the ultimate force.'

Feeling transcends logic, as we all discover when we yearn for that new car that we *know* we cannot afford, or believe that a new tennis racquet is going to transform our game. Feelings are priorities, preferences and prejudices that create the politics of business. The primary block to developing business is insensitivity to the people politics and feelings around you – your own and your customer's people.

Table 7.7 attempts to identify these feelings – or motivations – in the decision-making unit. It is based on your observation of the behaviours of the members of the unit and is essentially a consensus assessment by the customer team about the interests and personal drives that are exhibited by unit members. What motivations are likely to influence the thinking of the individuals in their relationships with suppliers?

Motivations may be evaluated under three headings:

- *function-based*: these motivations are the more tangible aspects of business performance that appear to interest the individual, which might include technology, quality, design, efficiency, safety, durability, simplicity, accuracy, comfort, economy, reliability, convenience, and so on;

- *need-based*: these may be described as those personal drives that subconsciously shape opinions and actions – they are the 'feel good' factors that afford special areas of satisfaction to the individual, the personal 'wins' that we instinctively aim for in everyday events;

- *role-based*: these cause us to behave in certain ways that we enjoy and which we perceive may help us to achieve our need-based motivations, so we are likely to regard favourably those people who create opportunities and encourage us to play our favourite roles; likewise, we are unlikely to seek relationships or enjoy relationships that inhibit this. Both buyers and sellers indulge themselves in playing roles. Sometimes these roles compliment each other and there is personal chemistry, but, on occasions, they

Table 7.7 Motivation analysis

Customer: Apex Corporation

Planned motivational strategies

DMU position Role	Job	Relations	Decision-making unit	Technical	Design	Quality	Economy	Durability	Safety	Finishing the task	Achieving – time	Control – responsibility	Personal visibility	Belong to groups	Affection and warmth	Innovation/change	Confrontation	Status and respect	Rules and conformity	Details	Work style	Decision – risks	Mental rate style	Physical rate style	Social style	Planning – thinking	Order – harmony	Emotional restraint	Opinion expression
				Functional						**Needs**											**Roles**								
DE	A	N	Southall	✗											✓					✗			✗			✓		✗	
E	P	N	West		✓		✗	✗					✓																	
S	R	B	Hinchcliffe			✓					✓					✓					✓							✓		
S	A	N	Unsworth	✓																										✓
S	A	C	Ferguson		✓			✓					✗		✓			✓		✓			✓	✓						
U	P	S	Parkinson															✗												
U	R	E	Watson	✓			✗		✓			✓			✓					✗				✗	✗					
S	A	S	Jackson							✓			✓		✓				✓											
U	R	N	Short				✓								✗		✓								✗	✓	✓			
S	P	E	Grant	✓																		✗								
U	P	N	Barmby			✓			✓					✗			✓				✓								✗	

conflict, generate friction and because these roles do not interact, the result is sterile.

Building relationships and motivation relies upon the ability of both parties in a relationship to be sensitive and tolerant to the priorities of others and to refrain from imposing their own excesses. More detailed analysis of this topic is given in Chapter 10 and at **www.business-minds.com/kcrm**

Tables 7.1 to 7.7 provide a comprehensive, structured approach to analyzing the people and the decision-making processes of your key customers. However it is recognized that not all customer business is conducted on such a scale and a more simplified approach can be justified. For these situations an abbreviated customer mapping document is shown in Table 7.8, which also incorporates the heart and mind analysis outlined previously as part of the 'executive summary'.

PERFORMANCE REVIEWS AND COMPETITIVE VALUE ANALYSIS

The very nature of a customer relationship means a regular (perhaps even daily) dialogue on your performance as a supplier. However, there should be more formal and structured feedback at prescribed intervals which may be monthly, quarterly, twice-yearly or annually, as appropriate. Whatever frequency is agreed, the opportunity for a *full* performance review should be taken at least once a year and, in the best relationships, will be a proactive, constructive tool for both parties as well as giving you valuable competitive information. In general terms, such a review will:

- concentrate on evaluation of the quality of your performance – not the price;
- be conducted at a time as far as possible from any annual price negotiations;
- have some value for your customer as a reward for sharing information;
- involve input from all relevant functions in the customer's organization;

Table 7.8 Simplified customer map

Customer ....

- list all influential people in the account
- Evaluator, Screener, User, Influencer or Decider?
- estimate % of influence in purchasing/listing decisions (column total = 100%)
- Active, Passive or Resistant
- Champion, Supporter, Neutral, Blocker or Enemy
- name friends (+) and enemies (-) amongst colleagues
- sources of influence – magazines, trade and competitor friends, seminars, competitors, demonstrations, clubs?

Business share	%	
Mind share	%	
Heart share	%	

Contact Name	Job title	Role ESUID	% influence	Attitude to change APR	Attitude to us CSNEB	Relations with colleagues	Sources of information/ influence	Other information including positive and negative contacts with us/competitors

- use your customer's evaluation of your competitors as a performance benchmark;

- give rise to an action plan in your organization.

The review should be set up as an open discussion either with a small group of your customer's relevant staff or as a series of one-on-one meetings with the individuals concerned. The discussion should be structured to take them through a process to evaluate their perceptions of your company's current performance compared with your main competitors for their business. To facilitate the process, limit the evaluation to your own company and, perhaps, two competitors. In the early stages of a customer relationship, the customer might be reluctant to discuss competition and your own performance might be the only topic on the agenda but as the review becomes accepted as a normal operational procedure, it is likely that the customer will see the value of more openness and assume a less negotiation-style response.

Your customer may have already installed a supplier review procedure as part of a quality control system but this may not cover all the aspects of your specific commercial relationship and this might have to be an extra procedure. Some companies regularly publish evaluations of suppliers who are identified only by codes. Each supplier knows their own code and can therefore identify how they rate against competition without knowing the names of the competitors (see Table 7.9).

If no review procedure exists it is an excellent opportunity for you to help your customer to install one and influence the format.

The steps in setting up a performance review system are similar to the methodology for evaluation and prioritization of customers as described in Chapter 3.

Step 1 - Agree with the customer a list of criteria to measure supplier performance – these criteria are called 'customer drivers' and usually include:
- *product technical performance* – how the product performs, quality of manufacture, matching specifications, handling properties, consistency, ease of use;

Table 7.9   Example of basic supplier rating system – result for third quarter 2000

Maximum score	Commercial performance						Technical performance						Overall result		
	15	15	10	10	50		15	15	15	5	50		100		
Supplier code	Price	Delivery	Supply flexibility	Admin- istration	Total	Rating	Product	Technical support	Speed of response	Design support	Total	Rating	100 max.	Q3 2000 rating	Previous rating
A	8	10	10	12	30	4	12	8	8	8	36	3 =	66	4	5
B	6	12	12	8	38	2	12	6	10	6	34	5	72	2	1
C	6	11	12	10	39	1	14	8	10	10	42	1	81	1	3
D	10	6	4	6	26	5	10	10	10	8	38	2	64	5	4
E	10	8	6	10	34	3	10	12	8	6	36	3 =	70	3	2

- *delivery performance* – accuracy of shipments, lead times, reliability of promises, 'just-in-time' facilities, dealing with small volume orders, split deliveries;
- *product offer* – range of products, availability, speed of response to special sample requests, TQM/ISO, environmental considerations;
- *technical support* – ease to work with, communication (progress information), technical competence, technical response;
- *commercial support* – promotional support, after-sales service and claims, salesforce usefulness, internal customer service helpfulness;
- *design support* – creativity, quality, development, competence (industry awareness);
- *business relations* – brand image, logistics match (geography?), stability, range and depth of personal relationships, enterprise.

Step 2 – The customer weights or ranks the importance of each of the customer drivers on a scale of 1 to 10

Step 3 – The customer rates your performance and, perhaps, your two main competitors, for each driver on a scale of 0 to 10

0 – atrocious
1 – bad
2 – very poor
3 – poor
4 – below average
5 – average
6 – just above average
7 – good
8 – very good
9 – excellent
10 – exceptional

Step 4 – Calculate the supplier quality table by multiplying the ratings by the weights for each criterion for each supplier. Add up the total score for each supplier and express as a percentage of total possible score (see Table 7.10).

The performances of your company and three principal competitors are shown in graphic format in Fig. 7.2a.

Step 5 - Using an index of 1 to 100, the customer rates the prices of each of your competitors relative to a positioning of your company at an index of 50. An example is shown in Table 7.9. The quality score and the price index for each supplier is then mapped on the competitive value analysis chart (see Fig. 7.2b) which compares supplier performance against price. Hopefully this will demonstrate to the customer your company's value position in a favourable light. If not, remedial action must be agreed; the extent by which performance has to be improved or price adjusted can be immediately calculated.

The purpose of the performance review and the competitive value analysis chart is:

■ to maintain a meaningful dialogue between customer and supplier staff;

■ to ensure that you are abreast of competitive activities and initiatives;

■ to provide a forum for improvement initiatives;

■ to check out your competitive position in the marketplace generally.

The dialogue is particularly effective if conducted with the customer in front of a computer screen using special software to facilitate the calculations and, most of all, to use a paired comparison method of weighting and rating. This works by asking the user to choose a preference between every permutation of pairings from a list of options, resulting in a set of ranked options. On a computer display, one can stack and sort the options visually by the simple 'drag and drop' method.

A typical template for the competitive value analysis process is reproduced in Exhibit 7b.

Table 7.10 The performance quality review – calculation example

Driver	Weight (1–10)	Max. possible	Your company		Competitor 1		Competitor 2		Competitor 3	
			Rating	Weighted score	Rating	Weighted score	Rating	Weighted score	Rating	Weighted score
Product performance	9	90	8	72	6	54	4	36	6	54
Delivery performance	7	70	8	56	4	28	5	35	2	14
Product offer	5	50	6	30	6	30	5	25	4	20
Technical support	6	60	7	42	5	30	3	18	2	12
Commercial support	8	80	7	56	5	40	3	24	4	32
Design support	4	40	5	20	6	24	2	8	5	20
Business relations	8	80	7	56	5	40	4	32	3	24
Price index			50%		55%		35%		45%	
TOTALS		470		332		246		178		176
Overall score				71%		52%		38%		37%

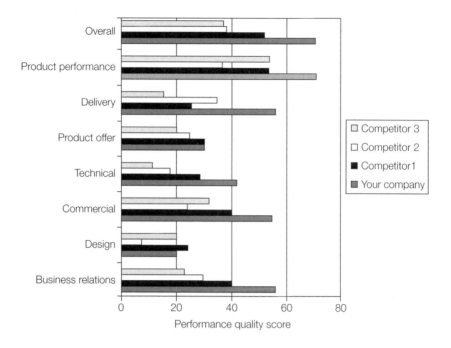

Figure 7.2a   Competitive quality performance profiles

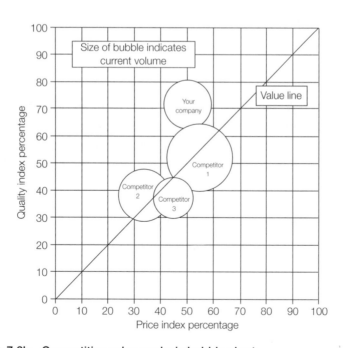

Figure 7.2b   Competitive value analysis bubble chart

CUSTOMER PENETRATION STRATEGIES

Inevitably, when involved continuously in building relationships with key customers, one develops a repertoire of *approaches, strategies* and *tactics* to pilot development projects through the political maze of people and priorities. This is not a manipulative process; it is adaptation to a given set of circumstances in order that the customer feels comfortable with and responds to proposals that will, almost certainly, mean change or departure from current practices.

In some supplier companies, where customer teams are well established, a kind of jargon may emerge to describe such strategies; it is a kind of shorthand which ensures that all members of the customer team understand the overall thrust of the plan for business development in specific customers. It may also serve as a creative checklist when reviewing options or dealing with particular obstacles to progress in a particular situation. The 13 most commonly used penetration strategies are *High Noon, Ho Chi Min, The Great Confession, Domino, The Wedge, Titanic, X-ray, Seeding, Disney, Trojan Horse, Popeye, The Atomic Bomb*, and *Stanley and Livingstone*, and they are detailed below.

■ *High Noon* is a well-prepared eyeball-to-eyeball confrontation with your most vigorous opponent in the decision-making unit. This strategy is not necessarily aggressive but seeks to identify the real *basic* issues behind any opposition and attempt to present counter-arguments. Success in reducing this opposition may depend on your ability to do something about the basic issues, which may not be easy if they are emotionally based.

> It is necessary to strip away the other person's formal behaviour mask which, to different extents, we all have and shelter behind.

Too often in business dealings the participants try to play the role that they think is *expected* of them. Buyers feel that they have to appear indifferent and focus on price as the main priority, while salespeople feel that they have to keep control of the interview and not credit the competition with any strengths.

The reality is that ongoing major business is built on an honest, realistic relationship where the principal performers know each other as people, not cardboard cut-out spokespersons for their company. For example, Stephanie, the buyer, deals with John, the salesman, as a human being and is not above rebuking him when he exaggerates (but with a smile on her face). Both parties occasionally fail to perform but make allowances for each other. They need each other: Stephanie may want that urgent shipment by this afternoon; at another time, John may have that production problem and need co-operation to reschedule deliveries. Disguising these problems in the relationship will serve no purpose and undermine personal credibility. It is necessary to strip away the other person's formal behaviour mask which, to different extents, we all shelter behind. However, we can only do this if we discard our own disguises and feel able to be more open with our real feelings, expectations and anxieties.

- Faced with a major opponent who may not respond to confrontation, the *Ho Chi Min* strategy is to concentrate on the friendly decision-making unit members around the opponent in order to bring pressure of numbers to bear on the antagonist. Eventually Saigon falls – but it could be a lengthy process.

- When the situation is blocked because of a bad experience for the customer in the past when dealing with your company, *The Great Confession* might be an effective strategy. This strategy involves a totally frank admission of your failings in the past. This can result in strong remorse from the customer and the declaration that perhaps it was not all your fault. Thus, with the conscience now clear, we can start again and give the relationship another try. *The Great Confession* is an effective way to heal old supplier– customer scars but it can only be used once!

- The *Domino* strategy is to effect penetration of the customer by targeting one department at a time. This is a particularly appropriate strategy for major customers with complex organizations or strong, decentralised, autonomous responsibility policies.

■ In situations where the competition is established and dominant, *The Wedge* – a product-by-product gradual penetration – might be appropriate. Instead of a head-to-head attack on the competition stronghold, which will only provoke a massive retaliation, an infiltration and gradual erosion of the competitor's position might give you a presence with the customer before the competitor has even noticed.

The objective in the early stages is not to be noticed by the competition, so focusing on the *minor* products might be appropriate. This strategy may also be considered when a customer has anxieties about not placing too much business with a single supplier.

■ *Titanic* is the favourite strategy of high-visibility companies with branded products faced with competition from manufacturers with lesser-known but lower-priced products. It emphasizes the security of the long-established reputation and the risk of changing allegiances. It is the added-value of the proven product and the uncertain future of the new entrant which is the main thrust of the supplier's argument. The survival of the global computer hardware manufacturers struggling against the low-cost assemblers may depend on how well this strategy works. 'No-one ever got fired by buying IBM' was a much-quoted axiom. 'No-one ever got promoted either!', the competitors responded.

■ Depending upon your industry, *X-ray* could be a viable strategy. It is based upon setting up surveys, analyses, investigation, and so on, into the customer's methods, in order to identify problems and opportunities to be addressed by your solutions. It is much favoured by consultancy and training service companies, whose initial aim is to get the customer's agreement to a survey or training needs analysis. Such an investigation can help the customer diagnose problems or become aware of opportunities. In addition, the supplier is able to participate in the preparation of specifications, which permits solutions to be tailored to the customer needs and negotiations to be based upon added-value rather than price.

The X-ray strategy is at the heart of customer management, because it builds up special supplier-customer relationships and establishes entry barriers against competition.

- The *Seeding* strategy is suited to a long sales cycle situation and calls for a disciplined slow release of benefits over a period of time. It is particularly appropriate when the customer is locked into a competitive contract which will not expire for some time and interest in new proposals to replace the competitor has to be sustained until change is possible. In all forms of negotiation, it is quite useful to withhold some particular advantage until the final stages – you might need it in order to gain preference over competition when the situation is finely balanced.

- The *Disney* strategy is a deliberate concentration on activities projecting warm, friendly relationships based on personalities and with, perhaps, a strong social emphasis. It might involve invitations to sports fixtures and entertainments and is based on the premise that business is fun and we are nice people to do business with.

  The use of this strategy depends upon an accurate assessment of the personalities involved. The strategy has to be a genuine projection of what the supplier believes otherwise it will be perceived as dramatically insincere and undermine all credibility in the relationship.

- *Trojan Horse* is a similar strategy to *Ho Chi Min* except that it is more directed towards finding champions in strategic places than towards any one specific opponent. For example, ensuring that decision-making unit members who favour you are part of any task force or committee appointed to review the current situation.

- The emphasis in the *Popeye* strategy is the big presentation and 'knocking their eyes out' with a high level of cosmetic dressing in all meetings, reports, samples and demonstrations in the process of winning over the customer. The message of success is projected at every opportunity with the invitation to the customer to join the bandwagon. Indeed, any alternative action would be unthinkable!

■ The *Atomic Bomb* strategy is the offer that cannot be refused. Usually price-based, this is a bottom-line strategy for the supplier if all else fails. Care should be taken to ensure that the competitor does not have a hydrogen bomb!

> The experienced salesperson always leaves an issue outstanding at the end of every meeting, which gives the reason and a purpose for the next meeting.

■ The *Stanley and Livingstone* strategy is probably the most common approach for penetrating the non-customer. It consists of patient, persistent exploration, looking for the problems and opportunities that will open the doors into the customer for you. The idea is to keep close to the prospect so that, when a competitor fouls up or new buying policies are decided upon, you are close enough to respond quickly to the changed circumstances. In this situation, real creativity is needed to find valid reasons for repeated meetings with the prospective customer, many of which will be covering the same subjects repeatedly. The experienced salesperson always leaves an issue outstanding at the end of every meeting, which gives the reason and a purpose for the next meeting.

SUMMARY

Information is at the heart of effective customer management – the more you know about the facts and feelings of your customer, the better able you will be to plan strategies and negotiate to your mutual benefit. A thorough understanding of the total corporate business plans both for your company and your key customers is fundamental to effectively managing customer priorities and relationships.

In addition, a structured approach to the customer development plan enables the collective experience of the customer team to be used. The development plan should always be focused on helping to support the customer's goals and embrace feelings as well as facts. But equally crucial to effective and constructive customer planning is understanding the customer's decision-making processes and the roles and influence exerted by the members of the decision-making unit.

8

How much do you really know about selling your ideas?

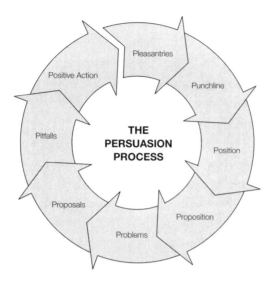

THE KCRM CULTURE SHIFT

Key customer management demands complete support from everybody in a customer-driven company. This enables key customer managers to spend the greater part of their time with customers, which is where, after all, the money comes from. It is a matter of some concern that straw polls conducted with managers over the past seven years suggest that less than 40 per cent of key customer managers' time is spent on external matters. So where does the other 60 per cent of time go? For the most part it is spent lubricating internal wheels of administration in order to fulfil promises to customers. Sometimes it is called 'fire-fighting' or 'trouble-shooting', but the ratio of internal activities to external activities is an interesting indicator of how customer-driven the organization really is.

For most companies coming fresh to concepts of key customer management, a significant shift in company culture is required. The key customer management team is the agent of change. It is no good thinking that you cannot change the culture. You have to, because if you do not, you are unlikely to win any prizes in your customers' preferred supplier programme.

The chief executive and every board member
should allocate at minimum 15 days per year
to field visits to customers.

How can the culture be changed, though? In the formation of customer teams, it has already been suggested that all functions, not just sales, should be involved. The chief executive and every board member should allocate at minimum 15 days per year to field visits to customers. Every department should be aware of who the key customers are and the degree of prioritization they enjoy.

Above all, the key customer manager has to exercise a high level of skill at persuasion. Now, that should not be too difficult if the manager has come up from the sales ranks. However, the internal selling job is probably the toughest influencing task that the manager has ever tackled and the emphasis is on a skill at which many salespeople do not excel – numeracy.

The chief executive probably has a dozen people a week bursting into the office with ideas for spending money: the data processing manager wants a new computer peripheral; the catering manager wants a new fryer ... In addition, there are probably at least ten outside salespeople trying to sell staff healthcare packages or sophisticated process control systems. All these entrepreneurs can demonstrate tangible benefits, payback time, return on investment, and so on, but in the final analysis, although *every* investment can be justified, there just aren't the resources to do everything.

Planning is about the allocation of resources and the key customer manager has to fight for a share of these resources with quantified and qualitative reasons. If a policy has to be changed, the change has to be fought for with a credibility and numeracy that generates confidence in the people in grey suits who make the policy decisions. The key customer manager needs a command of persuasion skills and an understanding of how money works in the organization, particularly when it carries the label 'profit'.

HOW CAN YOU MAKE COMMUNICATION MORE EFFECTIVE?

Communicating effectively is putting your case over in the manner that corresponds with the way people think when they are asked to make a decision. If there is any logic in the process, it is a simple four-step logic:

1   what is the situation?
2   should anything be done about it?
3   what are the options?
4   which is the best option relative to the risk involved?

It is a basic decision process that is with us every day of our lives, whether in business or at home: 'I need to wash my hands; should I do it now or later? There are washrooms on the first floor and in the basement; I'll use the one in the basement because it is usually less crowded.' It makes sense that we, as communicators and persuaders, should attempt to communicate in a pattern of thinking that is recognized by the person we are trying to communicate with, and from whom we need a favourable decision. That pattern is: 'Here is a situation; it is a high priority situation; what are the choices of action we have in this situation? The best choice is this because ...'. Remarkably, this is exactly opposite to the pattern that many salespeople use to try to influence customers. The usual sequence in these situations is: 'Here is a solution; it is better than all the other choices: by the way, do you have a problem for my solution to solve?'.

> The executive presentation quite often is bursting
> with features and benefits without having first really
> pinpointed the problem or opportunity.

The 'solutions-chasing-problems' syndrome is no less evident in the executive presentation – internal or external – which quite often is bursting with features and benefits without having first really pinpointed the problem or opportunity. This emphasis on the presentation of features and benefits sometimes leads to the belief that selling services is different to selling products. There *are* differences (selling services may be easier because the intangible solution can be much more customizable than the physical specification of a product), but selling is more about identifying customers' needs, and motivating them to put a high priority on satisfying their needs, than it is about presentation of solutions. On that premise, whether it's a product or a service doesn't really matter.

The logical decision-making sequence can be broken down into an eight-part structure for persuasive presentations – *pleasantries, punchline, position, problems, possibilities, proposals, pitfalls* and *positive action*. This structure is designed to take the listener (or reader, if this presentation is in written format) through the argument in a way which corresponds with normal thinking processes. Let us now look at these elements individually.

a. Pleasantries

This is the opening greeting which sets the tone of the meeting, effects introductions, and acknowledges the time contribution of all those present. Never underestimate the importance of this opening stage; your audience is making up its mind whether or not you are worth listening to.

Avoid the humorous start (especially early in the morning) and keep it short. Depending on the size of the group, greet by name and acknowledge any contributions by group members of the data which you are going to feature in your presentation – this helps to establish the credibility of your figures even before you start.

The pleasantries afford the time for the audience to settle in and get used to your voice. On an international level, the further east you go around the world, the longer you will spend on pleasantries. In Japan, for instance, the pleasantries will be accompanied frequently by a flurry of business card exchanges.

b. Punchline

In all presentations and reports, the way in which you start determines how the remainder of the presentation will go. You need a short, sharp stimulus to wake everybody up and get them leaning forward with interest. You want them to feel *curious* enough about what you have said to pay attention. You want them to feel a sense of *involvement* in the subject of your presentation and your aim is to accelerate their *confidence* in you, both as a human being and as a business person. Curiosity, a sense of involvement and confidence are your target responses at this stage.

Confidence accelerators include dress and manner appropriate to the situation; firm handshakes; well-prepared visual aids and figure charts (anything in writing enhances the legitimacy of your case);

discreet name-dropping of your supporters; and occasional use of technical jargon which signals your experience (but only if the group understands the jargon).

The punchline is sometimes known as the 'elephant'. We have all seen those American movies in which, when the circus comes to town, it advertises its presence with a procession through the town led, always, by ... an elephant. The punchline should be no more than three or four sentences and should contain a *number* or a *statement* which will arrest the attention of the group, such as '... and if the recommendations are accepted, I believe that it will be possible to achieve a revenue growth from our major customers of up to 25 per cent, or £3.4 million in the year ahead.'

c. Position

If you have been working on your presentation for the past three weeks, the current position will be clear in every detail to you but do *not* assume that your audience will be equally clear about it. They may have come from a crisis in their own departments and only be half concentrating on what you are saying. You have to recapitulate and update on the situation. Make it as detailed as you need to but keep it as brief as possible.

Although this is a summary, it is also the beginning of the critical phase in a presentation that aims to persuade and determines the awareness and the priority with which your audience is going to consider your proposals. Reviewing the position establishes what you expect to happen if the situation continues unchanged.

d. Problems

A problem is a discrepancy between what you *expect* to happen and what you *want* to happen. An opportunity is a possibility of a better outcome than you expect to happen in the normal course of events. If there is a defection of one of our key customers which means that we have a potential 25 per cent deficit on budget for the year, then we have a *problem*. If one of our *competitors* has had a major problem on supply which has weakened relationships with their key customers, there is an *opportunity* to exceed our budget for the year. Problem or opportunity – it is the *urgency* and *size* of the discrepancy or possibility that is going to influence the significance that is attached to the situation and the resources that will be made available.

The size of the problem or opportunity needs to be quantified in terms of revenue, profit, volume, lost production, downtime, sales costs or whatever the presentation is about. The implications need to be spelled out and, if necessary, extrapolated. If the situation is like this now, what will it be like next year, for example?

The key mistake that is made in presentations is not defining the problem. This stage is frequently not fully developed in the presenter's haste and enthusiasm to get to the proposals.

e. Possibilities

The purpose of this stage is to address the audience's need to review and choose between the options rather than be faced with the take-it-or-leave-it choice presented by a single proposal. By setting out the possible courses of action to correct the problem or seize the opportunity, you are demonstrating that you have investigated the situation and options fully, thus reinforcing the credibility of your eventual proposals.

Three possibilities should be indicated (more than three can confuse, while two options may not appear to be enough). Of course, one of the options will be to do nothing – to leave the situation as it is. This permits you to reiterate some of the implications of the problem or opportunity that were covered earlier. General advantages and disadvantages for each possible course of action should be listed.

f. Proposals

Having developed the case, you say which of the possibilities you have selected and are proposing. General advantages should be repeated and developed as specific benefits for each member of the group, if practical. Financial benefits should be directed at the controller; volume benefits at the production director, efficiency benefits at the general manager, and so on. The proposals should include the fine details and benefits of your recommendations but only those aspects for which you need approval for a fresh mandate.

Too much detail can confuse and promote disproportionate discussion on minor issues.

g. Pitfalls

In theory, once you have taken your audience through a logical decision-making process, they should be approving your recommendations wholeheartedly. In reality, a decision is a major commitment and not taken without some trepidation.

To alleviate anxiety, you recapitulate some of the *disadvantages* you mentioned when reviewing the possibilities. By admitting the snags in your recommendations, you are realistically acknowledging that no solution is 100 per cent perfect. A decision is a process of weighing up the pros and cons.

At this stage, establish that the advantages considerably outweigh the disadvantages. This gives a third opportunity to reinforce the benefits of your proposals. Perhaps leave out one minor disadvantage so that it can be picked up by your audience. Doing this should counter any impression that you know it all, which may have been created by your thoroughness, and allows the group to feel that they are contributing, not just being led.

h. Positive action

Finish with a clear definition of the approvals you seek and the actions you need endorsed. Make it easy for the group to say 'yes' by clarifying any qualifications and not complicating the issue with choices. If there are any details to be worked out after the presentation, get approval 'in principle'. If the details need further consideration by individuals in the group, agree a precise deadline or the time of a follow-up meeting. You must end the presentation on a positive note (perhaps by repeating that major benefit with which you opened) and be specific in what you are asking the group to do. Resist the temptation to reiterate any minor negative issues. It might be quite acceptable, in view of all the positive benefits you have indicated in your proposals, to exclude them completely from your thinking. This avoids distraction from the main thrust of your presentation.

As soon as agreement is secured, use body language to close the meeting. Sit down, stand up or close your document case, whichever is appropriate, and depart as quickly as possible or move on to the next topic on the agenda.

Internal or external presentations are made on a variety of topics in an infinite permutation of circumstances. In all cases, the presenter must know the objective – whether it be to inform, to secure approval, to explain, or whatever. The achievement of the objective can *only* be measured in terms of *response* from the group. The action of the audience will indicate that they have understood, agreed or accepted the explanation. It is simply not purposeful enough to express the objective as 'the presentation of the sales plan'; the purpose is to secure the agreement of the board to the strategies, policies and resource requirements of the sales plan.

Examples of presentations in this format are shown in Exhibits 8a and 8b at the end of this chapter.

MAKING WRITTEN PROPOSALS MORE EFFECTIVE

The same decision sequence format applies to the written word, but take care to limit the main body of the report to the basic argument, presented concisely in the eight main sections described above. All figures and technical detail should be contained in separate appendices, identified by the specific interests of individual members of your target audience. As in a verbal presentation, the opening section is critical; it has to persuade the reader to invest time in reading the rest of what may be a voluminous report.

MAKING BETTER ONE-TO-ONE PRESENTATIONS

These presentation techniques also apply to one-on-one persuasion situations except that, of course, the dialogue is likely to be more of a two-way discussion. The principle is the same, though. You are trying to help the other person think through a situation by means of a discussion sequence which fits in with natural thinking processes. You should keep asking yourself 'Which stage in the thinking process are we currently at?', 'How can we progress to the next stage?' High-pressure persuasion happens when the persuader is out of sequence with the 'persuadee's' decision-making processes.

THE SKILLS OF THE EFFECTIVE COMMUNICATOR

Effective communication with the senior management of both your own company and that of your key customers needs:

■ *accurate empathy*: showing relevant respect and concern for the other party's attitudes and beliefs;

■ *non-possessive warmth*: creating rapport without favouritism or subjectivity;

■ *authenticity*: feeling and appearing open and relaxed with genuine reactions and no defensiveness.

Effective presentations need:

■ competence in the subject

■ conviction about the subject

■ communication skills.

Strong ability in all three factors will make you a truly professional communicator. Weakness in one or more of these aspects will place you in one of seven other communicator categories: the oblivioius competent, arrogant charlatan, shallow persuader, endearing bumbler, boring lecturer, cold presenter or humble expert.

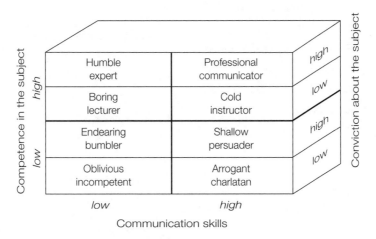

Figure 8.1   The communication grid

SUMMARY

No matter how good your ability to analyze and make plans for key customers, your success will depend upon your skills in communicating effectively with those who have to approve the ideas and those who have to implement them. Influencing people's opinions and motivating them to act needs an understanding of how people think when they are making decisions and the individual differences which generate dissimilar responses. The skill is helping your audience to think through a natural decision-making sequence and ensuring that the problem (or opportunity) that your proposal addresses is fully quantified. People do not buy solutions that are more expensive than the problem they solve.

Exhibit 8a

Presentation to directors: Farmhouse Foods Ltd

Farmhouse Foods Ltd are a leading manufacturer of packaged groceries (such as pastas, rice, sauces, ketchup, salad cream and soups) supplied to all major retail food outlets including Megabuy Stores – the largest and fastest-growing supermarket chain in the country.

Farmhouse Foods enjoys good branded business with Megabuy on all its products, with the exception of packaged soups, where it has less than 2 per cent of the total soup business. Farmhouse Foods is the number three supplier, well behind Knorr and Batchelors who, between them, have about 42 per cent of the business. Most of the other 56 per cent of the soup business is taken by Megabuys' own-label brand packaged soup, which sells at 50p per packet – about 17 per cent below the price of the branded product (60p). Megabuy purchases own-label soup at 37.5p, which gives them a 25 per cent margin on sales or 12.5p per unit. On branded products Megabuy enjoys a 20 per cent margin (12p).

Megabuy's superstores are designated 'S' outlets. Other stores are classified from 1 to 8 according to size (1 being the largest). Farmhouse makes 16 varieties of soup but only 8 varieties are 'listed' in the larger 'S' and class 1–3 Megabuy Stores. The smaller shops carry only three varieties. A new product, 'Chunky Main Meal Soup' is not stocked at all by Megabuy.

Soup sales at Megabuy have grown by 5 per cent annually, despite an overall market decline of 3 per cent per year. That growth has been mainly in the own-label brands which, of course, are not supplied by Farmhouse Foods. For all food lines, the growth of Megabuy has outstripped that of its competitors, mainly due to the success of its good quality own-label products, which now account for over 60 per cent of their total sales.

Megabuy have twice invited Farmhouse to become a supplier of own-label packaged soups. The first time the invitation was declined on principle, but the most recent request has coincided with a 30 per cent increase in soup-manufacturing capacity at Farmhouse's factory. After reviewing the new position, the key customer manager believes that the invitation should be accepted, given certain conditions. This would, of course, represent a major change of policy on the manufacture of own-label products for Farmhouse and so needs approval at the highest level. The key customer manager has to present proposals and secure the approval of the board, which includes the directors of finance and production. The presentation follows:

- *Pleasantries*: Good morning, ladies and gentlemen. Thank you for giving me your time for this presentation, which will take about 30 minutes and which involves a matter that I believe is crucial to the continued growth and profitability of Farmhouse Foods. In particular, I would like to thank Mrs Ellis and Mr James, whose departments have furnished the financial and production data used in this presentation.

- *Punchline*: The purpose of this presentation is to seek your approval to pursue a £6 million sales opportunity which could generate up to £750 000 extra net profit for Farmhouse Foods over the next three years. That opportunity is with Megabuy Stores – the largest supermarket chain in the country.

- *Position*: Megabuy Stores is the fastest-growing grocery chain in this country and it is estimated that they will be one of the ten major retail food distributors that will dominate Europe in the future. They are particularly strong in packaged grocery products – our market sector – holding 22 per cent market share of an overall market which is currently declining by 3 per cent yearly.

Although Farmhouse have excellent sales with Megabuy in most branded products, with up to 40 per cent share of their business in pastas, salad cream, and so on, we have not succeeded with our packaged soup products, where we have only 1.9 per cent of the business.

Whereas soups represent 10 per cent of our total sales nationally, at Megabuy Stores they are only 1.7 per cent of our overall business with them. Our varieties are not fully listed at the branches and they are not stocking our new 'Chunky' product at all. Of Megabuy's packaged soup sales, 56 per cent are own-label and this unbranded share is growing at the rate of 2 per cent per year. They have two suppliers, whose identities are secret, but they have invited us, for the second time in three years, to become one of their own-label suppliers. We believe that this is because one of their current suppliers is being dropped.

I accept that such a move would represent a significant policy shift for Farmhouse Foods but it does warrant serious attention at this moment and full consideration of the implications – both of accepting or declining the opportunity. Let us review some of our current difficulties at Farmhouse and with our relationship at Megabuys.

■ *Problems*: There are two difficulties at the moment. First, we are losing ground rapidly with soup products at the largest and fastest-growing potential customer.

Not only have they declined to stock our new products, but it is likely that our current branded products will be gradually 'de-listed' as the number of suppliers is rationalized over the next two years. This might be accelerated if we refuse to participate in this 'own-label' venture.

Second, our 30 per cent increase in production capacity is due to come on steam next month but, with current market conditions, it is estimated that only about one third of the extra capacity will be used over the next three years.

In the first place, although the total loss of Megabuy soup business might not be dramatic, it would exacerbate our capacity problem and do no good whatsoever for our market image. In addition, it might weaken our position with Megabuy for the pasta and salad cream products.

In the second place, although the new capacity will ease our immediate supply difficulties, it is calculated that under-utilization will cancel out any financial benefits accruing from the planned sales growth over the next three years. In a sentence, although we forecast sales will increase by up to 10 per cent over the next three years, profit will be static.

The current issue with Megabuy could give us the opportunity to address both of these problems.

■ *Possibilities*: There are three options. First, we decline the invitation and resign ourselves to the lack of profit growth for the next three years.

Second, we accept the offer. This would significantly improve our position with Megabuy, albeit in unbranded products, and utilize our spare capacity to the full. The disadvantages are that we would become more dependent on unbranded products with a single customer and that the full utilization of capacity might not allow for the modest growth in existing branded products and any new products that we wish to develop.

The third option is that we accept the invitation but on a limited basis and with conditions designed to improve the position of our branded products with Megabuy.

■ *Proposals*: Having considered the implications of these three options (which are set out in the charts which I have shown you), it is recommended that we take the third option.

We are prepared to enter a contract for supplying own-label packaged soups to Megabuy Stores as a *secondary* supplier for a period of up to *three years* and to a maximum volume of *two-thirds* of the new capacity. In addition, we will expect listings for *all* of Megabuys branches with *all varieties* in 'S' and class 1 shops and at least half our varieities in the remaining outlets. This will include the new 'Chunky' brand.

This contract, if we can agree these terms, will give us an estimated £6 million in extra sales over the next three years at today's prices, and £1 million of extra contribution to profit and overheads which after taking into account the utilization of capacity, is the equivalent of £500 000 extra bottom-line profit. In addition, we stay in touch and strengthen the relationship with our largest customer.

■ *Pitfalls*: I believe that the advantages of such a contract would significantly outweigh any disadvantages, but those disadvantages must be recognized and minimized.

There are three issues: reduced profit margin per unit, reservation of manufacturing capacity for the future growth of branded products and the principle of manufacturing for own-label which we have long resisted.

First, with reference to reduced margin, our manufacturing cost is 22.8p per unit. The own-label price currently paid by Megabuy is 37.5p, which would give us only 14.7p per unit contribution to overheads and profit. This compares with 25.2p contribution generated by the branded product. As the overhead (direct sales, distribution, R&D costs and fixed) is estimated at 22.5p per unit, branded or unbranded, we would appear to make a net profit of 2.7p per unit on branded products and, at first, it might seem that we would make a loss of 7.8p per unit on own-label for Megabuy.

I would suggest that many of the costs included in the branded soup overhead costs are not appropriate in the calculation of own-label product contribution. Advertising, for example, accounts for 10.2p per unit or over 45 per cent of the 22.5p overhead, but is hardly relevant to own-label products, the promotion cost for which is entirely paid for by Megabuy. The research and development cost of 1.3p per unit is also irrelevant.

Taking these two items out of the overhead allocation results in a net profit of 3.7p per unit on the own-label product – more than the profit on the branded product.

In addition, I believe it may be possible to negotiate an increase of 1p per unit on our unbranded selling price to Megabuy and, in order to maintain their same low retail price of 50p per unit, they may agree to accept a reduction in their current margin

Table 8.1 Farmhouse Foods – product cost structure

	Branded Product	Own-label product	Option 1	Option 2
Retail price	60.00	50.00	50.00	50.00
less retail margin	12.00	12.50	12.50	11.50
Megabuy price	48.00	37.50	37.50	38.50
less manufacturing costs	22.80	22.80	22.80	22.80
Direct sales costs	3.55	3.55	3.55	3.55
Distribution costs	2.10	2.10	2.10	2.10
Advertising costs	10.20	10.20	–	–
R&D costs	1.30	1.30	–	–
Fixed overheads	5.35	5.35	5.35	5.35
Total costs	45.30	45.30	33.80	33.80
Net profit	2.70	(7.80)	3.70	4.70

from 25 per cent down to 23 per cent. However, this 1p is negotiable and whatever split is agreed our net profit will be improved.

Of course, it might be pointed out that all the overhead cost is budgeted to be recovered from the branded products and these own-label soups should be treated on a marginal costing basis.

The second point concerns availability of production capacity for future growth of branded products. By releasing only 66 per cent of the new capacity to Megabuy, we are ensuring that enough capacity is retained for anticipated branded product growth for two years. There is a margin of error of 10 per cent built into that calculation.

If the contract with Megabuy works out as

planned, we must consider further extensions of capacity for year 3. That decision will not have to be taken for at least another 18 months.

The third and last point is the matter of principle. We endorsed the principle of not manufacturing for own-label three years ago when Megabuy first enquired, but circumstances change. policies, by their very nature are decided by the directors of the company and can be *changed* by the directors of the company. There is nothing to say that policies are carved in stone. I believe that the time has come to review those policies in the light of the changing market situation.

I accept that there is a possibility that once the own-label relationship is established, Megabuy will press for similar own label supplies on pasta, rice and our other branded products. I believe that our brands in these ranges are much stronger than our branded soups and we are in a better position to refuse, if we wish. However I do not feel that Megabuy will want to commit themselves to that extent with one own-label supplier.

- *Positive action*: Therefore, I would ask you to endorse my proposals and give me the authority to negotiate with Megabuy within the parameters so described. Have I your approval to proceed?

Such a presentation would, of course, take much longer than the simple outline given here and would be accompanied by charts and documentation, but the principle is the same. Make everybody sit up and listen, explain the position, fully develop realization of the problem, cover the options, present your proposals, deal with the negative issues and then move forward positively.

Exhibit 8b

Presentation to customer: Pennyweather Paper Mills

Pennyweather Paper Mills manufactures high-quality paper and packaging with a stable customer base but a rather conservative policy towards innovation. Their paper output has been increasing over the last three years – indeed, the withdrawal of a major competitor from the market place has necessitated an increase in capacity by 20 per cent but this will not be available for two years because of long lead times on new machinery. Pennyweather's annual sales are currently £120 million with a 20 per cent contribution to overheads and profit.

One of the materials used in paper production is lubrication oil for the machines – Pennyweather purchases, in total, 100 tonnes per year and uses 5 different specifications of lubrication oil in about equal volumes. Annual expenditure on lubricants is £150,000 (before discounts) evenly divided between all five oil specifications in cost and volumes. Stocks are kept at about £50,000 which is quite high because of some supply problems about 10 years ago.

Pennyweather has 10 large machines on continuous production and 4 engineers are fully occupied on oil-changes which take two engineers a full day on each machine every week. Allowing for a three-day annual overhaul and a 14 day holiday shutdown, this means there are 48 changes per year and 51 days downtime on each machine.

Each of the five lubricants used is specific to two of the ten machines and Pennyweather has a policy of never buying materials from a single source. They organise their purchases on the basis of particular specifications to each supplier and split the business between three suppliers; *International Petroleum* (specification 1 oil), *Global Oil* (specification 2) and *Universal Oil* (specifications 3, 4 and 5).

International has been doing business with Pennyweather for many years but, although thought of as a good supplier, they are not considered as the primary supplier. *Universal* have distribution centres very close to the Pennyweather Mills and give a 10 per cnet discount on list price. International's current list price to Pennyweather is £1500 per tonne. To increase their share of the business would require the price too be reduced by 10 per cent initially but Universal would almost certainly counter-attack and they might need to reduce price by a further 7 per cent to have any chance of increasing their share. At these discount levels, there would be no profit for International even with an increase in volume.

However, International's research and development have developed a new lubricant that is about a year ahead of competition. P36 is a universal oil that covers all the current five specifications, could reduce Pennyweather's inventory and the possibilities of costly mistakes due to the wrong oil being used. It also lasts 20 per cent longer between oil changes so therefore reduces machine downtime.

International's key customer manager can demonstrate financial savings (see Table 8.2) but believes the key issue for Pennyweather will be the prospect of nearly £4 million extra production per year at a time when they are actually buying in paper from other mills to meet the demand until their extra capacity is available in 2 years time.

To achieve this, they would have to give International *all* the business on all ten machines and the real obstacle is Pennyweather's 'no single-sourcing' policy. After discussing this with Pennyweather's buyer, International's key customer manager is invited to make a presentation to their purchasing committee.

■ *Pleasantries*: Good morning, ladies and gentlemen. Thank you for giving me your time for this presentation, which will take about 30 minutes and which may be a possible solution to one of the current issues that is restricting the continued growth of your company. In particular, I would like to thank your chief buyer, Mr Bond, who has furnished the financial and production data used in this presentation.

■ *Punchline*: The purpose of this presentation is to demonstrate how Pennyweather can generate more than £7 million extra production over the next two years before your additional production capacity comes on stream. At present rates, that means up to £1.3 million extra contribution.

■ *Position*: Currently each of your ten machines runs, after 51 days routine maintenance downtime, for 300 production days per year generating £40,000 production per day. Your capacity is 100 per cent utilised and will be for the next two years until extra machines are installed.

■ *Problems*: The main difficulty is that you are too successful. You have secured most of your old competitor's business

Table 8.2 Basic Pennyweather data and financial advantages of P36

Basic Data Summary

	Data	which means
Oil usage	£150 000 annual lubricant expenditure over 10 machines (480 oil changes)	£15 000 per machine per year (£312.50 per oil change)
Production days:	Mill runs 351 days per year (365 – 14) Each machine is down 51 days per year	Each machine has 300 production days
Production:	Production annual sales value = £120 million. Each machine produces £12 million per year	£40 000 per day (300 production days)
Inventory:	Current inventory of 5 oils is £50 000 which is £10 000 of each oil or 160 oil changes across the 10 machines (4 months stock	£50 000 inventory at 12% overdraft interest, is costing about £6 000 per year

Benefits

Extra production:	20% reduction in oil changes (480 days) = 96 days saving on oil change downtime	= 96 days more production @ in oil cost (£15 000 – £13 200)
Oil saving:	20% saving on oil usage per machine. P36 oil usage per machine is £15 000 x 80% x 110% (P36 higher price) = £13 200 per year per machine	= £1 800 per machine saving in oil cost (£15 000 – £13 200)*
Inventory:	With P36 stock could be reduced to 1 month which, because of less frequent oil changes, works out at 32 oil changes (40–20%) at £343.75 (£312.50 ≠ 10% higher price).	Total stock necessary is £11 000, which is £40 000 less stock than at present. At 12% overdraft interest, this is worth about £4 800 per year.
Manpower:	Currently 10 machines x 48 oil changes x 2 engineers = 960 man days per year operated by 4 engineers	Reducing oil changes by 20% = a saving of 192 man days per year (960 x 20%)

* one competitor could give up to 17 per cent discount on 6 machines that lowers the oil cost per machine to £12 450 or £750 less than P36 cost. This might be countered by a 5.7% discount on P36. However, even at list price, the total cost of oil for ten machines (£132 000) is still less than current cost with discount on 6 machines (£134 700).

and your factory is now running at 100 per cent capacity with little scope for improvement as your levels of efficiency are among the highest in Europe. You are even buying in product to meet the demand until you get your extra capacity.

■ *Possibilities*: So what can be done? There are three possibilities – first, do nothing

and try to keep on top of the situation for the next two years in which time you might lose some of those new customers because of difficulties with third-party suppliers. Second, try to bring forward your expansion of capacity – which, at best, is likely to be only weeks rather than months. Third, adopt a newly developed product – P36, that, by lasting longer, can reduce your machine downtime for maintenance and give you an extra 192 production days over the next two years, which, at £40 000 per day, I calculate at £7.6 million extra production in total.

■ *Proposal*: In view of these benefits, I suggest that you approve, in principle, that P36 should be adopted for all ten machines and that this additional production capacity should be available without delay. I do not anticipate any difficulties on specific contract details.

■ *Pitfalls*: However, there are some issues which I feel we should consider. To achieve all the extra production, as detailed, we are talking about all ten machines using P36. This will mean a rethink of your 'no single sourcing' policy. I believe that this arose because of oil shortages ten years ago. I do not believe that such fears are still valid but we would be prepared to put in a small consignment stock to reassure you on that point.

I should also point out that although the price of P36 is 10 per cent higher than the current specification, the reduction in volume used will mean a lower overall cost of oil without counting the savings in inventory and, maybe, maintenance labour.

■ *Positive Action*: So, therefore, I would ask for your approval to finalise contract details and implement without delay.

In addition to a sound structure, there are some other aspects of the presentation that may be noted:

■ the extra production is calculated for two years – a quite legitimate extrapolation because it will be two years before Pennyweather's capacity is increased and the larger number has more immediate impact

■ there is a considerable measure of understatement in the presentation. If you can deliver more than you promise the customer is pleased, so resist the temptation to overstate your case. Phrases such as 'I believe that' and 'it may be possible to' add a measured credibility to your claims

■ keep it simple – the only issue that is likely to persuade the committee to change its policy is extra production. Savings on oil purchases, inventory and manpower are secondary and may deflect attention from the key advantage

■ note the use of the phrase 'in principle' which seeks agreement on 'what' needs to be done rather than the 'how', and avoids the meeting getting bogged down in too much detail at this stage;

Of course, this presentation would only be the preliminary to a detailed negotiation between the supplier and Pennyweather

9

How much do you *really* know about CRM information technology?

SELF EVALUATION

Check out the following statements about your organization; the issues and implications are discussed in Chapter 9. Tick your answers as appropriate.

	NO	?	YES
Do you really have a fully integrated IT system – all functions from field sales to production and finance?			
Do you think such systems are (will be) necessary to stay competitive in your business?			

What are (would be) the primary objectives of such a system in your company?
   – *to increase sales revenues*
   – *to increase win rates*
   – *to increase margins*
   – *to improve customer satisfaction ratings*
   – *to decrease sales and marketing administration costs*			

To which aspects of your operation is CRM technology most relevant?
   – *sales management*
   – *telemarketing/telesales*
   – *time management*
   – *customer service and support*
   – *marketing*
   – *executive information*
   – *e-commerce*
   – *field service support*			

What problems might an effective CRM system address in your company?
   – *systems that don't communicate with each other*
   – *multiple system entries of the same information*
   – *transporting data back and forth to a central storage point*			

	NO	?	YES

*– proliferation of 'mini-applications' disconnected from
  everything else*

– 'black holes' where data disappears

– manual processes that can be automated

– paper reports (which indicate disconnects in data flow)

STRATEGY BEFORE SOFTWARE

The stunning advances in information technology have been a major force in advancing customer relationship management (CRM) into the forefront of corporate strategic thinking during the late 1990s. CRM software market comes from two directions – the front office and the back office. The back office, more readily known as enterprise resource planning (ERP), is the well-entrenched veteran in systems integration, which has already embraced manufacturing, purchasing, inventory control and various other back-office systems including financial infrastructure. The front office is the upstart challenger, ostensibly uniting under one banner all three varieties of front-office automation: sales automation, customer service automation and a repackaging of best practices database marketing called 'marketing automation'.

ERP (Enterprise Resource Planners) seeks to extend its information management methods out into the front office – forcing sales, service and marketing to work within rigid, systems-driven, back-office style parameters. The front-office vendors insist on maintaining the flexibility required to accommodate customers who care little about your system and insist you adapt to theirs. This means influencing how back-office systems manage data tied to specific customers. They see the future as one customer record used by every functional area – but, managed by front-office relationship managers.

We are seeing alliances, mergers and buy-outs between back-office and front-office system vendors in the pursuit of the totally integrated package – integrated not only functionally but globally. SAP and Baan have already made incursions onto front-office turf.

Oracle, a back-office player through and through, is so confident of its success that it is broadcasting its invasion plans and touting up-to-the-minute, worldwide sales forecasting by permitting sales reps to enter, via browser into an Internet database, their 'best guess' about size and probability of projected new orders. Never mind that those best guesses are likely pie in the sky.

Front-office vendors may seem undermanned for the fight and they have many more outsiders in positions of influence in their customers' hierarchy than insiders. Despite the melding of sales, service and marketing automation under one flag, together they'll be hard pressed to limit the ERP vendors. ERP has far more power, more influence, more experience – plus it is already the undisputed champion of the back office.

However, front-office technologists have been rather slow to grasp the full breadth of Customer Relationship Management. The three principal front-office technologies – sales, service and marketing automation – are only part of the equation. Top-level marketing is undergoing a transformation from being product- and media-based to becoming customer-based; not the automated database communication stuff but *strategic* marketing, which commands exponentially more dollars, influence and media coverage than just front-office automation.

In the past, strategic marketing has been content to lay back and remain aloof from front-office because, as long as sales, service and marketing automation could only operate separately, they remained tactical tools that traditional marketing could (and usually did) ignore. But when integrated, these systems provide a potential so huge that the new breed of relationship marketing has a vested interest in protecting and nurturing them. And it turns out that integrating disparate sales, service and marketing automation systems is virtually impossible in the absence of a relationship-marketing strategy to guides our overall dealings with customers. Suddenly, there's a synergistic relationship between strategic marketing and front-office automation.

FRONT-END SALES AUTOMATION SYSTEMS

CRM is the latest in a series of acronyms that evolved in the 1990s.

- *SFA – Sales Force Automation*

- *TAS – Technology Assisted Selling*

- *ERM – Enterprise Resource Management*

- *ERP – Enterprise Resource Planning*

- *TERM – Technology Enabled Resource Management*

CRM may be described as a concept, or management discipline, concerned with how organizations can increase retention of their most profitable customers, simultaneously reducing cost and increasing the value of interactions, thereby maximizing profits. In managing relationships with customers, organizations can, where appropriate, employ a range of technology and processes. One of the most important of these is front-office software – a system to automate sales, service and marketing processes, providing access to all information required to service customer needs while maintaining consistency across all access points, customer-facing functions and customer data. Once achieved this has two benefits – a holistic view of the customer by the organization and a holistic view of the organization by the customer.

This clarity on both sides enables much improved interaction with customers by the organization, which contributes to the goals of CRM. Where sales, service and marketing functions are automated without consistency then these goals cannot he achieved.

Front-end software (SFA and TAS) may be divided into the following three categories:

1 Personal information managers (PIM)

As their name implies, these programs are best suited for keeping track of all the little things that help you get through the day. In general, these programs cannot be recommended as a primary strategic solution. However, many of them can work well in tandem with your main program.

2 Contact managers

These programs are best suited for individual sales people working alone. They provide varying contact and calendar management capabilities and may provide a wide array of additional capabilities to increase sales impact. Most of these programs provide 'user-defined fields', but they usually aren't very flexible.

3 Integrated sales and marketing systems

These programs work best if you work with more than one person. A team can consist of two people or two hundred people. These programs should provide the full range of capabilities provided by the better contact managers. In addition, they should provide networked versions and database synchronization, so that team members can exchange and share information. These programs should also be flexible enough to adapt to a wide range of selling scenarios.

The programs referred to here range over the full continuum from the simplest single-user PIM to sophisticated automation of sales and marketing activities. Some developers might disagree with the classifications, but there can be no absolute demarcation lines between categories.

Salespeople face many challenges as they pursue new customers, discover their requirements, develop quotations or proposals, present their solutions, close orders and ensure good customer service. As the sales automation software category continues to mature, many sophisticated programs are emerging to solve specific problems encountered in the sales cycle.

There is no magic formula here. The trick is to look for ways to use technology to leverage your efforts to develop the business, take better care of and retain your customers.

However the new generation of CRM systems goes beyond the sales and marketing functions. These newer programs are referred to as 'enterprise solutions'. They should provide all of the capabilities provided by the better contact managers and sales and marketing automation systems as discussed above. In addition, they should provide a client/server version based on a robust database

Table 9.1   Three basic categories of front-end sales automation systems

	Personal information managers	Contact managers	Integrated sales and marketing systems
Supports:	individuals	individuals	individuals or teams
What do they do?	basic contact management	contact management	campaign management
		basic word processing	sales management
		merge facility	contact management
		automatic dialling	telesales, scripting
		typically flat-file or proprietary databases.	reporting and analysis forecasting
		basic database replication for remote workers	computer telephony integration
		minimal opportunity for customization	highly customizable
			run on popular relational databases
			integrate with existing systems
Benefits:	cheap, timesaving	low cost systems suitable for smaller companies	potentially huge return investment due to:
		useful productivity tools	increased efficiency
			improved effectiveness
			better-quality leads
			better forecasting and management
Points to watch:	only benefit individuals	limited functionality	do not automate bad processes
	extremely limited functionality	poor integration with systems	can take long time to implement (three months +)
		little opportunity for customization	expensive
			consultancy probably needed
Average cost	free to low	low to medium £100–£1000 +	medium to high £40k +
Representative vendors/products: *(this is not an exclusive list)*	Microsoft/Card file Schedule + PSA Software/ PSA Cards	Symantec/Act Goldmine Tracker Modatech Systems/ Maximiser	Aurum – Sales Trak Integrated Sales Systems/Oxygen Market Solutions/ Market Force

Table 9.1 continued

Personal information managers	Contact managers	Integrated sales and marketing systems
	Eurosmart/Salesmartz	Siebel Systems/Siebel Sales Enterprise
		Unitrac software/ Unitrac
		Saratoga Systems
		Caspian Partners
		Greystone Systems/ Contact 2000

management system (DBMS), such as Oracle, Sybase or Microsoft SQL Server. These systems must be easily customizable to support a wide range of complex selling environments. They should also provide the flexible communication capabilities needed to put the right information at the fingertips of whoever needs it so that you can take great care of your customers from design and production to the point of sale. Technology is enabling the concept of multifunction key customer teams to be made a reality.

HOW DO YOU EVALUATE CRM SOFTWARE?

So where do you start? You have read about sales automation, been mailed by the vendors and heard some of your colleagues, or perhaps competitors, discussing its merits. You have also recognized areas of your sales operation that could be improved by the application of the technology and have considered the commitment. Now you are ready to go forward, the question is *how*? If, like most senior sales management, you have never been involved in purchasing a major IT solution, you would probably welcome some guidance regarding the procedures to follow.

Customer relationship management currently means different things to different people. Moreover, the definition of CRM will evolve and change over time. Nonetheless, CRM software will usually consist of the following 11 components. Your initial CRM system will consist of one or more of these components, and is likely to grow over time to include additional components from this list and new components that will emerge as the CRM industry matures.

1 Sales – contact management profiles and history, account management including activities, order entry, proposal generation

2 Sales management – pipeline analysis (forecasting, sales cycle analysis, territory alignment and assignment, roll-up and drill-down reporting)

3 Telemarketing/telesales – call list assembly, auto-dialling, scripting, order taking

4 Time management – single user and group calendar/scheduling (this is likely to be Microsoft Outlook), e-mail

5 Customer service and support – incident assignment/escalation/tracking/reporting, problem management/resolution, order management/promising, warranty/contract management

6 Marketing – campaign management, opportunity management, Web-based encyclopedia, configurator, market segmentation, lead generations/enhancement/tracking

7 Executive information – extensive and easy-to-use reporting

8 ERP integration – legacy systems, the Web, third-party external information

9 Data synchronization – mobile synchronization with multiple field devices, enterprise synchronization with multiple databases/application servers

10 E-commerce – manages procurement through EDI link and Webserver, and includes business-to-business as well as business-to-consumer applications

11 Field service support – work orders, dispatching, real-time information transfer to field personnel via mobile technologies

WHAT ARE YOUR OBJECTIVES IN CRM SYSTEM IMPLEMENTATION?

It is important to understand the benefit of CRM for most companies. These generally fall into three categories: cost savings, revenue enhancement, and strategic impact. Based on successful CRM implementations, the following benefit objectives seem reasonable.

■ *Increased sales revenues*

An increase of ten per cent per annum per rep during the first three years of the project is reasonable. Increased sales result from spending more time with customers which results from spending less time running around chasing needed information (i.e., productivity improvement);

■ *Increased win rates*

An increase of five per cent per annum during the first three years of the project is reasonable. Win rates improve since you withdraw from unlikely or bad deals earlier on in the sales process;

■ *Increased margins*

An increase of one per cent per deal during the first three years of the project is reasonable. Increased margins result from knowing your customers better, providing a value-sell, and discounting price less;

■ *Improved customer satisfaction ratings*

An increase of three per cent per year during the first three years of the project is reasonable. This increase occurs because customers find your company to be more responsive and better in touch with their specific needs;

■ *Decreased general sales and marketing administrative costs*

A decrease of ten per cent per year during the first three years of the project is reasonable. This decrease occurs since you have specified your target segment customers, you know their needs better, and thus you are not wasting money and time on, for example, mailing information to all customers in all existing and potential target segments.

TEN IMPLEMENTATION SUCCESS FACTORS

Remember that the people doing the job know ways to do it better.
Take the time to work with them
and you will learn what needs automating.

To take advantage of the benefits of a CRM system, a company must undertake a structured process that ensures the automation venture does not become the automation adventure. There are ten critical success factors that are essential for the success of any CRM system.

1 *Determine the functions to automate*

Effective automation at a company starts with a CRM automation audit, which identifies the business functions that need to be automated and lists the technical features that are required in the automation system. While there are several different audit methodologies available, the usual approach uses questionnaires, face-to-face interviews, visits with sales reps in the field, quantitative matrices and a final report with recommendations. If the audit is not performed properly, you will most likely be unable to implement an effective CRM automation system.

2 *Automate what needs automating*

Automating an inefficient business process can be a costly mistake. To ensure that you automate what needs to be automated, your CRM automation audit should address a 'wish list' of how salespeople, marketing personnel, customer support staff and management would like to improve their work processes. Remember that the people doing the job know ways to do it better. Take the time to work with them and you will learn what needs automating.

3 *Gain top management support and commitment*

Companies who successfully automate CRM functions view CRM automation systems more as a business tool than as a technological tool. Keep this in mind as you approach top management for support.

Top management commitment can be secured by demonstrating that:

■ automation supports the business strategy (i.e., automation delivers the information required to make the key decisions that enable business strategy to be realized);

■ automation measurably impacts upon and improves results (e.g., improved win rates, improved margins, higher sales revenues, and higher customer satisfaction ratings);

■ automation significantly reduces costs (e.g., lower general sales costs) and thereby pays for itself over a specified time period. Document your case for automation based on business impact.

4 *Employ technology smartly*

Select information technology and systems that utilize open architecture, thereby making it easy to enhance and enlarge the system over time. Look for software applications which are modularized and can be easily integrated into, or interconnected with, your existing information databases. Ensure that the technology you select complies with international standards.

For firms conducting business between the field and regions or headquarters, or across regions, select software applications that are network compatible and that permit easy data synchronization between information held on field computer and information held on regional or headquarter computers. To accommodate future changes, be sure the technology you select can easily be customized as well as modified. In other words, let the technology help you to grow. As an example, Mobil first implemented a standard computing environment on a worldwide basis and then implemented specific CRM automation software applications.

5 *Secure user ownership*

Get users involved early to make sure that your CRM automation system addresses their needs. A large information technology manufacturer automated their sales force using the recommendations of a corporate headquarters sales and marketing automation task force. Unfortunately users were not sufficiently represented on this task force and ended up revolting against the system which they felt was yet another 'big brother' idea. Users have a vested interest in making 'their' system work in practice. Don't be afraid to hand over 'ownership' of the system to the users.

6 *Prototype the system*

Prototyping your CRM automation system facilitates the phasing in of new technology, allows experimentation on a smaller and less costly scale, tests the system's functionality, highlights required changes in organizational procedures and, most importantly, demonstrates that automation objectives can by met. Emerging rapid prototyping software development tools reinforce the importance of 'testing before you leap'.

7 *Train users*

Training includes, for example: demonstrating to users how to access and utilize needed information, ensuring that users are provided with understandable user documentation and that this documentation is frequently updated, offering online tutorials, which can be customised for each user, providing a telephone helpline to support your user, and training the 'trainers' to ensure that new users can quickly be up and running on the system.

Over the life of your sales and marketing automation system, training will end up costing on average 1.5 times the cost of the sales and marketing automation system hardware/software. Budget for training accordingly and remember that the best way to change work habits and to ensure systems success is via effective training.

8 *Motivate personnel*

CRM automation succeeds when users are motivated by the system's ability to help them obtain their objectives, and when users understand the strategic importance of CRM automation – from improved user productivity to the impact on the company's bottom-line. Trends come and go within an organization and it is critical that you determine ways to maintain individual motivation and commitment towards the CRM automation system. Show users their importance and their impact. This may mean launching an internal marketing campaign including an intranet site for sales and marketing automation effort.

9 *Administer the system*

One person/department must be held responsible for overseeing the welfare of the CRM automation system. This person/department includes an information 'gate keeper' who is responsible for ensuring the information is timely, relevant, easy to access, and is positively impacting on users' decision-making needs.

It is a strong demotivator to be out in the field and use your sales and marketing automation system only to find out-of-date or incorrect data. Be disciplined and pay careful attention to information and systems details.

10 *Keep management committed*

Set up a committee that includes senior staff and users as well as the information systems department. This committee should brief senior management quarterly on the status of the CRM automation project.

AN ACTION PLAN FOR IMPLEMENTING A CRM SYSTEM

Providing automated support for the customer relationship management (CRM) functions of your business can be an expensive decision not just in terms of software and consultancy costs, but also in the time and commitment needed from your staff. It will affect the working practices of the customer-facing employee in your organization – the very people you rely upon to get new and repeat business. To implement CRM successfully you will need solid support from the management team. With this support you can review the broad business processes you need, the role of CRM automation in the whole scheme and the objectives you expect to achieve when your system is operational. Objectives might include:

- increasing new customer business;
- decreasing customer losses;

- reducing the elapsed time for the sales cycle;
- improving lead qualification;
- introducing new channels to market.

By putting these objectives in order of priority and quantifying them where possible, you will have the road map for your system selection activities.

Make a short list of what you need, don't need, constraints and priorities

Decide which CRM features you need

With your objectives and broad business procedures in mind take a high-level view of common CRM capabilities, such as intranet access for your distributors, telesales, field service and monitoring campaign effectiveness. Aim to map your business priorities onto priorities for functionality.

Decide what you don't need

For a cost-effective solution, it is equally important to determine which features you don't need so that they can be discounted in your selection process. It is likely that vendors whose CRM systems are strong in areas that you consider unimportant will have future development plans which are also out of sync with your needs.

Too many buying decisions are based on the designer-label approach – 'if it is so expensive and has all these features, it must be the best and I can't go wrong'. This approach nearly always leads to an expensive purchase of a system that has too many features for your staff to assimilate.

Define your constraints

You must make sure that you are aware of internal and external constraints. Some will be obvious, but others may be of a political nature and unstated, or they may develop and change as the project progresses.

Define your priorities

Prioritize the criteria you have chosen. Keep this list in mind when you focus on CRM product presentations, but also keep your mind open for product features that are not on your list but which spark your imagination.

Now find out how the different CRM systems deal with your requirements. This will help you shortlist the products that best suit your needs.

Make a system shortlist

There is no single best tool for CRM – but there is a best tool for you. Having gone through the processes above, you should be able to produce a list of vendors who have a tool that suits your requirements.

A good way to get it wrong is to call just one supplier. This seems like the fast-track route because it cuts out the need for comparing products, visiting users and having long committee meetings. Even if you have a strong bias at the outset, take a look at equivalent products to see how they compare. All products evolve over time and you might he able to get the capability you want at a lower cost in an alternative product.

What to look for in CRM software for the front office

Relationship management

This represents the core functionality of a CRM software product, and is what distinguishes a CRM product from single functionality (sales automation, marketing automation or customer service) products. The distinguishing feature of a CRM product is its ability to maintain a single cohesive view of the customer across customer-facing functions of sales, service and marketing.

It is relationship management that determines whether it is possible for all sales, service and marketing staff to have one universal view of the customer across all transactions and, conversely, whether customers can initiate any kind of process (sales or service) regardless of the method of interaction chosen.

Sales, marketing and customer service

Naturally, CRM software for the front office automates functionality for front office operations (sales, marketing and customer service). So it is important to look at how well the products under consideration perform this automation. However, it is important to do this in a focused way. The product providing 'best' sales functionality is not necessarily the right product for you. You need to think carefully about what benefits you are looking for the software to provide and what functionality is required to provide this.

Productivity

If CRM products offer few productivity tools then there is little incentive to use the CRM system, which then reduces the overall effectiveness of a CRM strategy. Productivity tools result in successes with the people that matter – customers and front-line staff. Try to remove some of the petty annoyances from their lives. For example, make it possible for customers to change account details over the phone without filling in forms. Reduce the amount of paperwork required of sales staff, by providing proposal and quote-generation tools. Without the buy-in of customers and customer-facing staff, CRM does not work.

CRM products are only as useful as the information they contain.

Usability is also particularly important for CRM products, because poor usability will prevent both customer-facing staff and customers from using the system. CRM products are only as useful as the information they contain – if people decide not to enter information on the basis of poor usability or productivity then the product soon becomes useless to all others in the organization.

Universal access

CRM software enables customers to interact with the company through a variety of channels. These include:

- call centres – for telesales, telemarketing, service/support
- face to face – for both field sales and field service

- e-mail – primarily for support or requests for information
- web – for self-service access to sales and support functions
- channel partners such as a value-added reseller, agency or distributor.

These channels are more or less well supported by different vendors of CRM software. Some have specialized in particular channels, such as the call centre or the field: some, in attempting to provide all, actually provide none at all. Others have put little thought into access at all, concentrating on functionality but not the means for its use.

It is not wrong for a CRM software vendor to specialize in one or a few particular channels. What is important is that the CRM software chosen by an organization provides support for the channels that the organization requires. For example, telecommunications companies tend to have little requirement for field sales yet very challenging requirements in the call centre. A CRM product that provides no support for field sales, but excellent support for the call centre will be better for a telco than a product that provides good field sales and merely good call centre support.

Customization and integration

Customization and integration are crucial to the success of packaged applications. They determine the extent to which an organization can meet its requirements by buying an application 'off the shelf' and tweaking it rather than needing to go to the extra expense and inconvenience of building its own application from scratch.

There are two aspects to customization:

- the range of changes that may be made.
- the ease with which change may be made and managed.

Customization uses layers by which change may be performed. The layers closest to the source code are more difficult to use; the code interface layer, for instance, is probably the layer that the vendor's own consultants would use to perform complex customization. Layers towards the top are simpler to use and do not require specialist knowledge of SQL, 4GLs, programming languages or principles.

The range of change that may be implemented tends to be inversely related to the ease with which change may be made. Using a point-and-click interface to make change is simpler than using a code interface. However, the degree to which the system can be changed is likely to be smaller.

Note that although you may not use the code interface layer directly, its existence means that complex changes can be made without interfering with source code. This is necessary for the ability to upgrade to a new version of the application without re-performing customization.

In general, the lower the level of expertise required to customize applications safely the better, but there will always be some parts of some systems that demand a high level of expertise for good reasons. Some operations are always best performed by outside specialists.

Integration is particularly important in the context of CRM for two reasons.

1 CRM may be new but customers are not. Organizations have always had customers, and indeed, have always had customer information systems. Ideally, an organization should scrap all of its existing information systems every time a 'better' way of doing things was invented – but in the real world, organizations need to find a way to access and use existing systems and data whilst moving to and using the new.

2 In order to have a holistic view of the customer, which is completely consistent across the organization, it is necessary for there to be interaction between front- and back-office processes and, correspondingly, front- and back-office software. Without sound integration capabilities it is not possible to support CRM.

Selecting the vendors

Vendors have different strengths and weaknesses in meeting the requirements of CRM software for the front office. There are not many vendors that provide consistency and the full range of *access*.

To assess consistency, look at the extent to which the core customer-facing functions of sales, marketing and customer service are provided on a consistent technology platform using the same data model. Is it possible to integrate with external systems to achieve consistency across all of your organization's business applications? To assess universal access, look at the extent to which the products support different channels and how well these are supported.

CRM means trying new methods of system design – in response to client challenges to 'create one customer record' for the enterprise; or 'use every work process to add value to the customer'; or 'help make this company revolve around the customer'. What makes this challenge so daunting is that designing the desired systems requires several radical departures from system design norms:

- designing from 'the front office in' rather than 'the back office out';
- storing data in the applications using it most, rather than transporting everything back to the legacy system;
- using integrated application programs across multiple functions;
- using 'forms' to carry data from function to function to support linear work processes;
- eliminating any and all system elements that cannot support cross-functional processes;
- supporting work processes rather than work disciplines;
- structuring the system around customer information, not 'mission critical' back-office functions.

Like every process, this 'front to back' approach needs both a clear starting point and a 'spine' or organizing principle to relate multiple activities. In this case, the starting point is whatever moment in time a customer or potential customer first flashes across our radar screen, but only as a result of some action taken by either the customer or the enterprise. That could be a customer response to marketing, or sales contact, or actual purchase – as long as some action is involved, as opposed to a customer name passively listed on a third-party database.

The spine is data mapping – identification of all possible paths that customer names can travel to and through the enterprise – followed by re-mapping to reflect adoption of more desirable work processes. In the initial mapping step, we look at everything from sales and service contact, to billing, to manufacturing processes tied to that specific name. By tracking information flow this way we can readily draw a top-line map of work processes. This initial map shows the path of current processes – many of which are so ingrained that we've lost sight of them and accept them as part of the order of the enterprise.

With our data map in hand, we next look for ways to change workflow – and hence data flow – to better serve the customer. Among the 'red flags' we look for are:

- systems that do not communicate with each other;
- multiple system entries of the same information (a symptom of design flaws, not just an indication of wasted data entry time);
- transporting data to a central storage point only to be transported back when next needed;
- archiving data needed for real-time processing in data warehouses (which are archives and archives only);
- proliferation of 'mini-applications' disconnected from everything else and hence doing work that is of value only to the user;
- 'black holes' where data disappears;
- manual processes that can be automated;
- paper reports (which indicate disconnects in data flow, not just wasted paper).

The typical response to first-cut data mapping is 'Why are we still in business?' The dysfunction and waste uncovered may be appalling to the point of being funny, even in well-organized operations. But the opportunities uncovered can be highly motivating with system design possibilities leading to such outcomes as:

- system shrinkage – a natural outcome of focusing on function instead of process. We move a tremendous amount of unnecessary data unnecessarily. We store even more unnecessary information unnecessarily. And, in fact, designing work processes and data flow around customers simplifies everything – because whether we like it or not, our processes and systems have to be designed around the customer in order for us to do business. By fighting to take care of our internal needs before customer needs, we complicate both our work and the systems that support our work;

■ true integration – not just trying to tie back-office functions together with ERP. We fumble more data hand-offs than not. And we lose data and accuracy every time we do. Not to mention losing the opportunity to work together on behalf of the customer rather than working separately on behalf of our departments. Designing workflow and data flow around getting work done the best way shifts our focus to moving and sharing data where it should be;

■ simplicity – few of us use even a fraction of the computing power available to us. And the fix for that is *not* taking all the unused capabilities away as the network computer devotees tried to do. The remedy is to design systems around the work we do, rather than fitting work around our systems. If we make our systems responsive to users' work environments, they will use the system capabilities available to them – and ask for more.

> Design systems around the work,
> rather than fitting work around the systems.

That's the punchline. There's a better way to design information systems for today's and tomorrow's business environment – designing around workflow that delivers value to customers. And that's what integrating CRM and ERP is all about. Integrating the two will never be easy – but taking seriously the challenge of melding them will force us to change our current approach to system design. That will make CRM/ERP integration *possible*, which it's not when we rely on traditional system design methods.

WHAT TO LOOK FOR IN AN EFFECTIVE CRM SYSTEM

It is important for a manager to understand the best way to align the intelligent use of technology to meet business goals. Therefore, it is important to know which characteristics of this new approach are worth looking for if an organization is interested in utilizing these new customer service philosophies as a way to gain market share and improve its business.

The areas that have the greatest impact on the success or failure of such an initiative in an enterprise are detailed below.

Ability to integrate interaction and fulfilment processes

Bringing together the front ends and back ends of the existing customer-centred processes is key to achieving successful customer relationship management. Therefore, look for a system that integrates the customer interaction and fulfilment processes under one framework, inter-operates with other systems and easily shares customer information with legacy or third-party systems to enable end-to-end customer service.

Anywhere, anytime, anyhow customer service

This refers to the ability to manage all interaction channels with the customer. Does a system provide the flexibility to manage calls, Web hits, faxes, correspondence, e-mail and any other media channel that a customer will want to use to interact with your company? Optimally, a solution will provide an easy mechanism for adding additional channels of communication as they become mainstream and integrating them into the defined business process. This ensures that your organization remains flexible and responsive to changing customer requirements. A good example is the expanding importance of the Web as a critical communication channel with customers. Increasingly, customers are looking to launch service requests and perform self-service activities over the Internet. As e-commerce evolves, many companies that have traditionally only serviced customers by phone, fax or in person will realize that they are being left behind by the competition because they lack a well thought-out Internet strategy. Without a planned approach that will integrate this channel without disrupting current business processes, companies can find that they have to revamp their infrastructure just to accommodate the growing volume of service requests generated from the Web.

Intelligent work management

There are two approaches to enterprise customer management: data-centred and process-centred. The data-centred approach applies application-specific logic against a single customer information repository, which may or may not be replicated from legacy data. Data-centred solutions work well in single purpose, *ad hoc*, single-departmental applications. Examples where data-centred solutions have had success include helpdesk and salesforce automation.

However, it is necessary to look beyond the initial appeal of such tools, as there can be hidden but considerable disadvantages to data-centred solutions. Most data-centred products only focus on a small portion of the customer management puzzle. Any customer management tool deserving of the label 'enterprise' should be able to lower costs of customer management, but most have failed to do so.

In contrast, CRM solutions are data enabled, but process-centred. By leveraging the appropriate customer or system information at each step in a given process, CRM systems facilitate the intelligent management of work across channels and allow individuals at all levels of the organization to serve the customer better. As a result, a company is able to develop loyal customers, optimize resources and consistently meet service-level objectives.

Global organizations, where a single customer interaction can trigger processes across multiple departments, must respond in a timely, accurate, and consistent fashion. For such companies, a process-centred implementation of CRM is often most appropriate.

Easy access to information

Because information is generally distributed across the enterprise in mainframe systems, enterprise resource planning (ERP) applications or standalone databases, accessing the data to route work intelligently can be a challenge. That is why another critical element of a CRM solution is having defined interfaces to these disparate information repositories that ease the process of accessing and updating information across multiple systems. The goal is not to just to map data from one application to another application, but rather to use it in the context of a business process so as to more effectively and efficiently manage how that work gets processed by a knowledge worker or automated agent.

Rapid application design, development, and deployment (RADDD)

Change is one element that any enterprise in today's competitive environment can count on. For this reason, the ability to design, develop and deploy a production system in an accelerated time frame becomes a mandatory requirement in selecting CRM applications. This enables an organization to respond nimbly to changing market conditions and also realize a faster return on its investment by getting its system into production sooner.

Customizable tool kit, including process definition tools

Whenever we talk about process automation we have to understand that no two companies are identical and there is no such thing as 'one-size-fits-all', 'shrink-wrapped', or 'out-of-the-box' solutions. Every company has its characteristic set of rules, differences in job descriptions and differences in policies and procedures, which must be reflected in the enabling technology. Therefore, any technology that is selected must be customizable, open and otherwise capable of being integrated with the organization's existing computing infrastructure, including the ability to define all processes in detail.

Flexibility and agility

Workflow and process automation tools have been described as tools which help to automate rules (business rules about how the company treats transactions), routes (how the work is passed around the organization), and roles (what the specific job functions are along the routes). Tools to implement these systems must therefore contain enough flexibility to allow an organization to deploy systems that meet the needs of that organization.

Scalability

Businesses grow, particularly if they implement these systems successfully. As they do so, it is important to know ahead of time that the installed system will be able to grow with the increased demands of the enterprise. Scalability of databases, of numbers of workstations, of scope of business rules, and so on, are critical for the long-term success of CRM projects. By choosing a CRM solution that is scalable, you can eliminate the risk of having a system that cannot evolve with your organization but instead allows you to leverage your current investment in hardware, software and technical expertise.

Manageability

Managing CRM at enterprise level is a difficult task that can be facilitated by technology. Good process-centred CRM systems will help by automatically balancing loads among resources, by intelligently routing the work and by providing specific quantitative feedback to management on the specific metrics required to run the business across the entire CRM process. By modelling and automating a given customer-centred process from beginning to end, all data for each stage of that process becomes available through reports that allow managers to effectively improve a given process to achieve best practices.

SUMMARY

CRM is about strengthening the relationship with customers through reliable, quality human interactions and the effective fulfilment of obligations using the most appropriate resources. Technology is the catalyst that makes this possible by enabling individuals across the enterprise to be more efficient and effective in the delivery of superior customer service.

In order to succeed in the implementation of CRM, we must first understand the customer interaction cycle, the moments of truth where opportunities exist to make a positive impression on a customer. We must realize that the effective management of the customer involves the integration of the appropriate activities and information at all stages of the cycle. This means an understanding of and an appreciation for the enabling role of technology as that integrating factor. We must supply our people with a solution that allows them to communicate with one another, share information, and work co-operatively to provide a consistent and reliable service experience throughout the customer life cycle.

For more information on CRM systems and software, refer to the website which supports this book: www.business-minds/KCRM

10

How much do you *really* know about

motivating people and

building effective customer teams?

SELF EVALUATION

This is not an intelligence test. It is a simple summary of your likes and dislikes, preferences and attitudes. Indicate with a tick in the appropriate column how true the following statements about you are – 'never' means that you would totally disassociate yourself from the statement, 'always' means that you feel that the statement about yourself is valid. Try to avoid the 50/50 option unless you really do not have responses either way.

There are no 'good' or 'bad' answers or trick statements; quick, spontaneous answers are best and, although many statements may seem repetitive, do not check back on previous responses. Try not to hesitate, work rapidly (it should take no more than eight minutes) and be truthful.

How true are the following statements about yourself? Tick the appropriate column

SECTION 1	Never	Sometimes	50/50	Mostly	Always	
I like to keep at what I am doing until finished						F
I like to work hard						A
I like to help people make up their minds						C
I like to get a lot of attention						X
I like to be with people						B
It bothers me when someone dislikes me						P
I like to meet new people and do new things						N
I tell people when they annoy me						G
I like to follow people I admire						D
I like clear directions for doing a job						R
I like working with details						K
I work very hard						W
I make decisions easily and rapidly						I
I work at a fast pace						M
I am told that I am practically tireless						V
I like to meet people						S
I think and plan a lot						T

SECTION 1 continued	Never	Sometimes	50/50	Mostly	Always	
I am orderly; I put everything in its place						O
I am slow to anger						B
I am assertive						L
I am very selective about whom I work with						J
People appreciate my good advice						H
I have good original ideas						Z

SECTION 2	Never	Sometimes	50/50	Mostly	Always	
I always stay with the task until it is done						F
I like to do difficult jobs well						A
I like to give others advice						C
I want to be exciting and interesting						X
I enjoy being part of the group						B
I like to make close personal friends						P
I like to experiment and try new things						N
I sometimes blame others when things go wrong						G
I like to please the people in charge of me						D
I like to be told just how to do a job						R
I like work which calls for details						K
I work hard						W
I take chances						I
I talk quickly						M
I have a lot of energy for games and sports						V
I have a great many friends						S
I think a great deal						T
I keep my things neat and orderly						O
I can restrain my anger						E
The group usually does what I want						L
I believe in reward according to merit						J

SECTION 2 continued	Never	Sometimes	50/50	Mostly	Always	
Nothing is too much trouble to me						H
I am highly creative						Z

SECTION 3	Never	Sometimes	50/50	Mostly	Always	
I like to work at one job at a time						F
I want to do things better than others						A
I like to tell the group what to do						C
I like to be noticed by people						X
I enjoy being part of the group						B
I worry when someone does not like me						P
I am quick to change when I feel it necessary						N
I strike back when someone hurts me						G
I avoid being different						D
I follow rules carefully						R
I like work that calls for accuracy						K
I am a hard worker						W
I make decisions easily and quickly						I
I work fast						M
I like work in which I move around						V
I make friends easily						S
I think carefully and long						T
I keep things neat and orderly						O
I keep calm in upsetting situations						R
People think I am a good leader						L
I do not tolerate fools gladly						J
I enjoy giving and advising						H
I like to make even good things better						Z

SECTION 4	Never	Sometimes	50/50	Mostly	Always	
I keep at a problem until it is solved						F
I try very hard to be the best						A
I like to show people how to do things						C
I enjoy talking about my successes						X
I like to fit in with groups						B
I try to get very close to people						P
I like to do new and different things						N
I enjoy arguing						G
I respect suggestions from other people						D
I like to follow directions given to me						R
I like work that has to be done carefully						K
I try very hard						W
I take risks						I
I work at a fast and steady pace						M
I have energy and vigour						V
I am very friendly						S
I plan far in advance						T
People think I keep things neat and tidy						O
I am pleasant to people						E
I get people to do what I want them to do						L
I believe that people should be carefully evaluated						J
People think that I am a generous person						H
I take pride in my creativity and imagination						Z

SECTION 5	Never	Sometimes	50/50	Mostly	Always	
I always finish work I begin						F
I want to be very successful						A
I like to make decisions for the group						C
I like to get attention						X
I'd rather work with other people than alone						B
I like it when people are close and friendly						P

SECTION 5 continued	Never	Sometimes	50/50	Mostly	Always	
I like new styles in clothes and cars						N
I like to stand up for what I believe						G
I like to please people whom I admire						D
I like others to make decisions for the group						R
I like to do every step with great care						K
I always try to do a perfect job						W
I take chances						I
I usually hurry						M
I like to play games and sports						V
I am quick in making friends						S
I think and plan a great deal						T
I like to organize my work						O
When I speak, the group listens						L
I think that people are either winners or losers						J
I like to be generous to people						H
I have strong creative urges						Z

SECTION 6	Never	Sometimes	50/50	Mostly	Always	
I want to do only one job at a time						F
I want to be successful						A
I like to be responsible for others						C
I enjoy attention						X
I like to belong to a group						B
I try to make close friends						P
I like to try new things						N
I take great pride in my good name						G
I like to do what is expected of me						D
I like to be told what to do						R
Details and little things interest me						K
I try very hard						W
I make decisions quickly						I

SECTION 6 continued	Never	Sometimes	50/50	Mostly	Always	
I do things quickly						M
I get exercise regularly						V
I get along well with all people						S
I like to theorize						T
I keep everything in its place						O
I am a good leader						L
I have earned some preferential treatment in my job						J
I like to use my experience to help people						H
People approach me for ideas						Z

Do not read this until you have completed the questionnaire

There are 23 statements in this questionnaire, each representing a motivational facet of your personality as discussed in Chapter 10. The questionnaire is divided into six sections and each section lists all the 23 statements identified by the code letter in the right hand column.

Score the questionnaire by allocating points for each of your ticks as follows: never = 0 points, sometimes = 2 points, 50/50 = 5 points, mostly = 8 points and always =10 points.

Collate your scores for each code letter in the six sections in the panel below. Low scores are 0–18, high scores are 42–60. 'Low' and 'high' does not mean good or bad but merely extremes of personality traits which are likely to shape behaviours.

Refer to the interpretations in Chapter 10.

Codes	F	A	C	X	B	P	N	G	D	R	K	W	I	M	V	S	T	O	B	L	J	H	Z
Section 1																							
Section 2																							
Section 3																							
Section 4																							
Section 5																							
Section 6																							
Totals																							

SHARPENING OUR SENSITIVITIES

The ability to motivate is probably the most significant attribute of any salesperson, sales manager or key customer manager. The salesperson motivates customers to buy; the sales manager motivates the team to apply itself, particularly in adverse market conditions. However, key customer managers not only have to motivate customers and the customer team, there is also functional and senior management within their own company to influence in order to fulfil their function as 'broker' between supplier and customer.

> The real problem is when the chemistry is neutral,
> when the reaction is neither love nor hate – it is inertia.
> We have to analyze and plan how we can bridge that inertia gap.

Perhaps the secret of the born salesperson is the ability to motivate, based upon a natural facility for adapting to different people reacting with different responses. Many of us fall short in this respect and have to sharpen up our sensitivities in order to build up relationships. We have to be sensitive to the priorities, likes and dislikes that serve to differentiate us all from each other. This is partly intuitive but can be enhanced by understanding the process and using some guidelines for analyzing the people around us. This said, knowledge of how the mind actually works is still limited, so if you have an intuitively good chemistry with another person, just get on with it and do the business! On the other hand, if you have an intuitively *bad* chemistry with a key member of the customer's decision-making unit, the sensible recourse is to have the courage to back off and delegate that contact to another member of your team, however bruised your ego feels. The real problem is not when the relationships have good or bad chemistry; it is where the chemistry is neutral, when the reaction is neither love nor hate – it is inertia. We have to analyze and plan how we can bridge that inertia gap.

BEHAVIOURS, ATTITUDES AND PERSONALITY

The rules of life imposed upon us in our childhood by our parents and peer pressure, together with subsequent experiences, have programmed us with beliefs and attitudes that constitute our personality and determine our reactions, biases and prejudices. Psychologists suggest that, for many people, this programming is fairly negative. It is focused on criticism of abilities and results in self-imposed constraints on behaviour. Fear of failure becomes more important than desire to improve. People are usually more motivated by the need to address problems than to exploit opportunities. This does not mean that people are always negative, just that they oscillate between positive and negative attitudes. The natural mode, if we believe the premise above, is fairly negative, with an expectation that the worst will happen. If this is too difficult to believe, eavesdrop on people in any public place. Conversation is laced with observations such as 'I never win anything in competitions' and 'I could have had that job but I couldn't move because of the family'.

> Fear of failure becomes more important than desire to improve.
> People are usually more motivated by the need to address problems than to exploit opportunities.

Positive or negative attitudes tend to be reinforced by other people's actions, which are often termed 'strokes'. Positive strokes may be complimentary words or gestures, or even a 'good morning' which acknowledges your existence. However, each individual will have a different appetite for positive strokes, ranging from a strong hunger (which means having to *solicit* praise from others) to a mere peckishness (when too much praise will embarrass). Negative strokes are criticisms or lack of recognition, which generate vicious downward spirals of confidence. They are doubly dangerous because, invariably, negative strokes are passed on to others. In this way the entire morale of the organization can quickly crumble. A positive attitude has to be self-induced to counteract people's natural negative tendency. Based upon these ideas, in working together as a customer team and with customers, we have to ensure that:

- we understand our own mental programming and do not force *our* priorities on others;

- we can assess our colleagues' and our customers' programming so that we get what we want by helping them to get what they want;

- we give the appropriate level of positive strokes to colleagues and customers in order to encourage a positive environment;

- we are aware of our own negative reactions and turn them into positive attitudes;

- we create an empathetic environment that permits colleagues and customers to offload negative reactions and occupy the vacuum with positive thinking.

Positive thinking, of course, has been one of the sacred cows beloved of the management gurus for 40 years. Norman Vincent Peale, the doyen of positive thinkers, begins the later editions of his classic book, *The Power of Positive Thinking* (Ballantine, 1996) on the subject with the alarming confession that he never expected his book to sell two million copies! Positive thinking alone may not achieve anything ... but without it you cannot even start!

A STRUCTURED APPROACH TO MOTIVATION ANALYSIS

We know a lot more about each other than we think. We absorb subconsciously a plethora of perceptions about each other that resolve themselves into feelings of liking, disliking or indifference. Sometimes we are unable to diagnose why we like or dislike – it is just intuitive. Like a computer, we have stored the data, but we need a system to retrieve the information in a format that can be used.

The pitfall is to think in terms of stereotypes. People are individuals and the variety is infinite. One constructive approach is to focus on needs and roles. *Needs* are the basic drives that a person is seeking to satisfy; the pump that makes the system work. *Roles* are the patterns of behaviour that the individual enjoys and prefers to use to achieve a purpose.

Before we examine these needs and roles, it will be useful to complete the questionnaire at the start of this chapter, which is a self-perception tool that will give you a benchmark for analysis structure in the following pages. Before trying to gauge the motivations of others, we have to examine the drivers which determine our own abilities to assess objectively.

There are 11 basic needs and 12 roles that are played. Understanding these needs and styles and using observation to analyze colleagues and customers will help you to put together effective customer teams and devise motivation strategies to build closer customer relationships.

The 11 basic needs are associated with: *finishing the task, achievement, responsibility, personal visibility, belonging to groups, affection, change, confrontation, status, regulations* and *details.*

The 12 basic roles are associated with: *work image, expressing opinions, decision making, mental activity, physical activity, sociability, planning, organization, emotional display, fairness, possessions* and *creativity.*

It is important that, in observing and assessing, these needs and roles are viewed more as a continuum rather than a simple either/or. For example, in considering the need for belonging to groups using a 0–60 scale, the normal score for most people would be 19–41, but a loner might score low (0–18) depending upon how strongly he or she avoided group activities. A gregarious person would score high, in the range 42–60. No criticism is implied by any of these 'scores'. A 60 is not better than a 0 – just different.

Of course, it is the extreme scores that differentiate us from each other. We all have perhaps four or five 'extremes' (highs or lows) that pull the strings of our reactions and responses. We are motivated by these needs and continually seek opportunities to play these roles. An astute customer manager adapts and creates possibilities for personal 'wins' for team members and customers. That is motivation.

A detailed analysis of the likely behaviour clues, problems and appropriate strategies for dealing with such traits and motivating people can be found on the website **www.business-minds.com/kcrm**

Table 10.1 Motivation structure

Extreme Low	Code	Needs	Extreme High
Butterfly	F	Finishing the task	Persister
Long-term consolidator	A	Achievement	Short-term striver
Follower	C	Responsibility	Controller
Introvert	X	Personal visibility	Extravert
Loner	B	Belonging to groups	Groupie
Alien	P	Affection and warmth	Affection seeker
Traditionalist	N	Change	Innovator
Ducker	G	Confrontation	Confronter
Cheeky chappie	D	Status	Respecter
Individualist	R	Rules	Conformist
Scanner	K	Details	Analyst
		Roles	
Leisure-driven	W	Work style	Work-driven
Cautious	I	Decision making	Impulsive
Laid-back	M	Mental style	Hyperactive
Relaxed	V	Physical style	Bustling
Shy	S	Social style	Garrulous
Doing	T	Planning	Thinking
Freedom	O	Organization	Precise
Open	E	Emotion expression	Closed
Reserved	L	Opinion expression	Assertive
Sharing	J	Fairness	Meritorious
Keeping	H	Possessiveness	Giving
Destructive	Z	Creativity	Constructive

MOTIVATION ANALYSIS 1: NEEDS

As we have seen, there are 11 basic needs that, in different permutations, affect relationships at work and in business. They may be identified by certain behaviours, although it is misleading to make an assessment based on one observed incidence of such a behaviour. Motivation analysis is an imprecise science and you have to consider a cluster of behaviours before making a diagnosis. Even then, any one behaviour can be derived from two or three needs. For example, the fastidiousness manner of an individual might be tracked back to a need to finish the task, a sense of responsibility or a plain obsession with detail. The most one can do is to build up a 'silhouette' of the *sort* of person whom you are trying to develop a relationship with and to conceive a strategy for getting closer to that person by considering the drives and motivations that influence their attitudes and reactions. Even if your observations and assessment are incorrect and you pursue strategies that may not fully succeed, it is likely that you will then be in a position to make a better *second* assessment and better *second* plan, because you have a reasonable understanding of *why* the first plan failed.

The guidelines given here may help to improve your observation skills, anticipate relationship difficulties and inspire fresh strategies in your key customer management.

The 11 needs and high/low score implications are described in Table 10.2 below.

Table 10.2   Motivational analysis of needs

Need	Low score (0–18)	High score (42–60)
Finishing the task: stamina and concentration **F**	The **butterfly:** a restless mind, easily bored; jumps, perhaps erratically, from point to point; changes direction and priorities quickly; many tasks attempted but probably few completed; highly flexible and adaptable to changes of situation.	**The persister:** determination, persistence; one track mind; doggedess; inflexibility; reliability, conscientiousness and commitment
Achievement: getting results within a timescale **A**	The **long-term consolidator:** geared more to long-term achievement than short-term results; may be suspicious of short-term expediencies; may lack a sense of urgency.	The **short-term striver:** results-orientated; perhaps pushy; may be more concerned with the ends rather than the means; has to score … and score frequently; meaningless long-term promises.
Responsibility: attitude to power and the direction of people **C**	The **follower:** high degree of tolerance towards people; no apparent aspirations for major responsibilities that might involve telling people what to do; probably averse to any suggestion of people manipulation.	The **controller:** strong self-confidence and real appetite for responsibility – possibly to the point of having a power complex.

Table 10.2   continued

Need	Low score (0–18)	High score (42–60)
Personal visibility: using test an audience to ideas **X**	The **introvert**: reluctance to communicate or draw attention to oneself; ideas developed by internal rumination with little discussion; may have good listening skills.	The **extrovert**: high personal visibility; needing an audience to confirm or develop ideas, which may be perceived sometimes as a 'performance' but it may disguise a need for approval.
Belonging to groups: attitude to team membership **B**	The **loner**: feels crowded by too much team activity; needs for personal space.	The **groupie**: gregarious – gets bored with own companionship; needs other people; shows team spirit.
Affection and warmth: people sensitivity **P**	The **alien**: a strictly business attitude with no personal issues involved; may fear that relationships might impair business judgment or obligate them.	The **affection seeker**: a need to develop warm relationships with people; anxiety if these relationships break down; does business on a personal basis; may not be good at breaking bad news or anything that will jeopardize relationships.
Change: attitude to innovation and change **N**	The **traditionalist**: has difficulty in appreciating the value of new ideas; over-enthusiasm may be inappropriate.	The **innovator**: 'if it's new … we'll buy it'; constantly working for new ways of doing things and fearful of getting behind with new developments.
Confrontation: attitude to difficult situations **G**	The **ducker**: reluctant to confront or to 'attack'; believes that most problems are made worse by interference.	The **confronter**: always has a fight on; seeks perfection and frequently has little sense of priorities.
Status: attitude to respect and authority **D**	The **cheeky chappie**: an irritation with formality and pompousness; the desire to challenge the establishment; may not be malicious; an impudence directed towards authority.	The **respecter**: extreme formality; difficult to relax; prone to father–son relationships with capacity to play either part.

Table 10.2   continued

Need	Low score (0–18)	High score (42–60)
Rules: attitude to supervision, procedures, confirmity **R**	The **individualist**: has to be different; takes pleasure in getting around the rules; probably has excellent self-initiative; spurns supervision.	The **conformist**: the fear of being different; the need for rules and guidelines; safety in numbers; supporter of the majority decision.
Details: attitude towards information and figure work **K**	The **scanner**: implies boredom with detail; a disposition towards decisions based on feelings, hunch or instinct – 'I like the sound of it', 'It looks OK to me'; decisions may depend more on the response to the proposer's personality than the facts of the proposal.	The **analyst**: addicted to details, facts and figures; perhaps believes that enough information will make the decision for them.

MOTIVATION ANALYSIS 2: ROLES

While needs are the basic rules of the game, roles reflect the manner in which we prefer to play the game. The way we approach our lives and the behaviours that we enjoy will give us the best chance, we believe, of fulfilling our needs.

There are 12 basic roles that recur frequently in interaction with people. Often we feel that the roles we choose are the most efficient way to do the job and it is difficult to appreciate how a different role could be as effective. For example, a salesperson can be successful on the basis of work rate or creativity or simply through good organization. Their sales manager, however, who relies strongly on social skills, might have difficulty understanding this and the result is incompatibility between the two. Of course, it is not quite as simple as that. A good practical doer may work well with a partner who is a planner – because *together* they make a good team.

To build up good relationships with colleagues or customers, we have to reconcile the roles we *like* with the roles other people play. If we want to achieve a constructive, collaborative working synergy, the swimming upstream against other people's wishes is not the way to do it. If we can use the momentum of their motivations, though, we can ensure that *they* get what they want at the same time as we get what *we* want.

The 12 roles and high/low score implications are described in Table 10.3.

Table 10.3   Motivational analysis of roles

Role	Low score (0–18)	High score (42–60)
Work style: the work image we project **W**	The **leisure-driven** person: there is aclearly defined line between work and leisure in life; not necessarily , lazy merely sensitive to giving up leisure.	The **work-driven** person: in extreme forms, a workaholic; enjoying effort, taking work home and totally immersed in the job (frequently at the expense of family).
Decision making: security and risk attitudes **I**	The **cautious** person: carefulness; lack of impulsiveness; reluctance to commit too quickly – perhaps because both sides of the argument need consideration (how noticeable this trait is will be relative to the seriousness of the situation).	The **impulsive** person: impetuosity; speed of decision-making; rashness; instinctive reactions; quite often kept in check because of environment, but can be quite dynamic; good in crises.
Mental style: reaction to uncertainty **M**	The **laid-back** person: relaxed; unfrustrated; easy-going; perhaps too unconcerned about time and deadlines; appears not to care; switches off at the end of the working day.	The **hyperactive** person: the worrier whose brain never stops thinking; might appear neurotic to more relaxed colleagues; thrives on anxiety but can be a generator of ideas.
Physical style: display of energy and vigour **V**	The **relaxed** person: the physical equivalent of the mentally laid-back person; a sedentary style; belief in conservation of effort.	The **bustling** person: high energy output; never in the office; always on the move; easily distracted; unlikely to sit still during conversations.
Social style: personal comfort with people **S**	The **shy** person: modest and unassuming; perhaps short on social skills and may be rather serious or earnest-minded; not too comfortable with people *en masse*.	The **garrulous** person: never at a loss for conversation and finds it easy to mix with people; because it is so easy, they may not take enough care about what they are saying.

Table 10.3   continued

Role	Low score (0–18)	High score (42–60)
Planning: attitude to forward thinking **T**	The **doing** person: bull-in-a-china-shop mentality; highly practical; essentially a doer who might be advised to think and plan more.	The **thinking** person: being a planner or theorist, they might well miss the opportunity through an excess of preparation.
Organization: attitude to harmony and order **O**	The **freeform** person: attaches more importance to comfort than order, contrast than harmony, functionality rather than 'looking neat'; may find it difficult to keep up organization standards.	The **precise** person: neat, tidy, organized approach to work; few people will attain the standard required; more concerned with organization than results; irritated by confusion or disorder.
Emotion expression: the display of feelings **E**	The **open** person: open and transparent with reactions; could be moody and may not be able to disguise feelings; perhaps not the most subtle negotiator.	The **closed** person: dispassionate; does not readily display emotions; may be a good card player or negotiator; behaviour might appear less than human sometimes.
Opinion expression: degree of assertiveness **L**	The **reserved** person: high degree of personal tolerance; reluctrance to impose ideas on others.	The **assertive** person: strong self-confidence and belief in opinions; wants to convince others; may not fully consider viewpoints of others; pushes own viewpoint hard.
Fairness: interpretation of justice **J**	The **sharing** person: behaviour based on the idea that fairness means equal shares for all; no meritocracy; reluctance to differentiate; expects high ethics and fairness from suppliers.	The **meritorious** person: fairness is 'winner takes all'; ranking order; everything allocated according to ability or capability; the best supplier gets all the business.
Possessiveness: attitude to giving and taking **H**	The **keeping** person: the acquisition and keeping of assets, experience, ideas; unwillingness to share with others based, perhaps, on fear of becoming expendable; reluctant to assist others unless there is something in it for them.	The **giving** person: the compulsion to assist, to give of oneself, the paternal approach; the joy of teaching; the pleasure of imparting advice to others.

Table 10.3 continued

Role	Low score (0–18)	High score (42–60)
Creativity: positive and negative ways of using imagination **Z**	The **destructive** person: negative use of imagination; high level of destructiveness; negative attitude without constructive suggestions.	The **constructive** person: the urge to be constructive; positive use of imagination; the enjoyment of adding, changing, enhancing.

It is because of the individual differences between customers that the marketing and sales functions exist, adapting the product message to whoever they address. Use the guidelines to think about your more difficult customers and colleagues who may not always match your priorities.

Detach yourself from your own viewpoint and consider how you can use the powerful force of motivation constructively to achieve an aim instead of swimming upstream against the tide. A group approach to motivation analysis can be most revealing.

- Focus the customer team on the individual in the customer unit with whom you are having relationship difficulties.

- Consider the list of 'needs' and 'roles' and agree high, low or middle ratings for that person.

- Select the two or three traits that might rate *extreme* high or low scores.

- Discuss how these extremes might explain behaviours and how they might conflict with any traits of specific customer team members.

- Agree a behaviour strategy that might avoid conflict and generate positive reactions.

Such an intensive group session might only be justified in extreme situations of negative relationships but it is surprising how much 'soft' information is carried around in the heads of a customer team without a means of releasing and structuring it into a meaningful format.

THE GROUP DYNAMICS OF KEY CUSTOMER TEAMS

Teamwork is everybody doing what I say.

Michael Winner, film director

A team is a group of people who share common objectives and who need to work together to achieve them. In earlier chapters, much emphasis has been laid on the growing importance of teamwork in managing key customers. Key customers are too important to be the responsibility of one person.

In ensuring the effectiveness of customer teams, one has to consider the group dynamics of the company, how the teams are selected and the contributions that can be made by the individual members to the team. Individuals are seldom good at everything, so their effectiveness is often dependent on the people they are working with and they may have more to contribute than their function may suggest.

An analysis of needs and roles might forewarn of personal conflicts in the close confines of teamworking, but teams also develop dynamics of their own – unique identities which are exercised when interacting with other teams, other people in the company, or the customer.

Such group dynamics are apparent in a classic business game called Starpower in which several teams are allowed to trade with each other but one team has a secret advantage which helps it to be significantly more profitable than the other teams. This better performance permits the successful team to change the rules of trading, which it almost certainly will do to its own advantage. This abuse of power always results in either opting out, resentment, hostility, or even open revolt by the other teams. The leading team becomes united in its defence of the new rules, but mayhem ensues. In the end, nobody will trade and everybody fails.

The people who play this game are nice people, but the group synergy can be both positive and negative in its implications and conclusions. Success may bring about arrogance and division, neither of which are the basis of mutually beneficial customer alliances.

We work in teams or groups, both within our organizations and sometimes in our dealings with customers. Key customer managers find themselves having to secure agreement from functional groups such as production, finance and distribution within their own organizations. Externally they are constantly involved with the customers' teams representing technical, management and purchasing interests. Increasingly they are likely to be operating within a customer team themselves.

Key customers are too important to be the responsibility of one person.

In this context, an understanding of group dynamics plays an important part in determining the success of the key customer manager. In order to examine conflict and co-operation between groups, it may be useful to look first at behaviour within groups and the consequent characteristics of the group.

Team members assume roles

In order to feel a useful, productive member of a group, many people adopt roles. For example, some people feel comfortable being the group comedian, know-all, or father figure. This helps to give them a sense of belonging. These roles are not only assumed by group members but also often assigned by the group.

Teams formulate group norms

Groups establish acceptable ways of behaving, usually unwritten and unstated, but nevertheless influential. They are the means of making group membership more comfortable and secure by clarifying what behaviour is acceptable and what is not. For example, in some work groups it is acceptable to be on first name terms or have flexible working hours, while in others it is not.

Group ceremonies and rituals

Most groups – especially those working together for some time – develop ceremonies and rituals to help them cope with certain events. Examples of group ceremonies and rituals are birthday celebrations to intensify the awareness of the value of group membership, or farewell drinks when a group member leaves the group. This helps the remaining individuals to cope with the loss and, again, asserts the value of group membership. Initiation rites demonstrate to a newcomer a feeling of the group's value and strength and re-establish group identity. 'In' language and jokes are a further example of an intensification rite.

What happens when groups have to work together?

When two (or more) groups are faced with a joint problem, they may try to solve it in isolation from each other, they may be forced together by a directive from senior management, or one group may win, possibly leaving the losing group very demoralized. By assuming that a real solution is wanted which satisfies both groups, then some kind of joint problem-solving process must take place.

As loyalty to our own group is important to all of us, it follows that intergroup conflict is likely to be especially acute. To direct our hostile feelings within our own group would invite rejection, but hostility directed outward not only relieves us, but strengthens our membership of our own group. Thus, any intergroup problem-solving situation is likely to contain some hostility, as well as genuine attempts at co-operation.

The more the intergroup situation is defined as win-lose, the more likely we are to see conflict, but the more it is defined as problem solving, the less likely become the chances of conflict. Conflict, however, never wholly disappears; the following happenings are typical.

What happens within a group?

- Each group pulls in close and sees other groups as enemies, so group loyalty increases.
- Each group sees only the best in itself and the worst in the other, and puts up a filter or screen on information coming in.
- Each group feels that it owns, and must guard, certain territory.

- Members close ranks and increasingly feel that their group is a good group.

- Each group demands more conformity from its members.

- The leadership changes and more control is accepted by group members.

- The group atmosphere changes from low concern with task to high concern with task and from high group maintenance behaviour to low group maintenance behaviour.

- Each group becomes structured and this may reveal cleavages between sub-groups.

What happens between groups?

- Members become hostile towards the other group.

- Bad stereotypes are formed of the other group.

- Interaction and communication decrease – one group does not want to see the other nor does it understand the other, so that, at best, one group assumes that they understand the other without checking to find out.

- Members do not listen to those from other groups; they hear only that which supports their own position and they may even appropriate points of an adversary's position which are supported by their own group's position.

- Members mistrust the other group (and their representatives), seeing them as sneaky, unfair, and so on, and there is a strong emphasis on strategy rather than solving the problem on its merits.

What happens to the winners?

- Cohesion increases within the group.

- They are complacent.

- There is a release of tension and no more fighting spirit.

- There is more play.

- There is high co-operation but little work.

What happens to the losers?

- The group splinters, fights, re-organizes.
- There is an increase of tension, they are ready to dig harder and are 'lean and hungry'.
- They blame their own leaders and organization; they find scapegoats.
- If future 'wins' are seen as impossible, they may blame themselves and become depressed.
- The group can learn a lot about itself.

What happens to judges, arbitrators or 'third parties'?

- They find it hard to divorce themselves from their group and they are unable to be neutral.
- They experience conflict between their loyalty to their own group and the impartial role of 'judge'.
- They are seen as being biased by the losing group but are praised by the winners.

What happens to representatives of groups?

- They experience conflict between their own strategies, goals, wishes, and so on and the mandate given to them by their group.
- There is tension resulting from being responsible for their group's success or failure.
- They are seen as heroes if their own group wins, and as traitors if they lose.

The effects of group dynamics

Effects like those described above are familiar enough – we can see them whenever groups or departments of an organization, competing organizations, cities, parts of a nation, or nations themselves must interact to solve problems.

Many of the effects occur between individuals when they see their relationship with others as competitive – there is hostility, suspicion, misunderstanding, 'closing in' under attack, refusal to communicate with others, and so on.

How can we reduce conflict or help groups out of deadlocked situations?

Some strategies include:

- *finding an overriding goal* – one that the groups accept as essential to achieve and which both *can* achieve so that win-lose changes to win-win. Such a goal is often of a higher order or more inclusive nature so that if one group wants X and the other wants Y and each sees the other as preventing them from getting what they want, then the way out involves setting things up so that they both get what they want and, although this is not easy, it does work. (A negative example of this is when two fighting groups join forces to defeat a common enemy.);

- *creating another group which contains high-status members* (not representatives as such) is often useful, but the task on which they work must be unrelated to the win-lose issue dividing the groups. An example would be all cultural groups in a poor area working together on concrete tasks to improve their neighbourhood – having to work together creates new norms and more positive attitudes, which the high-status members then carry back to their own groups and help to spread;

- *intergroup maintenance operations* work if the groups wish to improve their relationship. In this procedure, representatives of each group meet to discuss the perceptions they have of the other group and have them clarified – no arguing or defence is permitted, only listening and clarification – then the representatives return to their groups, report, discuss and return to the other representatives for further clarification and discussion so that the process is analogous to giving and receiving feedback between individuals and tends to build more of a common language between the groups;

■ *the criss-cross panel* seems especially helpful: each group makes a list of nominations for representatives from its own group, and then gives the list to the other group. Each group then votes for representatives from each list, hence the representatives have the confidence and support of both groups so they can then negotiate more directly without worrying about problems of loyalty, attack, suspicion, and so on.

INTERNAL TEAM DYNAMICS

No matter how geographically spread or what their purpose may be *all* teams have internal dynamics.

As we have seen, people adopt preferred roles or styles of behaviour; research suggests that certain combinations of styles make for more effective teams. This effectiveness is enhanced if the individual members of the team perceive the specific contribution they can make and are ready to work to their strengths rather than allow their comparative weaknesses to affect their performance. The key to successful working relationships lies in the understanding of individual team roles, their scope and their limitations.

EVERYBODY HAS A TEAM ROLE

Research suggests that, to work effectively, there are eight roles, or jobs, to be done in a team. This does not mean that a team *must* consist of eight members as one individual may fulfil a number of roles in the team.

The eight jobs to be done are:

1 *Creative thinking*

This needs an innovator or ideas person with a fertile, fluid mind and a capacity for original thought, whether it be for new products or problem-solving strategies.

However, there is a danger that such a person will opt out of the team if the ideas are rejected, which could make for a difficult and uncomfortable colleague. Careful handling and generous positive encouragement by the team may be necessary to get the best from the creative thinker. Without such a person the team is likely to get bogged down, lack sparkle and will seldom excel.

2 *Critical thinking*

This requires the ability to analyse ideas and suggestions, both from within and outside the team, and to evaluate their feasibility and practical value in terms of the team's objectives.

Such a person may bring a serious attitude, astute perception, caution and objectivity to the job, but the critical thinker needs the ideas, knowledge of resources and perspective provided by other team members to be able to make full use of these critical faculties. In a situation where there is conflicting information, this team member can help to evaluate options clearly and help colleagues to reach the optimum decision. However, the serious, critical nature of the role may reduce team morale and dampen enthusiasm.

3 *Setting objectives, deadlines and priorities*

This involves elements of leadership from the front and a capacity for overcoming obstacles with a few sharp, incisive decisions and words, which can sometimes irritate the team. This activity pushes the tempo and urgency of the team and usually is contributed by an action-minded individual who likes to exercise authority and who wants to get the job done without being distracted. This contribution is essential to the success of the group but, if pursued in an unskilful way, might challenge the leadership of the team and upset members' feelings. The job requires considerable self-discipline and diplomacy.

4 *Maintaining team relationships*

This is a people-oriented task which must counter the conflicts generated by the critical-thinking and objective-setting activities. It requires a perception of the feelings, needs and concerns of the people in the group, together with the skill to promote individual strengths and underpin any weaknesses. The contribution may be low key but will minimize the bruising, friction and potential antipathies between team members. The objective is to hold the team together and maintain team spirit, frequently using humour to do this. The result is improved communication, co-operation and a generally positive outlook.

5 *Getting the work done*

This means getting down to the task of translating general concepts and plans into a practical working brief and carrying out that brief in a systematic fashion. It is not too concerned with generating ideas and innovations, considering options and devising strategies. It is more about clear-cut objectives, practical working routines and tangible results achieved with care, thoroughness, determination and common sense. This activity is the backbone of the team but may have negative elements of innate conservatism, lack of flexibility and limited vision.

6 *Investigating and getting resources*

This is a job best suited to an extrovert 'people-oriented' person with a restless, enquiring attitude to life. The task is about exploring resources and ideas, both inside and outside the team, and developing a wide range of useful contacts. Innovative skills are not necessary but the ability to stimulate ideas in others and to persuade and motivate is relevant.

Such a person needs variety and challenge but may lack self-discipline, be impulsive and, if the job loses impetus, can become bored and demoralized. Without this contribution, though, a team can become too inward-looking, defensive, cautious and out of touch. In some ways, this activity fulfils the function of 'team public relations' with the other teams and the rest of the company.

7 *Progress chasing*

This keeps the team on its toes with the objective of getting jobs finished to a high standard in good time. Without this activity, projects may fall behind schedule, mistakes may be made in specifications, less urgent matters may be put off (for ever) and complacency undermines team spirit.

The job calls for self-control, strength of character, an eye for detail and a sense of purpose. It requires a form of nervous energy channelled into nagging, communicating urgency and fighting inertia. The activity can irritate people, increase tension or bog people down in detail if not controlled, but it does not allow them to become careless, over confident, procrastinatory or tardy.

8   *Co-ordinating activities*

This is primarily (but not always) the job of the team leader, who should be adept at recognizing and using the resources within the group and balancing its strengths and weaknesses. The downside is that this might be perceived as manipulative by team members.

Ideally the leader will have many of the skills which figure in the other seven team jobs and should be prepared to adapt to the particular needs of the team, fulfilling those activities in which the team is weak, knowing which part to play and when. Co-ordinating does not necessarily demand intellectual capacity. It is more about making the best use of each team member's potential, together with the ability to command respect, inspire enthusiasm and to communicate lucidly.

The combination of team roles

So far only 'pure' team jobs have been discussed in terms of required abilities. While nearly everyone fits *one* of these eight jobs, they are also naturally disposed towards one or more of the *other* activities, though to a lesser degree; and there are some combinations more common than others.

The co-ordinator role is the most versatile, but there is a wide variety of possible role permutations. These possible combinations are particularly important in allocating team members to jobs other than their natural jobs, for the sake of achieving a better team balance. For example, maintaining team relationships may be more easily doubled up with resource investigation than the job of progress chaser.

Some tasks are limited by actual talent. For example, critical thinkers *must* have good critical thinking ability. The possible range of job combinations and emphasis within them reflects the range of management style itself. A co-ordinator and critical thinker will behave differently from a co-ordinator and creative thinker. An individual's main job, however, tends to determine the basic pattern of their potential contribution to the team, while the subsidiary jobs affect more that person's style, approach, and relationships within the team.

The picture is complicated by the learning of additional tasks and flexibility in the role that is necessary to a person's growth and, usually, survival. This learning and development is more effective, however, if it is based on an understanding of an individual's personality, basic talents and versatility.

What makes a good team?

The team jobs described are closely associated with personality characteristics and reasoning ability, but they owe their existence as definable styles of behaviour to the priorities and processes of the task.

Each job or role contributes towards the success of the team and it follows that a well-balanced, flexible and all-round successful team will have all the roles represented. The need for a co-ordinator, for example, is obvious; the need for a creative thinker may not be recognized for some time (and may need to be pointed out), and a progress chaser may not be missed until small omissions have built up into big problems. Some roles can be duplicated as needed but some should only be represented once in a team, as more than one tends to lead to confusion or competition. If possible, the co-ordinating role and the role of setting objectives, deadlines and priorities each should be be undertaken by only one person in the team.

Gaps may occur when an analysis of primary roles in the team may reveal that one or two activities are unallocated. It may be, however, that a review of the team members' secondary roles will show that they do, in fact, between them cover the full range of team roles. If not, some judicious role allocation can achieve an effective balance.

Overlaps mean that two or more team members share roles which are best represented only once each in a team. Again, there may be the possibility of achieving a balance by making use of their secondary roles, but this will need an act of 'role sacrifice' by at least one team member; an act of heroism that should not be underestimated, but one which can pay rich dividends in team effectiveness.

Finally, the team members should have an understanding of all eight team roles, not only to enable them to understand the unique nature of their contribution but, also, to demonstrate the need for tolerance towards the negative aspects of each role.

HOW DO YOU BUILD EFFECTIVE CUSTOMER TEAMS?

A manager seldom has the opportunity to choose from a full range of resources in building a project or management team. Much more likely is that there will be limitations on skills available, a diversity of interests and sheer lack of choice in terms of team roles. The emphasis of team management, therefore, is on making actual teams work rather than constructing ideal but unrealizable models.

In principle, each team role needs to be performed by the team member best fitted for the job. The problem is ascertaining the team role capabilities of each member or potential member. Where the manager knows the individuals well, all that is necessary is to become thoroughly familiar with the team role descriptions and principles and quickly check on the likely team role resources available. In choosing individuals for the team, it is advisable to give them personal briefs that correspond with the appropriate role specifications.

In the course of this exercise, inevitably a manager will come up against the realization that certain individuals will be unable to discharge certain responsibilities and that some adjustments to the intended team may be necessary. It may not be possible to create a well-balanced team but, forewarned, it is more likely that plans can be made for the way ahead.

This approach can yield excellent results but in other instances will not be practicable. A manager's personal knowledge of the individuals may be inadequate, for example. In such cases, various assessment methods may be tried to establish team members' roles. Fundamental to any approach to self and team assessment is a full understanding of the team roles and their implications.

When team members know each other well enough, members can assess their colleagues and the results pooled. This works even better when self-assessments are thrown into the mix and discrepancies explored. The process requires a lot of trust and openness, but the results are invariably good and are far superior to a purely mechanical slotting of people into roles. Knowing what to expect and what not to expect from colleagues avoids many mistakes and leads to less tension.

Effective teams are the key to the creation of synergy – when the whole is greater than the sum of its parts. There are two types of synergy in customer management: *external* synergy with the customer and *internal* synergy within the supplier's own team. People have great resources of energy, invention, creativity and enthusiasm to be harnessed, if given the opportunity to flourish. One of the main reasons for employees' reluctance to contribute fully is the feeling that their abilities are being underestimated. Managers too often see themselves as the main engine of the team and organizations tend to over-manage their people.

An apocryphal memo, allegedly circulating within the British Airways organization, was reported in the London *Sunday Times* in March 1999. It goes:

> Once upon a time BA and Virgin Atlantic decided to have a boat race on the Thames. Both teams practised long and hard to reach their peak performance. On the big day they were as ready as they could be and Virgin won by a length. BA became discouraged and senior management set up a project team to investigate the problem.
>
> Its conclusion was that the Virgin team had eight people rowing and one person steering. The BA team had one person rowing and eight people steering. Senior management immediately hired consultants to study team structure. Millions of pounds were spent and several months later they concluded that too many people were steering and not enough were rowing.
>
> The next year the team structure was changed to four steering managers, three senior steering managers and one executive steering manager.
>
> A performance and appraisal system was set up to give the person rowing more incentive to work harder and become a key performer. 'We must give him empowerment and enrichment – that ought to do it', they concluded.
>
> The next year, the big day arrived and Virgin won. BA laid off the rower for poor performance, sold off the paddles, cancelled capital investment and

halted development of the new boat. Then they gave high performance awards to the consultants and distributed the money saved among senior management.

A note on the bottom of the memo reads: 'This would be funny if it were not true.'

Characteristics of good teamwork

- Open and honest self-expression
- A group with balanced skills and abilities
- Mistakes used as learning experiences
- Conflict is used constructively
- Open confrontation of difficult situations
- Collaborative *not* competitive relationships
- Pride in team success
- Personal development is rated highly
- Team ownership of decisions
- Agreement of clear objectives
- External help and advice are welcomed.

Characteristics of poor teamwork

- Wrong balance of skills and abilities
- Limited self-expression and job satisfaction
- Interdepartmental political bickering
- Focus on recrimination and blame
- Protectionist attitudes (keeping yourself fireproof)
- Burying difficult situations and creation of an unofficial grapevine
- Line-drawing – not my job!
- Stampede to the exit at finishing time
- Isolation of the leader

■ No personal development plans

■ Rejection of external advice or help.

THE GAMES PEOPLE PLAY – PLANNING AND LEADERSHIP

One of the classic management exercises which has been played all over the world for many years is the Mast Contract. It comes in many versions, but the basic and original exercise calls for a team to build a structure from a boxful of interlocking toy bricks, with the objective of earning more profit than competing teams.

Profit is calculated on the basis of amount of time and number of bricks used and height achieved. Maximum profit is earned by using as *few* bricks as possible, building the structure as *quickly* as possible and achieving as much *height* as possible. The structure can be of any design – the only stipulation is that it should be self-supporting and should stand long enough to be measured and counted.

Each team consists of between five and seven members and an appointed leader, who is given a written brief and three graphs depicting the payments and penalties for bricks, time and height. The competing teams are given 30 minutes (the planning phase) to plan and rehearse the project, at the end of which a budget plan has to be submitted, indicating how many bricks they plan to use for their structure, the time it will take to build and the height that will be achieved. Then all teams assemble in the main room and, under competitive conditions, the teams erect their structures simultaneously (the construction phase).

The financial ramifications are straightforward. Using 100 bricks or fewer will earn a team $20 000, but every brick over this number will mean a deduction of $200. Completion of the structure in one minute will earn $30 000 with a penalty of $100 for each second over this time. In height, every single inch over 40 inches will earn $1000 but every inch under 40 inches will incur a *deduction* of $1000 from the total profit. Obviously the three ways in which profit can be earned counterbalance each other and the successful team has to make some choices in its grand plan as to whether it will go for time, height or bricks to achieve profit.

The exercise can be used to demonstrate teamwork, communication, leadership or planning skills. One lesson particularly relevant to customer relationship management is the realization that enthusiasm alone is rarely enough to win the day! Success is usually based upon analysis, selection of priorities, organized teamwork, leadership, motivation and a bit of luck in the form of having a creative individual in the team.

The observations on and conclusions about team behaviour drawn from conducting this exercise many times fall under the headings that follow.

Planning

Only one team in five will make an organized effort to analyse and identify the *key success factors* of the exercise. *Height* is the critical issue and will generate more profit than either economy of bricks or time. This can only be worked out by establishing how many bricks are needed for each inch of height and making a timed trial of how much time is needed for one player to assemble so many bricks. This is rarely done in a scientific manner and, frequently, sweeping assumptions are made based upon the visual degree of slope on the graphs (irrespective of the units of measurement on the axis of the graph).

Only two teams in five will try to plan the use of the 30-minute planning phase, but it is especially beneficial if a fully timed rehearsal is scheduled – three out of five teams go into the actual construction phase without having had any form of practice. Teams that practise can usually reduce the construction time by up to 20 per cent for each rehearsal they hold.

Although most teams leap in with insufficient planning, there are other teams who delay the action and indulge in wide-ranging discussion (not planning). Some teams will spend as much as 50 per cent of their planning time with the bricks untouched in the box whilst they theorize (usually with a flip chart). On one memorable occasion, the leader reduced the entire exercise down to a mathematical equation that I really could not understand and had no motivation to try to understand since the team concerned returned perhaps the lowest score ever recorded.

Much of the discussion usually revolves around the indication in the brief that 40 inches is the minimum height requirement. This objective is usually greeted with apprehension and confident assertions from the engineers in the team that it is impossible. Discussion usually gives way to experimentation and, even when the structure *does* stand up above this height, it has been known for the engineer to kick the table and bring the mast down, thus 'proving' that it will not work.

There are times, however, when the unguided discussion simply meanders on and, on one famous occasion, the team even *voted* on the motion that 'this team does not think it possible to build a structure of bricks more than 40 inches high'. The vote was carried and the game was lost.

Teamwork

Although this exercise generates activity and enthusiasm, much of this is dissipated through lack of direction. People focus on whatever aspect of the game interests them and, as a result, some areas – notably the arithmetic – are neglected.

Some individuals withdraw from the group and play with the bricks in their own private independent projects. Occasionally a team member will indicate through body language that handling and assembling the bricks is a somewhat lesser-status activity although, in the final analysis, almost invariably they are drawn into the physical excitement of the task.

Individual contributions tend to be spontaneous and, as such, tend to be regarded with as much seriousness as the assertiveness with which they are declared. Indeed, more assertive team members may find ready acceptance of their ideas without question if they sound knowledgeable. For example, quite often the team works with a creativity constraint that no more than 100 bricks must be used because someone has made that assumption in the first minute of the planning phase. This happens in 80 per cent of all teams.

Happily, although real synergetic teamwork is not usually apparent during the first 25 minutes of the planning phase, tremendous strides in co-operation and decisiveness are made in the last five minutes. Designs are finalized, objectives are set and roles allocated in the last 60 seconds before construction and, ultimately, 60 per cent of teams achieve the $50 000 minimum possible profit mentioned in the written brief. Altogether, 25 per cent of teams exceed $60 000 profit, 5 per cent exceed $70 000 and fewer than 1 per cent achieve genius level of $80 000+.

Leadership

To be fair, the chosen leader in this exercise has no specific knowledge or time for preparation for the role. After a minimal verbal introduction, the leader is given a written brief and finds that there are just 30 minutes to solve a problem, organize a team and prepare a plan.

In theory, the ideal leader will:

- read the brief carefully and decide how the preparation time will be best utilized *before* confronting the team;

- brief the team both verbally and by giving each of them full copies of the written information;

- identify any relevant knowledge and abilities in the individual team members and delegate specific tasks, such as counting and sorting the bricks, exploring possible designs, analyzing the figures, and so on;

- ensure that each team member will have the opportunity to contribute and that no one team member dominates the thinking with their assumptions or ideas;

- try to identify the key issues that contribute to the objective of the exercise;

- make positive decisions on the planned course of action after 20 minutes of the planning phase and allow a final ten minutes for practice and rehearsal before the actual construction stage;

- at all times try to *manage* the group activities rather than be a part of them.

In practice, it is rare for a leader to initiate *any* of these actions, although some of these actions will happen because of the suggestions of team members or, more often, the natural, unspoken dynamics of teamwork.

The brief is rarely actually read by the leader and never distributed as copies to the team members. Attempts are made in 40 per cent of instances to identify specific skills but sub-groups form more by self-delegation than anything else.

Many good suggestions are lost because they are not heard or are dismissed without consideration by more assertive team members. Key issues are not analyzed and are dealt with more on an intuitive than quantified basis. Most of all, the leader tends to become so involved in brick assembly, that no co-ordination or plan ever gets formulated. At times, the leader can be observed doing everything, with his entire team standing around as wry observers.

The exercise demands a classic demonstration of the complete range of leadership styles. On one hand, the lack of knowledge and the need for ideas calls for an open, participative style in the team, but, on the other hand, there is a 30-minute deadline that demands authoritative, decisive, perhaps autocratic, action by the leader. After all, when the office is on fire, there is no time to hold a participative brainstorm to decide on a reaction.

Ideally, the planning phase calls for a highly participative opening ten minutes, gradually moving towards the last five minutes of strong, decisive, autocratic leadership to finalize the plan. At this stage, any drastic new design ideas from any members of the team should probably be killed, because there is simply not enough time to plan their implementation.

The messages of this exercise for key customer management are clear:

- focus on key success factors;
- teamwork is more creative but has to be actively managed;
- good communication requires access to information by all team members;
- good strategy depends upon generation, and real consideration of, multiple options in the context of understanding the assumptions that are being made;

- there has to be a realistic balance between planning and action;
- it is beneficial to be able to test out one's ideas before implementation.

SUMMARY

Every individual is a unique combination of priorities and needs that drive the behaviours and roles that they play in interacting (or not interacting) with others. We are programmed by our past experiences, good and bad, and it is a measure of our maturity whether we can recognize and manually adjust our more basic instincts or prejudices. Subconsciously we are continuously observing and absorbing these behaviours, matching them against our own set of priorities and experiencing comfort or conflict accordingly. What is needed is a mechanism for organizing that information in a way that enables us to make sense of it and use it to enhance comfort in the relationship, whether it be with customers or colleagues. This does not mean pretending to be another person; it is a question of manually adjusting our priorities in areas of trait conflict. If there are too many conflict areas, perhaps you should withdraw and put another person into the relationship.

In effective teams each individual will have a functional role, but will also adopt a natural interactive style or 'team role'. The combination of 'team roles' will in no small measure contribute to the productivity of the team and should be a key aspect of selection and team building.

11

How much do you *really* know about negotiating with key customers?

THE BEST GAME IN TOWN

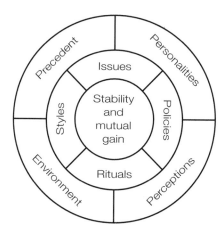

The fabric of negotiation

The Latin origin of the word 'negotiation' is *neg* (not) -*otium* (leisure) and certainly, if you are negotiating for hostages or bargaining for peace, there are unlikely to be too many smiles around the table. But negotiation can and should be pleasurable. Negotiation with key customers is more likely to be about prices, terms, conditions, payments, deliveries, and so on, which may have a considerable effect on the fortunes of your *company* but are hardly likely to stop the world spinning on its axis. For most of us, the seriousness of negotiation is more about bruised egos than making headlines on news bulletins. This should not be taken to mean that business is not serious. The consequences if our negotiations *consistently* fail might be very dramatic, but there is a tendency for negotiations to be approached by both parties with a high awareness of the potential negative implications.

This results in defensive strategies, constrained creativity, and, ultimately, competitive tactics – all of which is the very antithesis of relationship building. Relationships are built upon open trust, mutual respect, fairness and energies directed at creating synergy for both parties. These factors call for positive attitudes in a relaxed marriage of interests. Successful negotiations can be inspirational and motivational for the participants: the team works well together and pulls off the deal; supplier and customer have united to face the common enemy.

The most effective negotiations result from relaxed, rational minds working together, looking for positive results rather than preparing post-mortems.

Several years ago, a colleague running a small, specialized team selling high-technology applications of industrial gas in the UK was transferred permanently to set up and run a similar operation in the US. I doubted whether this rather conservative Yorkshireman would settle in the different culture of New Jersey but, within a year, the operation was making real breakthroughs and he reported:

> It's remarkable. In Europe we would have two opportunities a year to sell a project; we would build up to the big meeting and, if the idea failed to sell, there would be inquests, recriminations and scapegoats. Our focus was on avoiding failure rather than on success. Here, in America, we have two opportunities to sell a month; there is no time for blaming anybody ... we are on to the next prospect immediately. The momentum is exhilarating and somehow we seem to sell the prospect nearly every time.

The sad truth is that when we are nervous about the outcome this will often jeopardize our success. We can negotiate anything when we do not need to succeed, but when the pressure is on, that is when we fumble and fail.

NEGOTIATION AS A PROCESS

Negotiation is not an event, it is a *process* of influencing behaviour; the process of changing a relationship. When someone has been resisting you and changes their mind, it is because the relationship has changed. It may be that you are now perceived as being more powerful, trustworthy or co-operative and that perception may have been moved by your actions and attitudes over a period of time.

Negotiation is an *action-orientated* process. We are continually in a state of negotiation because, as key customer managers, we are continually trying to influence the relationship with our customers.

Awareness that you are operating in a continuous process is essential to the achievement of better outcomes.

Negotiations begin at, or even before, the first contact with your customer. If you are a supplier with a high-visibility, long-established company name or brand, the customer will have perceptions (and expectations) long before discussions begin. However, even if no such perceptions precede your first sales visit to a potential customer, the *positioning* of those perceptions starts immediately the contact is made. The supplier tries to project an efficient, confident image to the customer, while the customer may choose a co-operative but somewhat disinterested posture that is designed to create a climate of limited expectations in the supplier.

Some time ago, whilst meeting with a prospective client company in London, I was introduced to a wealthy American proprietor who was visiting. On shaking hands, I enquired, courteously, about his journey from the US. He related to me how, on the car journey to Newark airport, he noticed that he was low on gasoline and ended up pushing the vehicle because he chose to ignore a gas station where the price was two cents higher than he usually paid. He finished his tale of thrift with the words 'and so … I believe you are here to sell us something'. My fee expectations were, most certainly, conditioned by his story.

In business, the entire relationship will be conducted like a *courtship* over a period of time. Both parties will try to condition each other's expectations and the *proposal* and final ceremony that consummates the *marriage* is merely a formal endorsement of all the exploratory experiences that have gone before.

If this whole process is 'negotiation', what is 'selling'? Is selling part of the negotiation process? Is selling the same as negotiation?

The willingness to negotiate will depend upon the existence of a *balance of needs*. The customer perceives a need for what the supplier is offering; the supplier has a need for what the customer can give in return, which is primarily money but can include long-term commitment, volume or, perhaps, a user base for developing new technology.

Negotiation, then, is the process of satisfying both parties' needs while preserving the balance. *Selling* is the process of getting to that point of balance where negotiation about the details can begin.

At the outset, the supplier's need to gain business from the key customer is significant but the customer's perception of how much the supplier is needed may be minimal. This situation has to be addressed by selling skills.

Selling is persuasion-oriented in that the objective is to get the other person to accept a point of view. There is little room for manoeuvre in selling. The persuader only achieves their objective when the other party accepts the proposition.

> The hallmark of a good agreement is that *both* parties have lasting satisfaction from the arrangement.

Selling explores the customer's needs and develops their *awareness* of how the supplier's proposed solutions can address that need. With skill and discussion, that awareness becomes *preference* leading to a willingness to act. At that specific moment, both parties enter the *formal* negotiation mode in which proposals are discussed in detail.

This moment should be signalled by one or other of the parties by securing a commitment that the idea or proposal on the table is acceptable *in principle*. This agreement helps to ensure that the negotiation will go forward on the basis of the details and that the other party will not start backtracking on the basic proposal as part of their negotiation strategy.

Finding defects or shortcomings in the proposal is a recurring theme of the negotiation process; devaluing the position of the other party gives them less to trade with and may reduce the movement *you* have to make in order to secure agreement.

Creativity not compromise

The negotiation process is about *movement* - the movement of both parties towards a mutually beneficial solution – but it is not necessarily about *compromise*. Compromise is necessary only when the creative exploration of options is exhausted. Such exploration attempts to ascertain the *value* of specific issues to each party – what is important and what is not so important.

Creative negotiation happens when both parties are able to concede on issues that are valuable to the other side but of little consequence to the giver. For example, a one-year fixed-price contract may give price stability to the customer for 12 months at no great sacrifice to the supplier. The same contract gives an assured flow of work for the supplier (the cost efficiency of which makes possible a fixed-price agreement) at the expense of a modest commitment from the customer. Creative negotiation requires openness and trust in order to pinpoint values and generate new, perhaps even better, alternatives and options. Aware negotiators have to keep working for agreement on *how* the process of negotiation is being conducted, without getting bogged down in trying to get everybody to have the same agenda objectives.

> Negotiation is the use of *power, information* and *time*
> within a delicate fabric of relationships, perceptions and expectations.

The continuous process of negotiation does not even end when the contract is signed or the agreement is made. The manner in which the negotiation is conducted and the agreement is implemented creates the climate for the *next* negotiation. The more enduring the relationship, the more relaxed the negotiation will be and the less time will be spent on manoeuvring, manipulating and positioning each other. The selling and negotiation expenses of key customer management should fall (as a cost per unit) as the relationship grows. (See Chapter 6 (Fig. 6.1)).

Ineffective negotiators miss the significance of post-negotiation consequences. They are so relieved to have agreement that they misread this as a commitment to implementation. They do not consider fully the implications of continuity in the relationship, which characterizes key customer management.

The hallmark of a good agreement is that *both* parties have lasting satisfaction from the arrangement. If one party believes or comes to believe that it has been disadvantaged by the deal, it has the power to administer retribution – buyer's remorse turns to buyer's revenge!

Customers can make life impossibly difficult for suppliers; suppliers can make hard work for customers.

Skilful negotiators are always looking to identify benefits from *continued* co-operation, perhaps by reminding the other party of the adverse consequences of a failure to agree, and by being alert to the long-term implications of a short-term 'victory'.

THE FABRIC OF NEGOTIATION

There are three timeframes in the process: *pre-negotiation, formal negotiation* and *post-negotiation.* The relative skills of the parties in using the pre-negotiation, or preparation, time is probably the most important in determining the outcome of the negotiation. It is during this pre-negotiation time that the effective negotiator creates the fabric of negotiation upon which the formal negotiation game will be played.

Negotiation is the use of *power, information* and *time* within a delicate fabric of relationships, perceptions and expectations. Skills in the use of power, time and information may afford short-term advantages but are no substitute for a real fabric of negotiation. The fabric is an intricate weave, specific to each situation and the strands are:

- desire for stability and mutual gain
- precedents set by previous experience
- nature of the issues to be agreed
- personalities involved
- perceptions of strength by both parties
- policies and negotiation styles favoured by the participants
- environmental climate of the negotiation
- rituals of negotiation.

These elements form the basis of negotiation strategy, which will be formulated in the pre-negotiation time and monitored throughout the formal negotiation.

The desire for stability and mutual gain

If this is strong both parties can only be satisfied if a constructive win-win policy is pursued. In a relationship, if one party gains a visible advantage over the other, the ultimate outcome will be lose-lose for reasons discussed earlier. Even a 'more winless win' relationship will be difficult to sustain, as winning is a somewhat relative concept. As this desire is central to the strength of the negotiation fabric, it must be actively demonstrated in thought and deed by both parties.

Suppliers must demonstrate knowledge of the customer's value chain and get involved with the customer's problems rather than their own difficulties. In the final analysis, a supplier's business can be only as good as their customer's success in their marketplace. The aim of negotiation is to have your needs met without someone else having to be wrong or disadvantaged. Bear in mind that the only way you can get what *you* want is to help others get what *they* want.

The precedents set by previous experience

These derive not only from relationships with the party with whom you are negotiating, but also from other dealings you may have had with other, quite separate, customers or suppliers. Losing experiences will encourage your aggressive urges; winning experiences may induce complacency. Precedent plays upon the fear of change and a break with precedent might even be interpreted as a breakdown of trust or a dissatisfaction with elements of the relationship.

The terms and conditions of a contract may set precedents for the future. For example, the *real* cost of yielding a percentage cash discount lies in the fact that it becomes part of the customer's normal expectation forever after. Precedents are set, not only for the contents of a negotiation, but also for the *process*. A history of competitive conduct between parties is hardly likely to generate creative, trusting strategies for the next negotiation.

The nature of the issues to be agreed

This, of all the elements, may have the greatest potential impact on the fabric of negotiation. The significance and implications of specific issues may arouse survival instincts where it is impossible to *avoid* having winners and losers.

The secret of preserving the fabric of negotiation is to have *many* issues on the table and clearly defined *parameters of movement* within each issue. Many issues help to ensure that both parties come out with some 'wins'. When there is only one issue (for example, price) to discuss, there will by definition be a winner and loser.

> The aim of negotiation is to have your needs met
> without someone else having to be disadvantaged.

When one aspect of the contract has been challenged, then every aspect is up for negotiation. 'What do you mean when you include free operator training as part of the deal ... one day? ... one week?... one month? What does emergency call-out service mean ... two hours? ... four hours? ... twelve hours? ... two days?'

Some issues to be discussed will be *genuine*, while others are *false,* deliberately raised as bargaining chips. The game is to identify 'chips', devalue and dismiss them without being seduced into movement yourself. The genuine issues, however, require all your creative energy to determine their importance, their urgency and alternative options that lie within the parameters of acceptability. This applies to both *your* genuine issues and the *other party's* genuine issues.

Central to the concept of establishing the genuine issues is to recognize that they are very rarely a fixed quantum. Usually people have a range, from their 'idealistic' aspirations to the point of 'resistance' where agreement is barely acceptable. Somewhere between the two is a point of 'realistic' expectation.

> Perhaps the single most common failure
> is not preparing what you believe the number and range
> of issues will be in *the other party's* strategy.

Of course, both parties then have a range of acceptance for each issue and a considerable part of the negotiation process is finding common sections or areas of overlap in the ranges of the two parties. The parties' perceptions of what is realistic are not absolute either – they will perceive possible trade-offs. For example, a two per cent discount on price may be traded for prompt payment terms.

Perhaps the single most common failure is not preparing what you believe the number and range of issues will be in *the other party's* strategy. So often, preparation for negotiations is based upon self-centred notions with no conception of what is reasonable, let alone serious consideration of any fall-back position.

The scale of negotiation for each genuine issue has four points. They are:

1   the 'ideal' agreement that quite often will serve as the opening 'bid'

2   the 'realistic' agreement that you believe is fair to all parties

3   BADEN – or the Best Alternative Deal Elsewhere Now

4   the point of resistance below which there can be no agreement.

BADEN needs some explanation. Your *ideal* price may be $100 per tonne (that is what is printed on your price list), but you expect that a *realistic* price will be $95 per tonne. If there were other trade-offs in the contract, $92 per tonne could be feasible, but below $92 is the point at which the relationship can continue no longer. However, there are concurrent discussions with another customer where, you believe, a price of $93 can be negotiated. The $93 is your BADEN.

BADEN is particularly important when assessing your customer's scope for movement on the serious issue of price. Although you believe that their idea of a realistic price is $95 per tonne, if you also know that their BADEN is $94 from a competitor, you have to make the decision as to whether your relationship can justify that $1 premium.

The personalities involved

The personalities involved in the negotiation process will determine, to a large extent, the degree of creative synergy that is possible.

Personality will influence styles and attitudes, which may complement each other or clash. Sometimes the only way out of conflict is to change the principal personalities and, even with reasonable accord, a negotiation may be helped by different members of the team taking turns to lead the discussions. Certainly when negotiating as a team, discipline should be exercised – there is nothing that looks as unprofessional as the clumsy kick under the table to silence the colleague who is revealing too much.

Discipline starts by deciding which member of the team is going to be the lead speaker. A simple system of hand signals can prevent the 'tower of Babel' syndrome when everybody speaks at once. Only two signals are necessary: a low-key prayer-like gesture asks to be invited to speak; a clasped fingers posture indicates when you have finished and want to pass the topic back to the leader.

Ego is an important personality factor in negotiation. People do not like having their egos bruised and so the effective negotiator has to provide opportunities for the other party to move or make concessions *with dignity*. Ultimatums, once delivered, become ego traps for the deliverer if they do not work. Even if they *do* work, such a move is seldom in the best interests of promoting a long-term relationship.

The perceptions of strength by both parties

These represent the fuel for negotiation because the process of negotiation is directed primarily at influencing those perceptions. Power is illusory: there are only *perceptions* of power and we have as much or as little power as we *perceive* we have. We encourage the other party's perceptions that are favourable to our negotiation, while a customer will always encourage the supplier's perception that there is strong competition for the business. The customer will rarely deny that, whatever the reality.

> Power is illusory: there are only *perceptions* of power
> and we have as much or as little power as we *perceive* we have.

The customer's perception in a discount hi-fi store is that displayed prices are non-negotiable – after all, the prices are already quite low. The store does little to discourage that perception. However, *assumptions* are the cancer of perception and we need to carefully check out the perceptions that pull our behaviour strings. We *assume* that there is strong competition; we *assume* that prices are non-negotiable; we *assume* that the main criterion for customer decisions is price. In negotiations, both parties make assumptions and this affects their perceptions, which, in turn, dilute their bargaining strength.

The policies and negotiation styles favoured by the participants

These will be affected by:

- the anticipated *duration* of the relationship; and
- their perception of *gain* in the negotiation.

Where both parties perceive that there is no need for an ongoing relationship, they will tend to act competitively and expect the other party to do the same. Where both see the negotiations as part of an ongoing partnership, they will tend to be co-operative. The problem occurs when the two parties have different perceptions of the duration of the relationship. The first party may act co-operatively but the second party (perhaps while posturing co-operation) will act competitively to the grave disadvantage of the first party.

Serious consideration of the likely style of the other party should be made in the pre-negotiation timeframe, and beware of your assumptions. The tendency is for people to assume that the other party will be competitive; this then gives self-justification for employing baser competitive instincts to pre-empt the other party's aggression!

People are more likely to act competitively when they perceive that the outcome will be one of winners and losers. They see the negotiation as being about a fixed resource, so that one party will gain at the expense of the other.

People will co-operate when they see the probability of joint gain. This win-win result occurs when both parties achieve their outcomes, perhaps even exceeding their original expectations. A history of win-win outcomes augurs well for the ongoing relationship and builds a climate of co-operation.

The early days of a relationship, however, may be difficult, with each party circling the other with closed, suspicious minds. It requires an act of courage, a positive, tangible gesture of good intent from one party to break this anxiety barrier. It also requires a rapid recognition of that gesture by the other party and reciprocal action.

The environmental climate of a negotiation

This can create a positive or negative atmosphere that can have a marked effect on the outcome. Three factors interact to produce the negotiation climate.

1 *Physical setting*: the location and setting in which the discussions take place. The general rule is that you start in the other party's place, which enables you to observe and gather information more easily – not only facts, but feelings. Room and furniture psychology is a major topic in itself but overall it is worth remembering that a small, crowded room will generate more discussion and, if your strategy is to cool down frayed tempers, then putting a minimum number of people in the largest room possible may do the trick.

2 *Timing*: there is a right time to start negotiation, to use tactics, concessions and for settlement. Formal negotiation begins only when both parties recognize that they have a need for each other. Agreement and movement in the early stages happens slowly because a concession given too early may generate too high expectations in the other party, while an offer accepted too quickly might appear, in retrospect, to be unnecessarily generous. There are specific moments for action and the effective negotiator listens well and uses silence adroitly.

3 *Behaviours*: the attitudes and emotions each negotiator brings to the discussion affect the other party and play a major part in influencing the ambience in which negotiation takes place. Aggressive, confrontational behaviour is contagious. Frequently poor morale, due to adverse trading conditions or cutbacks, will

result in this aggravation being offloaded onto the negotiation table. Bad feelings beget bad feelings.

Not all behaviours are genuine. For example, head-shaking and wincing at any suggestions from the other party may be designed to lower their expectations and make them try harder, or the reluctance in giving concessions may be designed to enhance the *value* of those concessions once they are agreed.

Negotiation does involve some play-acting behaviour, usually with the aim of enhancing or devaluing concessions. The aim is that both parties go away believing that they achieved the best settlement possible.

Of course, this play-acting *can* reach absurd extremes, but such tactics are featured more on negotiation training courses than in real life! While these methods *may* be practised in one-off deals, professional buyers are far too involved with continuous supplier negotiations to play games like the 'Chinese Crunch' or rig door handles to come off in the other party's hands in order to undermine their confidence.

'Good guy–bad guy' tactics – in which one member of the negotiation team is made to appear more friendly in contrast to their over-aggressive colleagues – are rarely set up deliberately. However, it is not unknown for friendly buyers to imply that they have an aggressive boss (unseen) who 'will have to be satisfied'.

Progress problems that are due to unreasonable behaviour can only be resolved by open discussion of that behaviour. A negotiation will benefit from the occasional switch from a concentration on the content to an appraisal of the process and the behaviours of the participants.

The rituals of negotiation

These can be seen as an orderly step-by-step process, which again pursues the situation/options/selection/decision-making process described earlier. However, this time the process is complicated by differences of interest between the parties involved. Although the objective is the same, how can we both work towards the common purpose of mutual gain?

A negotiation can be (but is rarely) a single meeting or many meetings conducted over several years. It may consist of one-on-one discussions or larger assemblies. It may be about a simple contract or a continuous trading relationship. In all these circumstances, a pattern or ritual of six negotiation phases may be discerned.

1 *Preparation*: by far the longest phase and the one that is likely to have the greatest impact on the outcome of the negotiation.

2 *Positioning*: when the parties meet a formal declaration of the opening position is made. Positioning has already started before the first formal negotiation session; each party's perceptions will have been influenced by prior events and discussions, consciously and subconsciously.

3 *Exploration*: when issues and positions are clarified, differentiated and prioritized. Creative solutions are discussed in a non-committing context.

4 *Integration*: when tentative ideas are formulated into positive proposals and key issues are resolved.

5 *Settlement*: when minor issues are bargained and the total package agreed between the two parties.

6 *Implementation*: when any omissions or unfair aspects of the agreement are adjusted; performance is monitored and relationships are consolidated.

It is important that each phase is allowed to develop and be fully played out. The effective negotiator is aware of these phases as they happen and prepares for them as part of the overall strategy. It is particularly important to consider them when planning the pacing of the negotiation and the timing of tactics, concessions and final settlement offers.

The essential skills of negotiation are in creating this complex fabric that serves as a backcloth to the strategies and tactics of the formal negotiation sessions. Strategic customer alliances depend on a strong, well-bonded fabric of relationships developed over a period of time. On this foundation, the cut and thrust of dealing can be enjoyed as a sport more than a life-and-death struggle.

THE GAMES PEOPLE PLAY – NEGATIVE NEGOTIATION

Successful customer management depends on open, trusting, collaborative partnerships between suppliers and customers. After so many years of competitive pressures, though, is it possible to sustain such human relationships? Can the temptation to take advantage of the other party be resisted when the opportunity is afforded?

For nearly 20 years, I have regularly used on training programmes and conferences a number of exercises and games to demonstrate patterns of human behaviour and reactions. One of the most effective exercises that, in some ways, gives rise to concern about the baser human instincts is a game called 'Price and Quality' – a simple negotiation exercise – which I have used over 500 times with different groups in many parts of the world.

The idea is simple. The group is divided into four teams, ideally each of about five to seven participants and given a very short written brief. Each team has to vote either for Price (P) or Quality (Q) in a series of ten rounds spaced over a period of about one hour. At a signal from the facilitator, each team displays a card showing P or Q according to how it has decided to vote; the cards are displayed simultaneously. Rewards or penalties are awarded depending upon which of the five possible combinations of price/quality is chosen by the four teams.

Pattern 1:   4 Qs – Lose 1$ each

Pattern 2:   3 Qs – Win $1 each; 1P – lose 3$

Pattern 3:   2 Qs – Win $2 each; 2 Ps – lose $2 each

Pattern 4:   1 Q – Win $3; 3 Ps – Lose $1 each

Pattern 5:   4 Ps – Win $1 each

The payouts are multiplied by a factor of three in round five, five in round eight and ten in the last round.

The objective of the game is never verbally declared by the facilitator, but clearly stated in the written brief are the words, 'The purpose of the game is to end up with positive scores'. The *plural* of the last word in this sentence is rarely noticed by the participants until well into the second or third round!

After a little thought, it will be evident that the only way for *all* teams to achieve positive scores at the end of ten rounds is to vote consistently P on each round. In this way everybody wins! However, there is a risk in making the obviously correct vote. If one team casts the P vote, it could *gain* $1 but, if the other teams choose Q, it could *lose* $3. Similar implications apply to all teams. Perhaps the safer bet is for a team to vote Q, which would mean they might gain $3 (if the other teams voted P) and *at worst* would only lose $1 if the all teams voted Q.

In the early rounds, predictably, the vote almost always goes for Q, with accumulating negative scores for both teams. Each team avoids the P vote simply because of the fear of losing $3. The comi-tragic outcome of all this is that both teams will resign themselves to negative cumulative scores building up, rather than take the risk of letting the other side 'win'.

The teams interpret the game as competitive and gradually, by round four, they realize that something has to be done to reverse the negative hole that they are digging for themselves.

Usually at this stage some kind of fragile agreement emerges that enables all teams to climb slowly back into a positive position by voting P and, ultimately, achieve the purpose of the game.

However, even when teams fully realize the implications of their votes and that they all need each other, it still frequently happens that one or two teams cannot resist the temptation to renege on any agreement in the final or penultimate round, with the purpose of finishing just ahead of the other teams.

The conclusion from this activity is that, in general terms, people are more concerned about avoiding failure than achieving success.

I have collated data on this exercise for many years and have observed many fascinating permutations of human interaction.

- The purpose of the game (all teams with positive scores) is achieved on only 64 per cent of occasions. Of the 36 per cent 'failed' games, 25 per cent will end with one or more teams negative. This leaves 11 per cent where *all* teams end up with negative scores. These are usually highly competitive sales-people, who are frequently heard to claim that they have 'won' because their score is *less* negative than the other teams. They are dead, but the other teams are more dead!

- Each team *expects* to be cheated and focuses on self-defence. By a strange distortion of logic, each team will feel morally bound to cheat first, because it believes the other teams will cheat anyway.

  Teams, not infrequently, believe that they are smarter and that the other teams are rather stupid or irresponsible. This thinking becomes yet another reason why a team will justify its action to cheat first: it is reckoned that, because the other sides do not know what they are doing, they are almost certainly going to cheat.

  The discussion within each team is mainly concerned with being cheated by or cheating the other teams. The question is not 'if' the cheating will take place but 'when'. To be fair, however, there is more talk than action and regularly integrity prevails, albeit on a very marginal basis. Most of the team will be undecided and an extreme stance either way by one or two team members will influence the outcome strongly.

- On two occasions during the game there is a formal opportunity for representatives from each team to confer and negotiate together. The first occasion, after round three, is optional and depends on *all* teams agreeing to meet. If one team declines, there is no meeting.

  On 44 per cent of occasions, no meeting takes place because one of the teams declines; on 28 per cent of occasions, no meeting takes place because all teams decline. The decision not to meet is always regretted later, mainly because the descent into joint cumulative negative scores drops beyond a recoverable position.

  But why is there this reluctance to meet? The usual reason is that the declining team or teams do not know what to say at such a meeting and maybe feel that they might be railroaded into an agreement that they do not fully understand. It scarcely ever occurs to them that, although *they* might have nothing to communicate, the other teams may have something to say to *them*. Communication is a two-way process.

The second meeting is mandatory and, by the sixth round, most teams have realized what needs to be done and are scrambling to get positive. However, if by this stage in the game some teams have managed to be slightly more positive (or less negative) than the other teams, they are usually reluctant to concede their lead in the interest of mutual success, and the game is almost certainly doomed to failure. If one team goes down it has the power to take the others with it.

- The choice of representative is intriguing. Very rarely does the most aggressive team member volunteer. Usually the chosen spokesperson is the mildest-mannered member of the group – selected, maybe subconsciously, to project honesty and integrity.

  Frequently, the team decides to renege on the agreement made by its representative and, on occasions, this has resulted in a personal withdrawal from the game by the representative with their integrity bruised. On one occasion there was a fist-fight between the team and its representative!

  The other team is always most interested in their rivals' choice of representative and draw ponderous conclusions based on personality stereotypes. Discussion is laced with opinionated, subjective character assassinations.

- Whether the decisions made jointly by the representatives at their meetings are implemented fully at the time of voting may correlate with the 'firmness' of the agreement. A verbal agreement between the representatives is almost invariably broken (especially after the second meeting). A handshake improves the chances of success by 150 per cent and a signed document is almost a guarantee of no foul play. On one occasion, a team did manipulate the small print and they absolved themselves of their guilty consciences when they did break their word.

However, *morality* does figure strongly in these activities and a team that has gained advantage by cheating will frequently concede their newly gained advantage deliberately in the next round. In the same way, teams brave enough to send a positive signal early in the game will often find that their courage is reciprocated in the next round with a positive vote returned by other teams.

■ Excessive *delay* in making decisions spreads alarm and reinforces negative suspicions about the other team. A careless word like 'perhaps' or a reluctance to make any forward commitment beyond one or two rounds ahead, generates expectations of evil intent. The frail cobweb of confidence and trust can be blown away in an instant by an unfortunate signal in the form of body language.

■ On one occasion only (out of over 500 attempts) has the full positive score been achieved by all parties. Even when the objective of the game is fulfilled, one can expect that not more than 40 per cent of the potential score will be realized, due to the negative expectations and defensive actions of the participants.

The results I have quoted arise from the reasonably relaxed and friendly atmosphere of a training course. One can speculate what happens in the real world when the implications may be more serious. Occasionally, when trust has been shattered, individuals will take revenge on members of the offending team days later in the training course during other exercises. When self-image is shaken, the pain appears to linger long.

In addition, these negative and conservative reactions come from participants who would, most probably, describe themselves as coming from the more positive sections of the population and who are most aware of the importance of positive attitudes in their jobs.

Conclusions

So what conclusions may be arrived at from these behaviours?

■ People expect the worst and this becomes a self-fulfilling prophecy.

- People feel morally entitled to be negative because they expect others to be negative towards them.

- People are preoccupied with defending their own position and do not consider the effect this will have on the position of others or how the needs and wants of others can be accommodated.

- Feelings and egos influence decisions more strongly than logic.

THE TOOLS OF NEGOTIATION

There are three key tools of negotiation – power, time and information.

Power

For many people the word 'power' has negative overtones – power is abused; power corrupts; power conjures up images of domination and subservience. The *Oxford English Dictionary* has 18 definitions of the word. In the context of negotiation, the definition I choose to use is 'a source or form of energy'.

Power is a negotiating energy that adds strength to your position or the other party's position; power enables you to get from A to B. Negotiation is not a power struggle, but an exchange and influencing of perceptions. Henry Ford said, 'Whether you think you can or whether you think you can't, you're always right'. Our strengths and weaknesses lie primarily in how we perceive ourselves and the other party. Their strengths and weaknesses derive from how they perceive themselves and us.

> Whether you think you can or whether you think you can't,
>
> you're always right.

Everybody has some power. In the prison service there is a delicate balance of power between the prisoners and their guards that is based on the realization that they can both make life difficult for each other. Power enables us to stop or disadvantage the other party in the pursuit of its objectives. More positively, power also enables us to assist the other party to attain or even exceed its objectives.

From where do we gain these advantages? What are the sources of such energies? There are ten generic sources of power in a negotiation relationship:

- competition
- knowledge
- expertise
- investment
- reward and punishment
- legitimacy
- commitment
- image
- morality
- persistence.

The power of competition

Each party has a degree of competition for its business. The customer is probably in the better position to demonstrate this, but a long-running relationship as a preferred supplier with good bonding and high entry/exit barriers will reduce the relevance of this issue.

Suppliers should never devalue the importance of competition for their services in the perception of their customer. In high-technology markets, for example, the customer will wish to stay in contact with the research and development activities of a major supplier.

Every customer has a vested interest in maintaining a choice of suppliers to ensure a competitive incentive in the marketplace. Whether you are a buyer or seller, you try to create competition for your business and are conscious always of your BADEN (Best Alternative Deal Elsewhere Now).

The power of knowledge

Knowledge about a product or service and its application to customers' needs or problems is a source of strength and confidence to any negotiator. Additional areas of knowledge will include competitive products, laws, regulations, industry intelligence and current trends in the customer's markets.

In turn, knowledge of the supplier's priorities, corporate objectives, working methods and business practices will strengthen the customer's position in a negotiation.

Traditionally suppliers have not given cost breakdowns to customers for fear that they would be subjected to negotiating tactics that gradually eroded their position. The new order of preferred supplier relationships with open-book dealings on a cost-plus basis may warrant a revision of such historic conventions.

The power of expertise

Most of us rarely question doctors, tax accountants, car mechanics, computer specialists, professors or plumbers because we are somehow convinced that they know more than we do about their specialities. Certainly it is impossible to be an expert in all areas. In general, however, the only kind of expertise required for most negotiations is the ability to ask intelligent questions and know whether you are getting accurate responses.

If you have specialist knowledge, use it to become the counsellor and adviser to the customer; if you do not have specialist knowledge, become an expert in finding someone who has. Ensure that you are constantly reinforcing the customer's perception of your technical and commercial credibility during the pre-negotiation time frame. An occasional experience story or the use of a discreet technical term may build up a more positive image than the most spectacular presentation.

When you are confronted by 'experts' on the other side of the table, do not be overawed. Show a little puzzlement and ask them to repeat what they just said in layman's language. Experts do not always communicate well and this tactic may serve to devalue their expertise.

The power of investment

After we have invested considerable time and effort in anything, we hate to give up on it without a struggle. Salespeople who have spent months trying to penetrate a new customer may tend to make concessions to salvage the sale if it looks like failing.

There is a direct ratio between the extent of the investment and the willingness to move in negotiation. The US found it hard to pull out of Vietnam after they had already 'invested' 45 000 American lives. If the share price goes down, we hang on for a while and might even buy more because, at the lower price, it is an even better bargain than before. For this reason, key issues should be scheduled towards the end of a formal negotiation after the other party has made a substantial expenditure of energy and investment of time.

The power of reward and punishment

If the other party perceives that you *can* and *might* do something to affect them (even though you cannot or will not), you will have an advantage in your negotiation. If you know that they *think* you have power over them, you *do* have power over them. If your boss calls the shots on your promotion, salary, company car and vacation, you will most certainly be very tactful in dealings with him or her. Your boss will never defuse your perception of his or her power unless something is given in return that benefits the relationship.

In a commercial relationship, you never actually declare that you would not implement that obscure legal clause in the contract (it would be too costly to do so anyway), or that you would never impose a stop on deliveries due to late payment of bills. If the other party believes that you might just do it, it will constrain their actions and expectations and may prevent them from exercising opportunities to disadvantage you. Even in a well-established supplier–customer relationship, the possibility (never denied) that the customer might just transfer their business to a competitor will keep the supplier on their toes.

The power of sanction is best left unstated in negotiation. It is best to let the other party's perception work for itself. Once you declare the sanction, it becomes a threat or ultimatum and is more likely to provoke retaliation or determination not to yield.

The power of legitimacy

People are conditioned to respect anything that is printed. Documents and signs carry authority and most people tend not to question them. Police officers and government officials carry proof of identification, which is rarely examined, let alone challenged. Discount stores have the prices written large and few customers choose to haggle with them. After all, that is the price – it's written there for all to see.

> Discount stores have the prices written large
> and few customers choose to haggle with them.

Anything that visibly supports your case has more credibility than mere speech. Speech is capable of being misunderstood or misinterpreted. Get into the habit of illustrating what you say in visible form. The existence of a price list gives your price some authority – even if it is discounted. Letters from satisfied customers give added weight to the value of your services and are particularly relevant to key customer relationships.

In communication courses, we are urged to communicate in visual terms. This is because it not only assists comprehension, it adds to your authority and believability. Pre-meeting letters, agendas, minutes – all are elements of legitimacy to enhance your credibility.

The customer will also use legitimacy to strengthen their case by the use of policy statements or maybe even by allowing you sight of competitors' quotations. (Buyers will rarely actually *show* you these because of ethical guilt, but they will leave documents around for you to see).

Legitimacy can be questioned and challenged. There are no *standard* terms and conditions of business, there are only the terms and conditions of business that are agreed for *this* contract or relationship. Use the power of legitimacy when it is advantageous for you but challenge it when it suits your case.

The power of commitment

The visible, committed support of those around you magnifies the impact of your words and gives you confidence. Conversely, if the other party perceives that the members of your team are all saying different, perhaps even contradictory, things, your position will be undermined.

Gaining the full commitment and involvement of all the members of your team will help to spread the overall risk inherent in any negotiation, reduce everybody's anxiety level and transmit awesome power vibrations to the other party. Spreading the risk puts you in the position to try more creative approaches because the danger for you as an individual is reduced.

Commitment is increased in other ways by the involvement of a team. By appointing one member of the team as a 'process observer', you can have an overall, relatively objective appraisal of the strategy and tactics of the game viewed from outside the arena. As individuals, we will frequently look back at some gesture, sentence or concession and wonder if we could have done better. The presence of another team member can restore our self-confidence and commitment with a few positive strokes or help to brainstorm for new options.

The power of image

Advantage is gained if the other party has a strong, positive perception of your company image in terms of financial strength, creativity, technology or whatever is appropriate to their needs. Image is a function of reputation, precedent and legitimacy in that the other party believes that any company with high public visibility must have a good track record and ethics that it will be motivated to sustain.

But watch out, image may have negative connotations for some customers who may think that they are paying a premium for a cosmetic feature of debatable advantage. Image can generate arrogant attitudes so companies become blinkered by their own feelings of superiority. Nobody is perfect and this arrogance can be undermined by an effective negotiator pointing out areas of imperfection in the relationship.

The power of morality

Most of us are imprinted with the ethical and moral standards of our culture so our concepts of fairness tend to be very much alike. The desire to do the right thing and feelings of guilt if, to achieve our aims, we sometimes do the wrong thing are present in all of us to some degree, especially if we can identify with the other party's position.

That is why, if you lay morality on people in an unqualified way, it may often work. Even if someone can crush you, you might say 'You can take your business away completely but would that be the right thing to do on the basis of *one* mistake after all these years?', and your appeal may have a fighting chance.

Faced with a dependant supplier, any customer could try to screw the price down, but would it be the right thing to do? Having given a commitment, any supplier who gets a better offer elsewhere might renege, but would it be the right thing to do? How often do we hear 'They won, but we were the moral victors'? The power of morality is still with us and it is as strong as ever in the twenty-first century, maybe because we know that, in the end, we all have to live together and there will always be another time, another negotiation.

International negotiators know, however, that we tend to measure morality by our own cultural benchmarks and that not every society has the same benchmarks. In some parts of the world, for example, personal commissions are quite ethical – it is the way that business is done.

The word 'promise' may not always denote the same long-term moral obligations that we understand in Western society. In many countries the word 'promise' means that 'I give my word *in the context of the present situation*, if the situation changes I am released from my promise'. In different cultures, you should deal with people based on *their* frame of reference.

The power of persistence

Tenacity frequently pays off in selling and negotiation because most other people give up too quickly. They present something to the other party and, if there is no immediate acceptance, they shrug their shoulders and move on to something else.

Persistence is related to the power of investment. The more you persist, the longer an investment you are creating both for yourself and for the other party. Persistence indicates your eagerness to do business and, even if the content of your offer is not outstanding, one has to admire your personal application to the job.

Persistence requires patience and, in an inverse way, can be rewarding because people will agree, if only to stop you persisting. Persistence, however, is not pestering, it is finding new ways to re-open old discussions, not just rehashing old material. Persisting is patiently probing needs and problems until you find one that is important and urgent enough to promote a response. Persisting is ensuring that the benefits of the relationship are fully appreciated and create bondings to sustain future dealings.

Information

Because we tend to regard negotiation as an event rather than a process, we seldom anticipate that we will need information until the event starts. Obtaining information under formal negotiation conditions presents enormous difficulties. It is a common strategy to conceal true interests, needs and priorities during negotiation. Knowledgeable horse traders, for example, never let the seller know which horse interests them because the price might go up if they did. If you knew the needs, limits and deadlines of the other side, that would give you a big advantage.

The effective negotiator goes into formal negotiation knowing all this because 99.9 per cent of all information is gleaned in the pre-negotiation time. During this information-gathering period, you quietly and consistently probe. Curiously, the less intimidating and flawless we appear to be, the more other people will tell us. This concept is at the heart of the classic TV detective series *Columbo*. Our hero bumbles around and, because the bad guys are totally deceived by his appearance, they are caught off-guard and tell him everything that he wants to know.

> Ninety-nine point nine per cent of all information
> is gleaned in the pre-negotiation time.

If you want to know about people, do not ask the people – ask the people around the people. This includes secretaries, clerks, engineers, janitors, technicians and even past customers. They do not see themselves as being in a negotiation situation and will tell it how it is.

People will answer questions but everybody has a *question quota* – the point at which friendly chat becomes interrogation and uncomfortable. Use your chat wisely and try to be precise in your questions – never having to use two questions where, with a little preparation, one question would have been enough. Build up your questions, starting with easy-to-answer queries that are usually straightforward *confirmation* questions verifying the data you already know. For example, 'Paul Johnson is still looking after the EDP budget?' or 'You're planning to open the new branches before the end of the year, eh?'

This leads naturally into *new information* questions that are aimed at updating and expanding your knowledge. For example, 'And what will happen to the old factory when the Rectory plant is expanded?' or 'And who will control the budget now that the project manager has resigned?'

The next move is into *attitude* questions that explore feelings rather than facts. These might be more difficult to answer because they seek opinions and should not be asked until the conversation has gained some momentum from factual questions. For example, 'And what do you think of the changes?' or 'And what are the implications of that?' or 'How well will these plans be received by the staff?'

In most cases there is more to gathering information than saying 'Help me'. Generally you have to *give* information in order to *get* information. People *share* information. The information each party gives may be designed to lower the expectation level of the other party. It depends on who you are talking to and whether that person knows that they are in a negotiation situation. This is where a customer team, with some non-sales people interacting with the customer's non-sales people, can be an invaluable source of information.

One way to test the credibility of the other person is to ask a few questions to which you already know the answers. In this way you can test for optimism, pessimism or just plain lying by the answers they give. People are reluctant to lie outright, but will fudge, circumvent or evade. When you hear generalities, start to ask specific questions in order to clarify what is actually being said.

The more information you have about your customers' needs, the more opportunity there will be to explore creative negotiation. The customer's needs, however, are not static; they are constantly evolving:

- internally in response to *market conditions* or *company priorities*

- as a result of actions by your competitors

- as a result of *your input* as you work with your customer to refine or shape possibilities to mutual advantage.

Key items of information will include:

- *the decision-making unit*: who are the members, what are their roles and how much influence does each individual have?

- *the decision-making procedures*: what are the timescales and budgets? committees and meetings? deadlines and approvals? political factors and corporate priorities?

- *customer needs*: what results are expected? how is performance measured? what attitudes are evident? will they be prepared to take risks? what is the urgency of these needs?

- *resistance*: what are the areas of potential customer resistance and who are the principal protagonists? is it personal or product-related? can we realistically turn it round?

- *pay-off*: what is our proposal worth to them in terms of benefits? what is the cost to them of not buying? how important is this negotiation to them?

Of course, asking questions is no good unless you listen to the answers; good listening can yield more information than just the content of the answer – the emphasis can make all the difference. Try it. Speak the sentence 'I did not say that you were guilty' eight times, each time putting the emphasis on a different word. You now have eight different meanings.

Listen for clues in negotiation. Phrases such as 'at the present time' or 'as things stand' added to a statement of rejection leave doors open for the proposal to be reconsidered. Negotiation is about giving and receiving signals indicating possible movement. Do not be so preoccupied with your next question that you miss these signals.

Signals are sometimes sent in a *pattern* of movement. If my opening bid is £1000 and my second bid is £1400, you will have difficulty in believing that I cannot go higher than £1500. The £400 leap forward in my second bid was too large and suggests that my third and fourth bids are going to be £1600 (an increase of £200) and £1700 (an increase of £100) respectively. The pattern of my bidding is heading for £1750. If I had wanted to signal £1500 as my top price, I should have started at £900 and then bid £1200 (+300), £1350 (+150), then £1425 (+75), and so on. The other party would be signalling in a similar way but downwards towards my £1500 target.

Body language

Of course not all information getting and giving is verbal. A great industry has grown up around the subject of body language, an even more specialized form of which is neuro linguistic programming (NLP). This is based on eye-movements and analysis of the different sensory channels of communication that each one of us habitually prefers.

In body language no single action stands alone as a valid indicator. Only *gesture clusters* are significant. Some of the attitudes revealed by body language are:

- *open (receptive)*: arms open, coat unbuttoned; hands open, palms exposed; body square-on, leaning forward;

- *closed (defensive)*: arms crossed, palms hidden; legs crossed, fists clenched; body more turned away;

- *interested (in offer)*: eyes/pupils widen slightly; eye contact increases, head tilts; facial expression lightens; arms uncross, palms open; legs uncross, feet flat on floor; body square-on, leaning forward;

- *not interested*: eyes/pupils narrow slightly; eye contact decreases; forehead/jaw stiffens; arms/legs/ankles may cross; leans back, moves away; body turns away.

When observing for possible deception look particularly for mixed signals or contradictions between the spoken word and body language. Note variations in the usual frequency of behaviour patterns. Deception is 'leaked' as follows:

- *facial expression*: 'poker-faced' (micro-expressions);

- *eye contact*: evasive (drops by half);

- *arms/hands:* decrease in gross gesticulations; increase in hand-to-face contacts (for example, covering the mouth or touching the nose);

- *body posture*: controlled (tight);

- *body orientation*: less immediate, turned away;

- *body movements*: decrease in overall body movements; increase in body shifts (squirms);

- *non-verbal speech*: note changes in pitch/speed.

Of course body language works for both parties so think about the image you want to project during sales negotiations.

The technique of *mirroring* is a way of enhancing the rapport between two people and involves maintaining awareness of the other party's current body posture and copying it discreetly. As the other person changes position, you adjust your position. It sounds unlikely but it can be very successful. Using this technique, it is possible to 'lead' the other party gradually over from a position of disinterest to a healthy leaning-forward, curious-for-more position.

To walk on the water you need to know where the stones are.

But, without solid information, negotiation skills count for little. To walk on the water you need to know where the stones are.

Time

The way we use time can be critical to negotiation success. A delayed arrival may be interpreted as evidence of confidence or hostility, whereas an early arrival may be viewed as anxiety or just plain bad manners. Time can favour either party depending upon the circumstances.

In general terms, the further east you go around the world, the less concerned people appear to be about time and deadlines. This is to the disadvantage of negotiators from the West whose lives are driven by time. They have their deadlines and their time manager systems and will almost certainly be outmanoeuvred by people with patience whose business plans are built upon 15-year payback periods.

The North Vietnamese resisted coming to the bargaining table in the Vietnam war because they had been fighting that war for over 600 years and they knew the Americans had a more immediate deadline. Just prior to a presidential election, they agreed to attend peace talks in Paris. The US rented a room on a week-to-week basis in the Ritz Hotel. The North Vietnamese rented a villa on a two-and-a-half year lease. In retrospect, we can now understand why those Paris peace talks did not resolve this war to the satisfaction of the US.

We have already discussed time as a key element in the context of the power of investment, but time also has another dramatic impact in the form of deadlines.

Negotiation is about movement and the maximum amount of movement (from both parties) happens in the closing stages of the negotiation – at or even beyond the deadline. Patience pays and the approach to the deadline calls for the highest levels of self-discipline under tension.

In competitive negotiation, one should try to ascertain the other party's deadline but not disclose one's own. Better still, as deadlines are the product of negotiation, they are more flexible than one thinks. Never blindly adhere to a deadline, but evaluate the advantages or disadvantages as you approach the brink and, if possible, try *not* to have a deadline. Moving the deadline is a tactic (sometimes known as the 'salami' technique) whereby every time it moves, another small slice of concession is yielded.

Generally, the best outcome cannot be achieved quickly. If it is, then one or other party might get the feeling, in retrospect, that they could have done better. Very often, as the deadline is approached, a shift in power will occur presenting a creative solution. In addition, with the passage of time, circumstances change; old options die, new options appear.

Time relates also to the pace of the negotiation. Give yourself time to assimilate what the other party has said because a long silence followed by a considered reply is far better than leaping in immediately with a counter-proposal. Such action shows scant regard for the other party's ideas and will probably fall upon listeners preoccupied with your hasty rejection of their thoughts. Neither side benefits.

After visibly demonstrating that you have considered their proposal, the manner in which you reject can have a bearing on the constructive progress of the negotiation.

> When rejecting an idea, it is better to give your reasons first,
>> before declaring your rejection.

When rejecting an idea, it is better to give your reasons first, before declaring your rejection. For example, 'I believe that, because of the volatile nature of our raw material prices and the fact that we have not really agreed volume figures yet, your proposal of a one-year fixed price contract is unacceptable ...'.

In this way, the other party is taken through the reasons for your rejection and could even come up with a refined proposal based upon agreed volumes with prices indexed to raw material prices. If rejection comes *first,* however, the other party, in thinking about the rejection, may not even hear your reasons for it.

Another device for slowing down the pace of the negotiation but ensuring good comprehension by both parties is to signal ahead that you are going to ask a question, make an observation, modify a proposal: 'I'd like to ask you a question. How much extra volume do you reckon you could achieve if you were able to market your product at a price ten per cent lower?'

In doing this, you are priming the senses of your listeners and adding weight and authority to your questions. In the same way, when answering questions from the other party, the *reflective question* gives the same attributes to your answer. It also buys you time. For example, 'So what you are asking is, would the increase in volume at a lower price offset the ten per cent we would lose in price per unit?'

The reflective question is an excellent way of coping with difficult issues in the negotiation. The fact that you do not resist and are not immediately evaluative creates rapport, increases trust and encourages further expression. Most of all, it slows down the pace at times when the discussion could become overheated due to major differences of opinion.

Evidence that the other party, by repeating what you have said, comprehends and is giving consideration to your viewpoint, goes a long way to inducing win-win attitudes.

NEGOTIATING STYLES

To some people, 'selling' is an uncomfortable word. It suggests verbal domination, aggression, manipulation and even trickery to get across an idea almost against the other person's better interests. To the same people 'negotiation' would appear to be 'upmarket selling', directed to the same ends but somehow with a more sophisticated element of deceit, subtlety and manipulation.

Negotiation can be all these things in the hands of different people. In some circumstances, the process can be tough with the two parties adopting very competitive tactics. These are usually situations where the relationship is perceived by both parties to be of short duration and the 'spoils' go to the winner. For example, buying a used car is usually a competitive process although, as a result of increasing regulatory measures, there is now a breed of dealer who depends on a core of regular customers for a living and is more relationship-orientated than in the past.

The whole concept of strategic customer alliances is geared to long-running relationships between preferred suppliers and customers. Although the bondings are designed to lock in suppliers and customers, abuse of power is scarcely to be contemplated, and the marriage can only survive on the basis of win-win attitudes.

The real tragedies of negotiating occur when the two parties are playing lose-lose tactics in a position where there is the potential for a mutually beneficial long-running relationship; where there is the opportunity to generate extra benefits for both parties by devoting energies to *collaboration* rather than *competition.*

Second only to this shameful waste of resources is the situation where sub-optimal performance occurs when one party cannot resist its primal urge to beat the other.

Lack of trust, which is brought about by a perception that one or both sides are withholding information, is a major determinant of negotiation style. All negotiators have developed, through their experiences, underlying attitudes that subconsciously influence their behaviour in a negotiation situation.

The basic stance that we are inclined to take when negotiating can be characterized as tending either towards a hard-line position (competitive) or tending towards a more soft-line position (co-operative). It is important to be able to recognize our 'natural' position, and that of the other party, in order that we may consciously adjust our behaviour as appropriate during the negotiation.

The effective negotiator makes a conscious style choice and does not merely behave reactively. In general terms, the choice of competitive or co-operative style is determined by the degree of concern each party has with the goals of the other party. The five negotiating styles are shown in Fig. 11.1.

- *Enforcers* use force, threats, demands and intimidation to get what they need from others. Their actions are wholly centred on achieving their own goals and the negotiation is perceived as a win-lose scenario. Often, if they cannot win they will withdraw.

- *Compromisers*, or scorekeepers, measure each concession and demand reciprocal movement, issue by issue. They are afraid of not getting their fair share and are usually suspicious of the other party's motives.

- *Peacemakers* neither clarify their own concerns nor probe the concerns of the other party for fear of creating trouble or confrontation. Their main aim is to have good relationships and to avoid, or even conceal, issues of conflict. As a result, nothing is

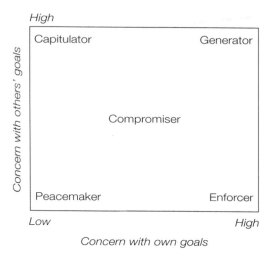

Figure 11.1   The five styles of negotiation

ever finalized and withdrawal may result without notice or explanation.

■ *Capitulators* are so anxious to please that they lose sight of their original objectives and have low perceptions of their own strengths. As a supplier, they may become 'the customer's friend' and rarely survive as negotiators in the longer term.

■ *Generators* are less defensive and more trusting and thus invite others to be less defensive and more trusting. As a result, both parties find it easier to function proactively and effectively. Generators believe that there are more than enough advantages in a good business relationship to satisfy everybody and they attempt to negotiate with others to find solutions to the needs of all parties. The other person's needs are as much the generator's problem as their own, if co-operation is the objective.

The objective in effective negotiation is to negotiate as much as possible in the generator style. People have a tendency to match the behaviours used by the other party so that if the enforcer pushes us, we push back. We can get sucked into other people's styles or we can draw them into more *productive* styles that will get us more of what we want.

Understanding the five different roles gives us a choice of *conscious* behaviour in negotiation. As generators we will practise enforcer, compromiser, peacemaker or capitulator behaviours as appropriate to the situation, not as *emotional* reactions but as part of a *conscious proactive* strategy.

Faced with the enforcer, we may *choose* initially to be aggressive in order to get the other party's attention. With the compromiser, we have to invest time in discussing the process of the negotiation, the criteria of a fair outcome for both parties and, perhaps, take a calculated risk by revealing our figures to establish trust.

The skill of dealing with different styles of negotiation is to be able to consciously operate in each different style long enough to secure attention but to keep on the generator level as much as possible. Individuals will move in and out of styles, depending upon how safe or threatened they feel. It is to your advantage to negotiate as a generator and create an environment safe enough for the other party to do the same.

Identifying the competitive style

In a long-term supplier–customer relationship, the preferred styles of individuals will soon become apparent. When thrust into a negotiation with individuals whose preferred styles are not known beforehand, watch out for the danger signals that indicate a competitive style:

- *extreme initial stance*: an opening position that is totally outside the anticipated parameters;

- *requests for secrecy*: in order to keep the competition out of the dealings; of course when it is to their advantage, competitive bidding will be encouraged;

- *limited authority*: never negotiate with anybody who does not have the authority to make a commitment, otherwise every new level of management coming to the table expects another slice of concession and enough is enough. From the other side of the negotiating table, never give anybody unlimited authority – whoever you delegate to, agree an attainable limit and grant the authority for them to commit as far as that limit, watch carefully how your delegate uses that authority and, if they handle it well and achieve agreement well within that limit, you might extend more latitude of authority next time. People earn authority in such circumstances by demonstrating that they can handle it;

■ *emotional tactics*: as all children can demonstrate, displays of emotion can work – they can get you sweets to keep you quiet or toys in exchange for no tantrums – and can only be countered by ignoring them or by a special kind of *sang froid* (Harold Macmillan demonstrated this when faced with Nikita Kruschev, at the height of the cold war, pounding his shoe on the rostrum at a session of the United Nations. While the world trembled at the prospect of what was perceived as a hysterical barbarian having the capacity to blow up the world, Macmillan politely requested a translation.) The moral is that, while ultimatums and dramatic walkouts are not really the stuff of key customer relationships, this does not mean that there is no room for some emotional display – reaction is a necessary part of creative negotiation, whether it is the expression of surprise, gentle teasing or even mild irritation;

> Reaction is a necessary part of creative negotiation,
>> whether it is the expression of surprise, gentle teasing
> or even mild irritation.

■ *slow, mean concessions*: not only is there an evident reluctance to move but, when movement happens, it is minimal with little regard for any patterns that you are signalling – in fact, any movement on *your* part is perceived to be a sign of weakness and might provoke absurd demands from the other party. They will always try to induce you to make the first concession and thereafter avoid any reciprocation (by practising forbearance, competitive negotiators strive to see that the size and number of times you concede is greater than theirs);

■ *ignoring deadlines*: everything may start on time but delays will be endless; deadlines are manipulated, building up stress in the other party and increasing the time investment in the negotiation;

frequently, deadlines will be treated like rounds in a boxing tournament with the 'reward' for surviving one round being permission to partake in the next and, of course, for each round there is a percentage deducted so the counter-strategy is to have your *own* deadline (which you do not reveal) and when you reach it, get up and walk away – life is too short (if you have the time and inclination, you can enter the next round and, if you really have the patience to go to the final bell, you might turn it into a collaborative encounter).

Walt Whitman wrote, 'you learn great lessons from the people who brace themselves against you'. There are two reasons why people oppose you. They may not like you, in which case your best recourse may be to change the negotiator. They may not like your ideas, in which case you focus on the ideas that you both like and perhaps probe the variables to find some more areas of mutual agreement.

Avoid making judgements aloud about people, which may only exacerbate the irritation, and check out whether the opposition is due to a bruised ego (have you damaged their self-image amongst their colleagues?) Use their ideas, take a moderate risk, discuss the negotiation process (and the difficulties that you are experiencing), demonstrate that you want to meet their needs and do things to establish trust.

You do not have to be great friends with the other party; do not take the opposition personally, it is only business. Develop the attitude of caring, but not caring that much.

THE SIX PHASES OF NEGOTIATION

The negotiation process breaks down into six distinct phases – *preparation, exploration (supposing), integration (proposing), settlement (bargaining) and implementation.*

Preparation

Preparation starts at the very first contact between two parties, perhaps even before that contact if a supplier has targeted the preferred customer as part of its key customer strategy. Preparation is concerned with building up a databank of information about the other party – not only the facts but the feelings as well.

Positioning

Positioning has already started before the formal negotiation begins in order to influence the expectations of the other party. However, negotiation ritual dictates that most formal negotiation starts with a declaration of position and an opening stance from each party in turn. This opening stance usually corresponds to the ideal settlement criteria that each party has planned. At this stage, little interest is usually shown in the other party's statement.

Positioning checklist

■ *Introductory style*
  - what will be the *other party's* introductory style? co-operative? competitive? unclear?
  - what will be *your* introductory style? co-operative? competitive? unclear?
  - how will you control the climate to produce your preferred introductory style? timing? verbals (questions or statements)? non-verbals? listening?

■ *Opening remarks*
  - who should initiate the opening remarks? you? other?

■ *Opening tactics*
  - what opening tactic do you expect the other party to use? how will you counter?
  - what opening tactic will you use? how will they counter?

■ *Moving on*
  - how will you manage the move to the exploration phase?

Exploration (the suppose phase)

This phase is second only to the preparation phase in its impact on the success or otherwise of the negotiation. It calls for clarification of issues and their priorities, together with creative input on resolving conflict. It requires open questions, good listening skills and regular summarizing to ensure that the discussion stays on track and that there are no misunderstandings.

Avoid talking too much or too fast, being too specific with your ideas or your answers, and check yourself for assumptions that are being made about issues and possible (or not possible) movement from the other party.

Exploration checklist

- How much differentiation do you expect between the parties?
- How will you seek clarification of issues and options?
- How will you check your understanding of the negotiation movement range?
- How will you avoid making concessions during this phase?
- What tactics will the other party use during this phase? how will you counter them?
- What tactics will you use during this phase? how will they counter them?
- What deadlock situations might occur during this phase? how will you break them?
- How will you manage the move to the integration phase?

Integration (the proposal phase)

At this stage the exploration of possibilities may be exhausted and both sides have perceptions about the relative importance to each party of the issues on the table. This is the stage of positive proposals with trade-offs or concessions, pitched at realistic levels. The focus is on win-win and results of the earlier preparation, positioning and exploration phases should begin to bear fruit.

Avoid reacting negatively to any last-moment attacks, or gloating if you feel you have won on a particular issue. Do not agree too quickly – make the other party feel that your concession was as much as they could have gained and, most of all, keep the discussion on track. The introduction of some minor but controversial issue at this stage can sometimes take the whole meeting back to the starting point.

Integration checklist

- What signals will you be looking for to indicate that the other party is willing to move to integration? repetition? shift in levels (for example, from organization to personal)? questions about process; non-verbals? change in formality?

- What signals will you be giving to show a willingness to move to integration?

- How will you show understanding of their needs? acknowledge any need that cannot be satisfied? employ listening skills? empathise?

- How can you change the negotiation style of the other party? show provocation? gradually model co-operation?

- How can you change the climate? change time? change place? change emotions? change negotiators?

- What process options can you plan? change levels? promote esteem? focus on common ground? shift time perspective to future? search for options? commence concession-making?

- From your list of alternative trade-off options for the other party how will *they* seek to manage the concession-making/gaining process? timing/rate? sequence? reciprocity? size? grouping?

- How will *you* seek to manage the concession-making/gaining process? timing/rate? sequence? reciprocity? size? grouping? uncertain?

- What concessions can you make to get concessions in return?

- How can you help the other party make concessions?

- How will you lock in concessions as they are made by the other side?

- How will you manage the move to the settlement phase? summarising areas of agreement? drafting heads of agreement?

Settlement (the bargaining phase)

This is usually a fast-moving phase where all the main points of agreement are recapitulated and summarized, minor issues are bargained for, final offers made and commitment pledged. Watch out for any last-minute, serious issues that appear. They may be introduced at this point on the basis of 'we've got this far, it would be a pity to spoil it now'. The opening up of new issues now invalidates any previous concessions and agreement and this should be made clear.

Sometimes small points are suggested almost as an afterthought. On a contract with indexed pricing, the date at which the index is started and the frequency with which it is implemented can make a substantial difference to the monies involved. On a volume discount agreement, does the increased discount apply to all the volume or just that part of it that exceeds the volume discount break-point? Professional buyers are well versed in slipping another goal in the net after you thought the final whistle had gone.

Settlement checklist

- How will you control the climate in the settlement phase?
- How will they make *their* final offer? how will you counter?
- How will you make *your* final offer? timing? content? verbals? non verbals? formality? how will they counter?
- How will the other side seek to lock in the agreement? written agreement? non verbals? personal/organizational? going public?
- How will you seek to lock in the agreement?
- Who is to draft any written agreements?

Implementation

The final measure of an effective negotiation is that everything happens as both parties agreed that it would. Therefore, an important part of the negotiation is to have mechanisms that will ensure compliance. Systems for measuring customer satisfaction have been discussed earlier, but the more co-operative the style of negotiation the more important it is to have a process.

It might be necessary to ensure compliance by using rewards and bonuses (the co-operative way) or by the use of penalty clauses and sanctions (the competitive way).

Most long-term agreements need renegotiation as circumstances change and the best time to set up a dispute resolution process is now, during this honeymoon period of agreement.

Implementation checklist

- How will the other party seek to ensure your compliance? How will you counter?

- How will you seek to ensure the other party's compliance? monitoring? sanctions/penalties? continuing contact? use of third parties? bonuses.

- How will the other party seek to maintain the relationship?

- How will you seek to maintain the relationship? sustained contact? renewal of mutual objectives? boosting esteem? review mutual benefits? recognise anniversaries? informal/personal contacts?

- What actions will you be taking to enhance the next negotiation?

THE NEGOTIATION AUDIT

Every negotiation should be used as a learning experience and, at the end of the day, it may be valuable to ask yourself the following questions, rating both content and process.

- What did the other party do well?

- What could the other party have done better?

- What did you do well?

- What would you do differently next time?

- What else have you learnt from this negotiation?

SUMMARY OF NEGOTIATION PRINCIPLES

- *Negotiation is the act or process of bargaining to reach a mutually acceptable agreement or objective*

  Both sides must feel they have won, but not regret what the other side has achieved – it must not be seen as gained at their expense. Each side achieves what it feels is most important.

- *Negotiation must take place between equals in each other's eyes*

  Although job titles may differ, the ability of both sides to make matching decisions is essential, as is the mutual respect between negotiators – both must see each other as equals.

- *Negotiation is based on a common respect for the rules of the game*

  Be yourself. Discuss rather than debate. Neither side must attempt one-upmanship. At the same time, neither side yields anything that is really important to them, although they may well indicate the opposite. Avoid domination.

- *Put your cards on the table*

  Do not pretend negotiating powers you do not possess. Declare what you *can* do and what you *cannot* do.

- *Be patient*

  In negotiation rushed decisions are rarely good ones that satisfy both sides. Be prepared to take time and do not hurry. Delay is better than a bad decision.

- *See the other side's case objectively*

  Being able to put yourself in the negotiation position of the person opposite you without being blinkered or emotional about it helps you to a better assessment of their position.

- *Communicate to advance relationships and negotiation objectives*

  Be open and disclose your motives and self-interest. Lay it on the line and let the buyer do so in turn. Do not be obscure.

- *Avoid confrontation*

  Do not put yourself in a position from which you cannot retract. If you have an argument, things are said that can make negotiating impossible. Avoid showdowns. Stand firm, but always state your position calmly.

- *If you disagree, do so as from a position of devil's advocate*

  Be prepared to discuss your case from the other person's point of view. This enables you to say things that do not force a confrontation.

- *Give concessions step by step*

  Never concede 'everything or nothing'. Give piece by piece but, for every concession you give, gain one in return: 'if you do this, I will do that'.

- *Know when to leave well alone*

  In negotiation there is rarely an ideal solution, so do not pursue one when it is beyond your reach, too costly or takes more time than you can afford.

- *Declare company strategies if you must, but not objectives behind them*

  Company strategies and plans become public knowledge as soon as they are implemented, but the objectives, personal motivations and needs that catalyze and maintain them should be kept secret.

- *Do not compromise your ultimate objectives*

  Set your highest and lowest negotiating objective, then do not settle below the lowest point. Lose rather than gain a worthless deal.

- *Never relax your guard*

  Stamina is one of the hallmarks of a good negotiator. Your opponent may stall for hours just to find out when you will crack. If you cannot bide your time in such duels, do not negotiate.

- *Always rehearse your case*

  Tell yourself what you are going to say, how you are going to say it and when. Then rehearse how your opposite numbers will do the same.

- *Do not underestimate other people*

  Many negotiators pretend not to know or to be foolish. Some *are* fools, but others may appear so to mislead you.

- *Respect confidences given when negotiating*

  Do not ever betray a confidence given during negotiation. The essence of negotiation is mutual trust.

- *Find out the complete extent of the other side's demands before responding*

  How can you start to negotiate until you know the full ramifications of meeting the other side's demands? In addition, a full list gives you control of the meeting agenda, the sequence in which issues will be discussed and options to link issues when the meeting becomes deadlocked.

- *Always start high and trade down*

  Use your highest figures first then trade down if you have to. You can rarely trade up from a lower figure.

- *Use silence*

  When an unacceptable offer is presented, silence is the best reply.

- *Be prepared to break off negotiation when the alternative is having to retract later*

  If the unexpected arises, it is better to confer with colleagues in your team and agree the next step, than to go on and then have to retract in front of your opponents.

- *Delay sensitive issues to avoid confrontation*

  If you risk a direct confrontation by raising a delicate issue early, either delay or, if necessary, defer meeting.

- *If a negotiation is deferred, decide the basis for the next meeting*

  Always agree the next step or objective if more than one meeting is necessary to reach agreement.

- *Do not exaggerate the facts*

  Never exaggerate what can later be verified about your company. Be frank.

- *Respect the buyer's conventions*

  Be watchful to ensure you do not offend: 'When in Rome, do as the Romans do'.

- *Use simple language*

  Negotiation, above all else, requires clear thinking and clear speech. Keep your language simple.

- *Do not be greedy*

  Everyone has a breaking point. If you push too far or too hard you may succeed once, but *only* once.

- *Record all points agreed as you go*

  Avoid the need to meet again to renegotiate what was not noted down.

- *Keep the negotiating team even*

  Do not be overpowered and do not overpower.

- *Choose the negotiating team carefully*

  How technical will the discussions become? Take technicians for technical advice only.

- *Do not assume anything*

  Clarify each point agreed, including the limits and the precise latitudes.

- *Do not send subordinates to speak for you if you can help it*

  As a rule, only equals should negotiate. Besides, what your subordinates *report* they said, and what they *actually* said, are frequently different!

- *Do not embarrass others who make mistakes*

  Do not draw attention to their errors and do not knock other people. If you make mistakes, do not over-react but do not make too many.

- *Avoid personal opinion about others*

  Unless you know people very well, your personal opinions can swing a finely balanced decision against you. Be sure that you understand the 'chemistry' of the relationship.

- *Expect negative reactions in negotiating*

  No one wants to give the impression of pleasure at decisions reached, in case it alters balance of advantage.

- *If you decide to be provocative or unpleasant, know what you are doing*

  Such actions should be very controlled. If you make someone lose their temper, they could cause you to lose yours and you may throw away all your negotiating advantages.

- *Watch for wandering eyes*

  Some people are very good at reading upside-down. They may read your next negotiating point and answer it before you are ready.

- *Do not sign anything in haste*

  Always read the small print. It can often contain unnegotiated surprises!

- *Avoid the hospitality trap*

  Try and negotiate *before* lunch.

- *Never appear to be superior*

  In negotiating stick to your objectives. If you cannot reach the minimum, the timing is wrong or your overtures are unwelcome. Better to lose with good grace and live to talk again on a better day.

- *End negotiations positively*

  Satisfactory negotiations should end when both sides can part without regret. Try to end all negotiations on a positive note, satisfying the needs of all parties.

For more on the 54 principles of negotiation see our website www.business-minds/kcrm

You don't bring me flowers any more

WHY ARE CUSTOMERS LOST?

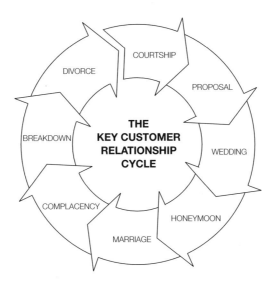

THE
KEY CUSTOMER
RELATIONSHIP
CYCLE

COURTSHIP · PROPOSAL · WEDDING · HONEYMOON · MARRIAGE · COMPLACENCY · BREAKDOWN · DIVORCE

'… I remember when you couldn't wait to love me …

now after lovin' me … when you feel alright …

you just roll over and turn out the light …'

'You don't bring me flowers any more',

© 1977 Stonebridge Music and Threesome Music

Barbra Streisand's classic duet with Neil Diamond may strike a chord in all romantics. Somehow the heady euphoria of courtship, wedding and honeymoon may, in time, give way to other priorities, resulting in a failure to notice obvious signs of restlessness and unease in our partner.

This reflection serves only to draw attention to the fact that many supplier and customer relationships move through the same patterns of ecstasy and complacency which inevitably culminate in breakdown and divorce. Considerable time, effort and expense is directed at new business and beating the competition, when perhaps a little more caring investment in the *existing* customer base might prove strategically more effective.

Why are customers lost? Alarmingly, research suggests the following causes:

- death 1%

- change of customer location 3%

- specific competitive offer 5%

- generally lower prices elsewhere 9%

- complaints not dealt with 14%

- lack of interest by supplier 68%

This data confirms a widely held belief that professional buyers are mainly interested in establishing mutually beneficial working relationships with suppliers at competitive, but fair, prices. Loyalties are important on both sides of the negotiation table and a very substantial price differential is necessary to persuade a buyer to change from using established suppliers.

The dangers of complacency

The only way a new potential supplier can enter the market is by changing the buyer's specification or working practices and opening up the whole purchasing method to review. Complacency by existing suppliers allows this to happen and the only protection lies in keeping close to your customer and their changing needs.

A disgruntled customer tells an average of 11 other people about the bad experience.

Other research suggests that the cost of neglect is compounded by the fact that a disgruntled customer tells an average of 11 other people about the bad experience, and reduces supplier profitability by as much as six times the cost of keeping that customer satisfied.

Clearly, apathy towards the customer is an expensive malaise and marketing strategy must embrace the investment of maintaining the magic of the stable marriage. An exploration of the earlier analogy might yield some clues as to what can be done.

Courtship and proposal

Sometimes the initial approach is turned down; after all, an attractive customer is bound to be courted by other interested parties.

This fierce competition spurs the suitor on to greater effort and persistence; getting the business may assume less importance than beating the competition – at any cost. Market awareness and market share rate higher than profit or customer care.

Although the visible participants in this projected liaison have reached an understanding, there are other interested parties on both sides who must be convinced that the marriage is right. A bride's parents may often want to be satisfied as to the prospects of the groom. The groom's parents may have to accept some initial scepticism about their precious child and make sacrifices in the short-term to help consolidate the marriage. In the same way, 'marriages' between buyers and sellers are set up with both parties weighing short-term sacrifices against long-term benefits. The buyer may well have to give up an established but static relationship with another supplier that could involve costs in re-specification, retraining, inventory and personal risk.

The seller may have to modify standard products and procedures to meet the more exacting specific desires of the key customer. If either party is too demanding or inhibiting of the other, the relationship will fail or may never even begin. In business this means flexibility in packaging, specifications and service. The two principal 'negotiators' must have the skill and authority to commit themselves and to ensure the support of their 'parents'.

The wedding and honeymoon

At this stage, co-operation is excellent and relations progressively less guarded leading to a period of high participation and satisfaction. The size of the 'dowry' from the buyer to the seller will occasion more than passing interest from the parents and other parties who will be anxious to protect their investment, but the participants themselves will be prepared to overlook minor teething problems.

Marriage and complacency

The two parties are conditioned to each other; favours are received and given. Seller complacency is particularly apparent during periods of high market demand on the seller's resources, when a new customer opportunity is perceived to be more important than a routine order. The seller may use license with the regular demand to meet such opportunities; telephone calls will be substituted for regular visits and changes will be made in the supplier's organization which impinge upon the customer's established procedures and relationships. More critically, the seller loses contact with the purchaser's business. Are the benefits still being realized? Are changes taking place in the customer's markets? Are new ideas being developed that may supersede the current methods?

Breakdown and divorce

Here, operational problems and personality clashes create doubts about what is being achieved in the relationship. Other priorities begin to take first place. Sometimes the seller is the last to know of the breakdown. The separation is gradual and the visible signs are subtle:

- key people become less available;
- the business is delegated to subordinates;
- the buyer meets you in the foyer, not in their office;
- hospitality is not accepted;
- telephone calls are not returned;
- invoices are paid less promptly;
- queries on details increase;
- names of competitors appear in the Visitors Book;
- meetings are brief, with frequent interruptions;
- telephones are not diverted during meetings.

It can be useful to brainstorm with your customer teams a list of such indications for your organization. Can this disastrous cycle be averted? There are two essential elements that keep the marriage alive: professional relationship management and customer-driven, rather than competitor-driven, marketing.

The idea of identifying the small number of specific customers who contribute, or could contribute, to the major part of revenue, profit, market share and volume, is well recognized. Unfortunately for many companies the concept stops there. A salesperson is given key customer responsibility and assigned to call there more frequently. Alternatively, the sales manager may 'keep their hand in' by retaining responsibility for large customers.

To do the job efficiently, a manager must have a sound basic awareness of business strategy, first-class negotiation skills, and the authority within their own company to effect changes of specification and operational procedures.

- *Business strategy awareness* refers to a thorough understanding of financial and marketing strategies within your own company, particularly in the areas of product margins, resource utilization and limiting factors. This will aid the creation of a profitability model, perhaps computer-assisted, for each major customer. This awareness must extend to appreciation and assessment of the customer's corporate strategy to permit the supplier to put forth suggestions and ideas that are of mutual benefit.

- *Negotiation skills* mean being able to play the ritualistic game in a rational way and assimilate the value of concessions to be traded by both parties. In particular, creative negotiation skills enable the relationship horizon to be opened up beyond mere price considerations.

- *Authority* is having the capacity to change and adapt standard services, staffing, and specifications in order to address the specific needs of a key customer more readily than competitors can.

CHANGING THE ORGANIZATION TO MEET SPECIFIC CUSTOMER NEEDS

The most significant obstacle to implementing effective key customer relationship management is the inability of suppliers to realize that many aspects of their own organization may have to be changed to meet specific customer needs.

By virtue of their size and organizational complexity, major customers often require a degree of customer service that is different from that required by smaller customers. Large suppliers, too, may have their own problems of communication, due to the numbers of people and layers of management. If costs are to be kept within bounds, and all parts of the organization to be co-ordinated properly, a certain uniformity of practice is essential. A company's procedures often deprive the first-line managerial levels of the need and the power to make independent decisions. Consequently, they tend to be of a lower grade, less well paid and more tied up in administrative duties than their counterparts in medium-sized enterprises.

The supplier who fails to recognize these particular organizational problems of large companies may become exasperated and financially disadvantaged by the inability of the system and employees to react with initiative and imagination to unforeseen customer needs. In short, unless the supplier ensures that all arrangements are properly defined, that all plans are clear and concise, and that the administration is as simple as possible, it is likely to find itself in periodic panics requiring an irritatingly high amount of skilled management intervention. This is not only costly, but, additionally, it diverts management attention away from other sectors of the business.

It is probable that, ultimately, both major customer and supplier would consider the relationship uneconomic: the supplier because they no longer achieve the same levels of prices and margins as they do with less-demanding customers; the purchasing company because of the disproportionate commitment of management resources and the losses occasioned by faults such as late delivery, faulty materials, poor maintenance facilities, and so on.

Hence, it becomes obvious that dealing with key customers is not a random task, but one that needs to be very carefully planned and controlled. That applies equally to sales and to customer services.

As far as the selling aspect is concerned, there is a need for a clear definition of objectives with regard to a particular customer, as well as for the development of a customer penetration strategy. The key customer manager cannot make independent decisions without understanding the impact on the capacity utilization, planned material requirements and stock levels of their company. Managers cannot, or should not, take on commitments whose full implications they cannot start to calculate. Such decisions must be made jointly between sales and corporate management and this requires the customer team to quantify and present the needs of the situation concisely.

In its contact with major customers, the supplier company cannot rely upon contact at only one level. All companies have staff turnover and the bigger the company, the greater the chances that one individual will leave, be moved, or retire. As continuity is of the essence, where major customers are concerned it is vital that employees at all levels within both companies have contact with their opposite number in the partner organization.

Once a negotiation has been successfully completed, it is essential that the negotiating team on the supplier's side defines the service level expected by the customer, communicates that information to all concerned and, in many instances, takes a hand in leading the team of people (technicians, analysts and programmers in capital equipment businesses; merchandisers, salespeople, depots and distribution management in fast-moving consumer goods) who will have to provide it. That calls for skilled planning, organization and leadership.

In a negotiation situation, both the buying and selling sides require a real understanding of the nature of costs and of costing systems, as well as some familiarity with balance sheets, and with the effect their actions may have upon their profit and loss accounts. They also need to be able to present their proposals to a group rather than to an individual. On the one hand, they have to present their ideas to their management; on the other, they may have to negotiate with a purchasing committee that consists of commercial and technical people. These presentations involve a number of expensive and very busy people.

Many suppliers' representatives enter a negotiation situation without realizing that it is different from a selling situation; the basis is different and the tactics to be employed are different. Negotiation is a process that must be learnt and practised skilfully if both supplier and customer are to gain maximum benefit.

THE DISTRACTION OF COMPETITIVE FOCUS

Michael E Porter's book *Competitive Strategy* (The Free Press, 1980) triggered a decade of competitive marketing which suggests all business life is about the problems of dealing with competitors. Many corporations have employees who are assigned to immerse themselves in a specific competitor, financially, technically and culturally. Marketing ploys are checked out against these 'clones' and, in IT companies, considerable effort goes into putting together what is believed to be the competitor's proposals on a contract for strategic comparison.

This competitive emphasis is regarded as *war*, with references to 'frontal attacks', 'encirclements', 'guerilla tactics', 'commando force', 'pre-emptive defence' and 'strategic withdrawal'. The law of the jungle prevails and full-blooded competition necessitates the Rambo approach!

A UK company in the print supplies field grew some 20-fold in seven years through a similar competitive focus. Key customers and target development customers were pinpointed and one full day per month was spent with each salesperson to assess progress and strategy. This single-mindedness was reinforced by a carefully nurtured intense hatred of the specific competitor who led the market – rather like Montgomery's focus on a photograph of Rommel during the Second World War. Perhaps the most unifying and motivating device in war, politics and business is to find someone to hate – there is no greater teambuilding formula. Ironically, this successful company then found itself in the position of being the target of hatred for its old, reformed competitor and other leaner, hungry, fast-growing companies. Sadly, it has now been broken up and its component parts sold to bigger, more global interests.

Is the military analogy in the best interests of all concerned parties? Competition is perceived to be a good thing; beating the enemy is more important than satisfying the customer and, in the long-term, this juxtaposition of priorities may be to the disadvantage of the customer. I know of an international company pouring thousands of dollars into a product that has limited potential, but has the attraction of competing directly against a company for whom the management team worked several years ago. Meanwhile, other more worthwhile projects are starved of funds for the sake of egos and revenge.

The good old-fashioned price war is one aspect of unfettered competition that might lead to the disappearance of the weakest participant in the market and thus reduce choice and quality. Airline deregulation in the US has made for reduced fares and better service paid for by fewer and less convenient, or more expensive, services on less attractive routes. In some cases, airline staff have been forced to accept pay cuts of up to 25 per cent to stay in business.

AN EXCESS OF QUALITY?

The alternative to reduction in quality is to give the customer an excess of quality – over-engineering or over-specifying products that do not serve customer needs. The latest cars have a fascia full of electronic microprocessor wizardry and hi-fi that is changed every year. I have the technology on my desk that, 30 years ago, was used to put a man on the moon.

This 'bells and whistles' syndrome applies to computers, wordprocessors, hospital equipment, video-recorders – and even popcorn and hotdogs at the local cinema where they are twice as big as you really want, at three times the price you were expecting to pay.

> Marks & Spencer loves you; Securicor cares.
> At Amstrad, we want your money!

Much of this frenzied competition is wasted and duplicated effort that ultimately leads to *less* customer satisfaction. It distracts and syphons energy from the real objective – profit through customer satisfaction. Amstrad's Alan Sugar has said, 'Marks & Spencer loves you; Securicor cares. At Amstrad, we want your money!' In its heyday, Amstrad made their money by giving customers what they wanted – even a fan in the back of a personal computer, which was deemed technically unnecessary. Perception is more important than reality. Although no longer a significant player, Amstrad's amazing early growth was achieved not by emulating the technical specifications of the hi-fi market leaders but by producing integrated units, which eliminated the tangle of power cables, and by building to a price attractive to the 'truck driver and his wife'.

The successful product developers are not startling innovators; they are the ones who study the customer's real needs and consumer system and adapt to it. Classic product development starts by identifying problems with existing solutions. Mr Dyson wrestled with the shortcomings of the traditional vacuum cleaner and went away to design something much more user-friendly. Trevor Bayliss addressed communication problems in Africa by developing the clockwork radio. The Japanese have been successful not only in innovation but also by speedily adapting products to suit customers' lifestyles.

The starting point for a successful business is *benefit for the customers*, however difficult this is to accomplish. The message is summed up in a single phrase – customer relationship management. It does not mean ignoring competition, but it does mean keeping close and responding to changing customer needs.

Customer

development

plan

CUSTOMER DEVELOPMENT PLAN

Prepared for

Plan period

Date of last update

Customer Co-ordinator ....

Customer relationships

Design a graphic to map the relationships between your operating units and the various departments and locations of the customer. Concentrate on mapping current contacts and potential relevant contacts. Use colour coding and, if not too complex, name individuals (supplier and customer) handling each link.

Customer profile

Customer		
Invoice address		
Relevant locations (include delivery points)		
Tel/Fax/e-mail/Web		
What is the type of business?		
Size (employees, turnover)		
Their products and markets served		
Their key customers		
Customer's competitors in their markets		
Key decision-making units and influencers		
Other contacts		
Purchasing policies		
Sensitivities		
Our main competitors		
Payment and other terms		
Delivery requirements		
Technology data		
Other technical data		
Executive summary	Heart %	Mind %	Business share %

Trading history

	Previous year	Last year	Forecast	Trend
Customer's revenue				
Customer's profit				

Current total annual usage and value – relevant products (all suppliers)	Your company		Competitor 1		Competitor 2	
	value	%	value	%	value	%

Three-year trading history with customer			
Top products	Previous year	Last year	Current year
Totals			
Explanation of variances			
Between last year and previous year			
Between current year and last year			
Key trends in relationships with us and other suppliers			

Performance audit

Key points arising from the last performance audit   Date........................

Agreed actions

Current usage of competitors' products

Product	Annual volume	Supplier	Year started	Trend → ←	Review date?	Success possible %	Price?	Current lead time
1								
2								
3								
4								
5								
6								
7								
8								
9								
10								
11								
12								
13								
14								
15								
16								
17								
18								

Customer strategy overview

Your relevant strengths (3)

1

2

3

Specific opportunities – Short term (2)

1

2

Identifiable opportunities – Longer term (2)

1

2

Vulnerability (1) that could seriously damage your current business

1

Customer's primary business goals

The customer – their three-year broad strategic goals		
This year	Next year	The year after

Your primary sales goals	Valid business reason

Business development initiatives

Objective	Current supplier	Estimated annual value	Price	Success probability %	First order expected	Who?	Action to date

Development initiatives in past 12 months

Date.........	Total Initiatives	Initiative successes	Failed initiatives			Extra value	
			Price	Technical	Other	For you	For your customer
Last 12 months total							
Add current quarter total							
Total 15 months							
Minus same quarter last year							
Moving annual total							

Objectives, actions and milestones

Customer ....

Objectives: a series of practical achievements leading to goal fulfilment

1 Select one objective (to be achieved within one year)
2 Establish milestones (action schedule to measure progress)

Template

We will sell, install etc. ————— (number, volume, quantity) of ————————— (product, service)

to ————————— (department, branch, division of key account) by ——————————- (date)

Example

We will place ten of our model E19 calibrators in their quality control lab by 15 September 2001 so that they can test the last quarter's production samples more accurately thus reducing re-test time and field installation callback costs.

Overall sales goal	
Objective (doable)	

Actions	*Who?*

Milestones (done checkpoints)	*When?*

Resources needed to achieve plan (linked to objectives)

Description	Quantification

Bonding initiatives

Customer ....
Focused investments to build relationships – leading from strengths
Your strengths
Building trust
1
2
3
4
Creating exit barriers
1
2
3
4
Creating entry barriers
1
2
3
4
Contribution to customer objectives
1
2
3
4

Account Team Matrix

Customer...

Name and numbers	Sales	Design	Tech support	Customer service	Production	Finance	Other

Competitive

value

analysis

Performance quality review

Customer ....

1 List the decision drivers by which the customer selects and measures supplier performance (exclude price)

2 Consider how significant each driver is and *weight* each driver on a scale of 1 to 10 (1=low, 10=high)

3 *Rate* your company and leading competitors *in perception of the customer* on a scale of 1 to 10 for each driver and calculate the weighted score (rating x weighting)

4 The maximum possible score for each driver is 100 (weighting x rating)

5 Add up total weighted scores for your company and each competitor and calculate as a % of maximum possible overall score

Driver	Weight (1–10)	Max. possible	Your company		Competitor 1		Competitor 2		Competitor 3	
			Rating	Weighted score	Rating	Weighted score	Rating	Weighted score	Rating	Weighted score
Totals										

Overall performance quality score   %   %   %   %

For your company and each competitor, calculate performance on each driver by expressing, as a percentage, each weighted score against the maximum possible score for each driver. Map on the competitive profiles chart below using horizontal bar graphs for each competitor on each driver.

Competitive profiles

Drivers

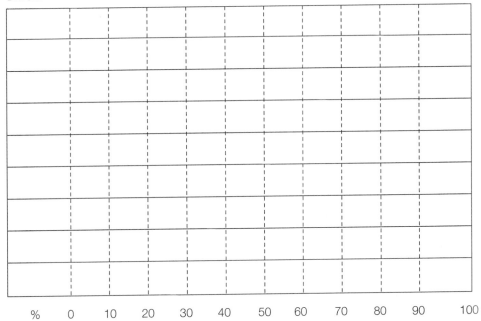

% 0   10   20   30   40   50   60   70   80   90   100

Competitive value analysis

Pricing index – Using a scale 0 to 100 with your company at a benchmark of 50 indicate the general pricing levels of your major competitors in this account

Your company	Competitor 1	Competitor 2	Competitor 3	Competitor 4	Competitor 5
50					

Map the overall performance quality percentage of your company and each competitor against their price index on the competitive value analysis chart below. Around each map point draw a circle the size of which represents the volume purchased relative to that supplier.

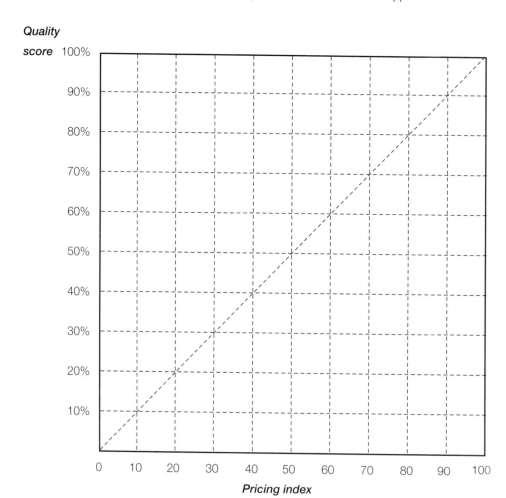

A worked example of this performance quality review is available on Website **www.business-minds.com/kcrm/**

Competition strategy and action plan

Main competitor strengths and weaknesses	
How do we *neutralize* competitive strengths?	
How do we *exploit* competitive weaknesses?	
What does this account need that the competitor is less good at?	
What do we have to do to win business from competition?	
What could competition do to win business from us?	

Index

–